Lecture Notes in Computer Science   10320

Commenced Publication in 1973
Founding and Former Series Editors:
Gerhard Goos, Juris Hartmanis, and Jan van Leeuwen

More information about this series at http://www.springer.com/series/7411

Lydia Y. Chen · Hans P. Reiser (Eds.)

Distributed Applications and Interoperable Systems

17th IFIP WG 6.1 International Conference, DAIS 2017
Held as Part of the 12th International Federated Conference
on Distributed Computing Techniques, DisCoTec 2017
Neuchâtel, Switzerland, June 19–22, 2017
Proceedings

 Springer

Editors
Lydia Y. Chen
IBM Research Zurich Lab
Zurich
Switzerland

Hans P. Reiser
University of Passau
Passau
Germany

ISSN 0302-9743   ISSN 1611-3349   (electronic)
Lecture Notes in Computer Science
ISBN 978-3-319-59664-8   ISBN 978-3-319-59665-5   (eBook)
DOI 10.1007/978-3-319-59665-5

Library of Congress Control Number: 2017941504

LNCS Sublibrary: SL5 – Computer Communication Networks and Telecommunications

Printed on acid-free paper

This Springer imprint is published by Springer Nature
The registered company is Springer International Publishing AG
The registered company address is: Gewerbestrasse 11, 6330 Cham, Switzerland

Foreword

The 12th International Federated Conference on Distributed Computing Techniques (DisCoTec) took place in Neuchâtel, Switzerland, during June 19–22, 2017. It was organized by the Institute of Computer Science of the University of Neuchâtel.

The DisCoTec series is one of the major events sponsored by the International Federation for Information Processing (IFIP). It comprises three conferences:

- COORDINATION, the IFIP WG6.1 International Conference on Coordination Models and Languages
- DAIS, the IFIP WG6.1 International Conference on Distributed Applications and Interoperable Systems
- FORTE, the IFIP WG6.1 International Conference on Formal Techniques for Distributed Objects, Components and Systems

Together, these conferences cover a broad spectrum of distributed computing subjects, ranging from theoretical foundations and formal description techniques to systems research issues.

Each day of the federated event began with a plenary speaker nominated by one of the conferences. The three invited speakers were Prof. Giovanna Di Marzo Serugendo (UniGE, Switzerland), Dr. Marko Vukolić (IBM Research, Switzerland), and Dr. Rupak Majumdar (MPI, Germany).

Associated with the federated event were also three satellite events that took place during June 21–22, 2017:

- The 10th Workshop on Interaction and Concurrency Experience (ICE)
- The 4th Workshop on Security in Highly Connected IT Systems (SHCIS)
- The EBSIS-sponsored session on Dependability and Interoperability with Event-Based Systems (DIEBS)

Sincere thanks go to the chairs and members of the Program and Steering Committees of the aforementioned conferences and workshops for their highly appreciated efforts. The organization of DisCoTec 2017 was only possible thanks to the dedicated work of the Organizing Committee, including Ivan Lanese (publicity chair), Romain Rouvoy (workshop chair), Peter Kropf (finance chair), and Aurélien Havet (webmaster), as well as all the students and colleagues who volunteered their time to help. Finally, many thanks go to IFIP WG6.1 for sponsoring this event, Springer's *Lecture Notes in Computer Science* for their support and sponsorship, and EasyChair for providing the reviewing infrastructure.

April 2017

Pascal Felber
Valerio Schiavoni

Preface

This volume contains the proceedings of DAIS 2017, the 17th IFIP International Conference on Distributed Applications and Interoperable Systems, sponsored by the IFIP (International Federation for Information Processing) and organized by the IFIP Working Group 6.1.

DAIS was held during June 19–22, 2017, in Neuchatel, Switzerland, as part of DisCoTec, the 12th International Federated Conference on Distributed Computing Techniques, together with FORTE (the 37th IFIP International Conference on Formal Techniques for Distributed Objects, Components and Systems) and COORDINATION (the 19th IFIP International Conference on Coordination Models and Languages). There were 23 submissions for DAIS. Each submission was reviewed by at least three, and on average 3.7, Program Committee members. The committee decided to accept 11 full papers, two practical experience reports, and two short papers.

The accepted papers represent a compelling sample of the state of the art in the area of distributed applications, services, and systems. There was great emphasis on data storage and security this year. The proceedings include contributions on optimizing distributed applications and systems (SQL streaming processing, and P2P) as well as novel techniques to store data (data deduplication, block placement, and executable choregraphies). The focus of the security area ranges from practical evaluation of cryptographic schemes, specialized hardware like Intel SGX, to emerging blockchain access control. In the area of distributed services, there are contributions on building collaborative services and packaging micro-services are included, and the techniques to process distributed graph.

The conference was made possible by the work and cooperation of many people working in several committees and organizations that are listed in these proceedings. In particular, we thank the Program Committee members for their commitment and thorough reviews and for their active participation in the discussion phase, and all the external reviewers for their help in evaluating submissions. We would also like to thank Maco Vukolic, our invited keynote speaker. Finally, we also thank the DisCoTec general chair, Pascal Felber, organization chair, Valerio Schiavoni, and the DAIS Steering Committee chair, Rui Oliveira, for their constant availability, support, and guidance.

April 2017

Lydia Y. Chen
Hans P. Reiser

Organization

Program Committee Chairs

Lydia Y. Chen   IBM Research Zurich Lab, Switzerland
Hans P. Reiser   University of Passau, Germany

Program Committee

Luciana Arantes   Université Pierre et Marie Curie-Paris 6, France
Carlos Baquero   HASLab, INESC TEC and Universidade do Minho,
                       Portugal
Sonia Ben Mokhtar   LIRIS CNRS, France
Alysson Bessani   University of Lisbon, Portugal
Robert Birke   IBM Zurich Research Laboratory, Switzerland
Andrea Bondavalli   University of Florence, Italy
Sara Bouchenak   INSA Lyon, France
Nikolaos Chrysos   Foundation for Research and Technology (FORTH),
                       Greece
Miguel Correia   INESC-ID, Instituto Superior Técnico, Universidade
                       de Lisboa, Portugal
Wolfgang De Meuter   Vrije Universiteit Brussel, Belgium
Jim Dowling   Swedish Institute of Computer Science, Sweden
Frank Eliassen   University of Oslo, Norway
David Eyers   University of Otago, New Zealand
Kurt Geihs   Universität Kassel, Germany
Karl M. Goeschka   Vienna University of Technology, Austria
Franz J. Hauck   Ulm University, Germany
K.R. Jayaram   IBM Research, USA
Mark Jelasity   University of Szeged, Hungary
Vana Kalogeraki   Athens University of Economics and Business, Greece
Evangelia Kalyvianaki City University London, UK
Ruediger Kapitza   TU Braunschweig, Germany
Attila Kertesz   University of Szeged, Hungary
Benny Mandler   IBM Haifa Research, Israel
Miguel Matos   INESC TEC and Universidade do Minho, Portugal
Rene Meier   Lucerne University of Applied Sciences, Switzerland
Alberto Montresor   University of Trento, Italy
Kiran-Kumar   Harvard University, USA
  Muniswamy-Reddy
Juan Perez   Universidad del Rosario, Columbia
Peter Pietzuch   Imperial College London, UK

| Altair Santin | Pontifical Catholic University of Paraná, Brazil |
| Spyros Voulgaris | VU University Amsterdam, The Netherlands |

Steering Committee

Alysson Bessani	Universidade de Lisboa, Portugal
Sara Bouchenak	INSA Lyon, France
Jim Dowling	KTH Royal Institute of Technology, Sweden
Frank Eliassen	University of Oslo, Norway
Pascal Felber	Université de Neuchâtel, Switzerland
Karl Goeschka	Vienna University of Technology, Austria
Rüdiger Kapitza	Technical University of Braunschweig, Germany
Kostas Magoutis	FORTH-ICS, Greece
Rui Oliveira	Universidade do Minho, Portugal
Peter Pietzuch	Imperial College, UK
Romain Rouvoy	University of Lille 1, France
François Taiani	Université de Rennes 1, France

Contents

Running System Efficiently (Distributed System)

Similarity Aware Shuffling for the Distributed Execution of SQL Window Functions

Fábio Coelho[1(✉)], Miguel Matos[2], José Pereira[1], and Rui Oliveira[1]

[1] INESC TEC, Universidade do Minho, Braga, Portugal
fabio.a.coelho@inesctec.pt, {jop,rco}@di.uminho.pt
[2] INESC-ID/IST, Lisboa, Portugal
mm@gsd.inesc-id.pt

Abstract. Window functions are extremely useful and have become increasingly popular, allowing ranking, cumulative sums and other analytic aggregations to be computed over a highly flexible and configurable sliding window. This powerful expressiveness comes naturally at the expense of heavy computational requirements which, so far, have been addressed through optimizations around centralized approaches by works both from the industry and academia. Distribution and parallelization has the potential to improve performance, but introduces several challenges associated with data distribution that may harm data locality. In this paper, we show how data similarity can be employed across partitions during the distributed execution of these operators to improve data co-locality between instances of a Distributed Query Engine and the associated data storage nodes. Our contribution can attain network gains in the average of 3 times and it is expected to scale as the number of instances increase. In the scenario with 8 nodes, we were to able attain bandwidth and time savings of 7.3 times and 2.61 times respectively.

1 Introduction

Nowadays, the scalability of database engines is paramount, specifically when it is targeted at large scale analytical processing. Systems must be able to support several computing nodes, enabling component scalability to possibly reach hundreds or thousands of nodes. However, reaching such scale introduces several challenges associated with data and request distribution and balance. Cloud computing infrastructures offer a nearly transparent environment where computation is available as virtually infinite computing nodes. However, commercial relational database engines (RDBMS) do not conform to such paradigm, typically offering a monolithic structure. Legacy-type servers are usually considered for running RDBMSs, limiting system scalability from the purchase moment or until they become economically unacceptable.

Window Functions (WF) define a sub-set of analytical operations that enable the formulation of analytical queries over a derived view of a given relation R. They are also known as OLAP Analytical Functions and are part of the SQL:2003

L.Y. Chen and H.P. Reiser (Eds.): DAIS 2017, LNCS 10320, pp. 3–18, 2017.
DOI: 10.1007/978-3-319-59665-5_1

standard. All major database systems like Oracle [7], IBM DB2 [14], Microsoft SQL Server [6], SAP Hana [21], Cloudera Impala [17] or Postgresql [20] have the ability to execute a sub-set of the available WFs.

WF are widely used by analysts as they offer a highly configurable environment together with a straightforward syntax. In fact, SQL WF are used in at least 10% of the queries in TPC-DS [22] benchmark, a benchmark suite aimed to evaluate data warehouse systems. Despite their relevance, parallel implementations and optimizations considering this operator are almost non existing in the literature. While [4,18,23] are notable exceptions, these works are targeted at many-core CPU centralized architectures that are substantially different from distributed architectures.

The nature of current centralized architectures do not typically take into account data distribution. This eases their processing models, but prevents them to scale beyond the limitations of the hardware that hosts them. The massively parallel nature that distribution approaches enable requires, however, to carefully address data distribution. Having the right grasp on data placement allows to improve data movement, but requires additional mechanisms to maximize network efficiency.

In this paper we focus on WF, particularly exploring opportunities for their distributed execution. We propose a technique that exploits *similarity* between partitions as a metric that can be used to judiciously improve the affinity of data and computing nodes, consequently minimizing the data movement between computing nodes.

Contributions: First, we demonstrate that it is possible to improve data forwarding by using partition *similarity* to chose the forwarding mechanism between Distributed Query Engine (DQE) workers. Second we present an experimental evaluation that confirms the merit of our approach. **Roadmap:** The remainder of this paper is organized as follows: Sect. 2 introduces WF. Section 3 introduces Distributed WF, describing their query execution plans and cost models. Section 4 presents our similarity technique, improving affinity between data and computing nodes. Section 5 evaluates our proposal. Section 6 presents related work and Sect. 7 concludes our work.

2   Window Functions

WF started to be largely adopted by database vendors from the 2011 revision of the SQL standard. These are powerful analytical operators that enable complex calculations such as moving, cumulative or ranking aggregations to be computed over data. WF are expressed in SQL semantics by the keyword OVER as shown in Fig. 1. In the next Sections we will analyze each part of the query.

```
select analytical_function() OVER( PARTITION BY A ORDER BY B ROWS BETWEEN
        UNBOUNDED PRECEDING AND UNBOUNDED FOLLOWING) from R
```

Fig. 1. Example of SQL query with WF.

Like other analytical operators, WF are required to reflect several concepts, namely: the processing order, the partitioning of results or the notion of the current row being computed. These design constraints are clearly translated from the syntax as seen in the previous example, and configure two main considerations as foundation for the WF environment. Firstly, WF are computed after most of the remaining clauses in the query (e.g., such as JOIN, WHERE, GROUP BY or HAVING), but immediately before any required final ordering (e.g., ORDER BY). Secondly, the analytical operator to be computed with the WF environment will create an output attribute that reflects, but does not modify or filter the input data present in the source relation. Therefore, the result-set will present the same cardinality of rows as in the source relation, but will have an additional attribute mapping the result.

2.1 Partitioning, Ordering and Framing

The WF environment can be decomposed into three stages, as depicted in Fig. 2, defining the processing order: the partitioning (1), ordering (2) and framing (3) stages. Each stage is defined by specific clauses namely: the PARTITION BY and the ORDER BY that respectively create logical partitions of distinct data elements and afterwards develop an intra-partition sorting. The logical partitions are regulated by the mandatory argument of the PARTITION BY clause, defining the column attribute or expression that controls the partitioning. The partition clause resembles the behavior of the GROUP BY clause, but does not collapse all group members into a single row.

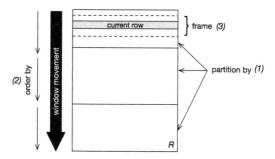

Fig. 2. Stages of the Window operator: partitioning (1), ordering (2) and framing (3).

The intra-partition ordering follows the partitioning stage and is also regulated by the mandatory column attribute or expression considered as argument for the ORDER BY clause. The ordering stage is very important for a set of non-cumulative analytical functions, that are the focus of our contribution, but also as it is the costliest operation in the environment [4].

Finally, the framing stage builds on the provided ordering, taking into account the current row being considered to introduce the concept of window or frame. The frame is built from a group of adjacent rows surrounding the current row and changes as the current row moves towards the end of the partition. The framing is set by either the ROWS BETWEEN or the RANGE BETWEEN clauses. The former considers n rows before and after the current row, while the latter restricts the window by creating a range of admissible values and, the current row is considered if the stored values fit in the provided range[1].

The WF environment allows to combine different clauses, enabling the inclusion or exclusion of each clause type. For instance, it is possible to declare a WF with just a partitioning or ordering clause. If no partitioning clause is declared, the entire relation is considered as a single partition. If no ordering clause is declared, then the natural ordering of the relations key, or partitioning clause (if present) is considered. Moreover, each available analytical function may or not change the computation logic. Due to space constraints we do not characterize all the possible configurations of the WF environment. The interested reader should consult the 2003 and 2011 revisions of the ANSI SQL standard for further information [1].

2.2 Cumulative and Ranking Analytical Functions

The analytical set of functions currently available in most Query Engines (QE) can be classified into Cumulative or Ranking. Cumulative analytical functions or aggregates, are a group of functions that are not order-bound. That is, when they are computed within a WF, an ORDER BY clause is not required. The $sum(x)$, $avg(x)$ or $count()$ are just some examples of this category of functions. Figure 3(a) depicts the result of computing a WF structured as "select analytical_function() OVER (PARTITION BY A ORDER BY D) FROM table", but immediately before applying the requiring analytical function to a given relation. Figure 3(b) depicts the result of computing the previous WF with the $sum(D)$ function. The result of a cumulative function is the same for all the members belonging in the same partition.

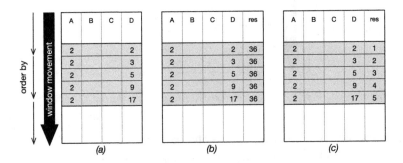

Fig. 3. WF query as: select analytical_function() OVER (PARTITION BY A ORDER BY D) FROM table. (a) WF where the partition by clause generated 1 partitions. (b) Cumulative (sum) analytical function over WF in (a). (c) Ranking (rank) analytical function over WF in (a)

---

[1] Typically, the use of this clause is restricted to numeric types.

Ranking analytical functions, on the other hand, are order-bound. That is, the function requires the data to be ordered according to some criteria in order to output a deterministic result, and thus, the ordering clause is always required. The $rank()$, $dense\_rank()$ or $ntile()$ are just some examples of this category of functions. Figure 3(c) outputs the result of computing the previous WF with the $rank()$ function, outputting a different result for each row in the partition.

The ordering requirement for the latter category of functions implies data co-locality in order to minimize the number of sorting steps needed to achieve intra-partition ordering [4]. In the remainder of this paper, we consider a WF computing a ranking analytical function with a single partition and ordering clause and no framing clause, since the rank function implicitly defines framing constraints.

3   Distributed Window Functions

RDBMS are built from several components, namely the QE and the Query Optimizer (QO). The former translates SQL syntax into a set of single operators. The latter considers several statistical techniques to improve the query execution plan of a query. In a nutshell, QEs split the execution of a query in two separate stages: the query planning and the query execution. During the first stage, the QE decides how the query is executed during the second stage, and which operators are used in such a query plan. This builds a complex multi-optimization problem that has to be executed in polynomial time.

The QO uses hints about data in the form of statistical approximations, allowing the query engine to optimize query execution based on the approximation cost of each individual operator in a given data set. When scaling from a single QE to a DQE, data partitioning techniques are necessary in order to distribute data among instances. The number of available computing nodes configures the installed Degree of Parallelism (DOP). However, non-cumulative analytical algorithms are order-bound, thus requiring that logical data partitions are co-located (i.e., they should live in the same storage node). If elements of a given logical partition are spread in a group of nodes it becomes impossible to sort each logical partition in just one step. The sorting in each data partition would induce a partial sorting that is not deterministic and that would prevent inter-partition parallelism. The QOs therefore need to adapt their cost models to reflect the data movement required in order to ensure co-locality of partitions during execution time of the operator.

3.1   Distributed Query Engines

The DQE takes advantage of data distribution in order to scale query execution. The present architecture is provided by a Highly Scalable Transactional PaaS [16]. Each node in the system is split in two layers, the DQE itself and the storage layer, holding the data partitions to be manipulated by a given DQE instance. Particularly, the considered DQE is based on the Apache derby

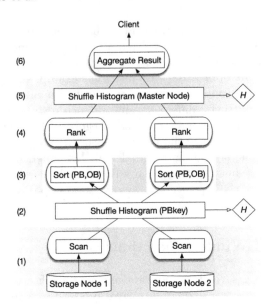

Fig. 4. Distributed Query Plan for Ranking WF. Round boxes represent individual stages of the WF environment. Arrows represent data flow in a process or over the network. PB and OB respectively represent Partition By and Order By attributes. H describes a statistical histogram. Numbers represent process execution order.

project [2] and the storage layer is provided by Apache HBase [11], working over the Hadoop Distributed File Systems (HDFS) [13].

The DQE instances are able to accept client query requests through a JDBC connection and generate the distributed query plan. This plan is then shared with all participating DQE instances. The data distribution in each Storage Node is typically accomplished by means of an Hash function, considering a single or a collection of attributes as key. The distribution of keys lies within the inner characteristics of the considered hash function, usually producing uniform distributions that evenly place tuples across all available storage nodes. Poorly chosen hash functions may result in data skew and should be tailored to each specific workload providing adjusted table splitting [8].

Figure 4 presents the simplified distributed query plan for a ranking analytical function. The following stage numbers resemble the ones depicted in Fig. 4. With data partitioned in several nodes, each one will scan (1) its local partition. The partial results found in each node derive from the data partitioning required to distributed data. Data movement is then required in order to ensure that each logical partition created by the partitioning clause will reside in a single node for computation. This is achieved by the shuffle mechanism (2). Afterwards, data is sorted according to the partitioning and ordering clauses (3), and results are submitted to the rank function (4). At this stage, each computing node holds partial results from each logical partition. The results from each logical partition are then reunited in a single location (5) before being delivered to the client (6).

Ranking aggregation algorithms are dependent on having full disclosure of the entire logical partitions. If the first shuffling stage (2) is not performed, the partial results in each partition will produce incorrect results. That is, if members of a logical partition are processed in the same node where they are stored (therefore in distinct DQE instances), the partial aggregation results produced will not be able to sort the entire logical partition. Thus, when the partial results of logical partitions are merged in the final result-set (6), they will need to be entirely recomputed. By considering the first shuffle stage (2), the results produced by stage (3) in each logical partition are globally correct since, independence from logical partitions ensures inter-partition parallelism, allowing computation to be distributed through several computing locations. The partition strategy considered depends on the mandatory argument of the partitioning clause. It is thus impractical to adjust the table splitting of the workload to a specific partitioning clause, since the ideal configuration may change with each query. Moreover, the environment allows the use of expressions as the arguments of the inner clauses, posing an extra hurdle to this abstraction.

3.2 Data Shuffling

Data movement during the execution of a WF query is required, ensuring that all the elements of each logical partition are in the same location. In order to judiciously forward data while minimizing at the same time the transfer cost, in [5] we introduced a mechanism that works together with the data transfer mechanism, a shuffler, promoting co-location of logical partitions. This is achieved by considering an histogram, characterizing the universe of elements present in each partition. Briefly, the histogram should hold the cardinality of each different element in each different column qualifier. The histograms referring to each node are then combined into a global histogram. The introduction of this mechanism along with the shuffler, allowed to forward data to the specific node that should process a given partition.

Consider Fig. 5 where a table similar to the table in Fig. 3(a) was split in two partitions on the storage layer. This initial partitioning is defined by hashing the value of the nodes ol_w qualifier and performing the arithmetic modulo between the hash result and the number of computing instances ($Hash(value\ in\ ol\_w)$ % #$Nodes$). Guided by the query in Fig. 1, the results were then ordered according to the qualifier ol_d (the partitioning clause). Both nodes of the storage layer hold elements from the available three partitions in ol_d ($p1, p2, p3$). According to the previously introduced, ol_d partitions ($p2$) and ($p3$) in instance $DQE\ w1$ will be relocated to instance $DQE\ w2$ and, ol_d partition ($p1$) will be relocated from instance $DQE\ w2$ to instance $DQE\ w1$.

On the one hand, hash forwarding a single row at a time prevents batching several rows in a single request. On the other hand, due to the asynchronous nature of DQEs, latency is usually not the bottleneck and thus, data movement can be delayed until network usage can be maximized [12]. This enables the use of batching in order to improve network usage. A batch payload is formed by grouping rows that need to be forwarded to a common destination and it is

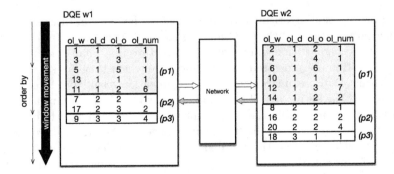

Fig. 5. Shuffling instances partitioned by ol_w. In WF context, they were partitioned by ol_d and Ordered by ol_num. The DQE instances will use the network to combine partitions during execution time. Instance w_1 will hold partitions $ol\_d = 1$, instance w_2 will hold partitions $ol\_d = 2$ and $ol\_d = 3$, respectively.

regulated by a buffer within the shuffling mechanism, whose size and delivery timeout are configurable. Nevertheless, the use of this mechanism can prove to be a misfit in cases where workloads do not benefit from grouping data (i.e., logical partitions with reduced number of rows). Therefore, not having to delay data transmission reduces execution time. To understand up to what level a given logical partition may or not benefit from batching, we considered a correlation mechanism to guide such decision, identifying the logical partitions that are good candidates for forwarding data in batch.

4   Similarity

QOs found in modern QEs use several statistical mechanisms to explore data features in order to improve query execution performance. Without them, independence assumptions between attributes are preserved, which commonly leads to under or over provisioned query plans, which is particularly undesirable in DQEs. As in real-world data, correlations between relation attributes are the rule and not the exception, the array of correlation or other algebraic extraction mechanisms in the literature is vast, namely [3,9,19]. Correlations can also be used in DQEs to improve how data distribution is handled. When logical data partitions need to be relocated in order to improve co-locality, the correlation between qualifiers in different locations of the storage layer can be explored to minimize the required data movement.

In this paper, we introduce a *similarity measure* to quantify to what level the partitions of a given attribute held by different storage nodes are alike. Data partitions with high *similarity* are good candidates to be shuffled within a batch payload. This is so as a high *similarity* implies a high common number of partitions. On the other hand, data partitions with low *similarity* are better candidates to be immediately shuffled for their destination. This is so as they share a low number of common partitions. This is efficiently achieved through Algorithm 1. The *similarity measure* quantifies in a universe between 0 (not

Algorithm 1. Similarity Aware Shuffling Mechanism

1: $P(r) = < r_0, r_1, r_2, r_n > \leftarrow partition$
2: $r_i \leftarrow current\_row$
3: $pbk \leftarrow partition\_by\_key$
4: $w\_id \leftarrow worker\_id$
5: $H \leftarrow histogram$
6: $t \leftarrow similarity\_threshold$
7: **procedure** SIMILARITY$(attr\_A, attr\_B)$
8:     $Sim \leftarrow \frac{unique(attr\_A \cap attr\_B)}{unique(attr\_A \cup attr\_B)}$
9: **procedure** BATCHSHUFFLING$(P(r), dest)$
10:    send $P(r)$ to $dest$
11: **procedure** HASHSHUFFLING$(r_i, dest)$
12:    send r_i to $dest$
13: **function** SHUFFLER
14:    $dest \leftarrow H(r_i.pbk)$
15:    **if** $w\_id \neq dest$ **then**
16:        $Sim \leftarrow$ SIMILARITY$(w\_id\_pbk, dest\_pbk)$
17:        **if** $Sim > t$ **then**
18:            BATCHSHUFFLING$(P(r), dest)$
19:        **else**
20:            HASHSHUFFLING$(r_i, dest)$

---

similar) and 1 (similar) how similar two attributes are, by considering the number of unique values in each attribute to compute the metric. The data required to compute this metric is already provided by the histogram introduced in previous work [5], bypassing the need to collect additional statistical data. This structure is characterized by a small memory footprint (few KB) and the update period dictated by the DQE administrator. This algorithm will be considered during the first shuffling stage (stage (2) of Fig. 5). It will consider each logical partition $(P(r))$, the previously introduced Histogram (H) and a configurable *similarity* threshold. Three auxiliary procedures are considered. The SIMILARITY procedure computes the *similarity measure* from the set of unique values in the qualifiers considered as arguments. The BATCHSHUFFLING procedure marshals all the rows of partition $P(r)$ and sends it to the destination worker $dest$. The HASHSHUFFLING procedure marshals a single row r_i and sends it to destination $dest$.

When the shuffler action is required, it consults the Histogram H to verify what is the optimal destination (DQE instance) from row r_i. When the destination is a remote instance (line 15), the shuffling mechanism computes the *similarity measure* between the local $(attr_A)$ and destination $(attr_B)$ qualifiers (line 16). The partition $P(r)$ is marshaled to the appointed destination when the observed *similarity* is above threshold t (line 18) (BATCHSHUFFLING), or each row r_i is otherwise sent to destination (line 20) (HASHSHUFFLING). The parameter t sets a threshold above which rows are forwarded in batch to the destination instance. This parameter defaults to 0.5 meaning that if not modified, rows are batch forwarded if the origin contains at least half the number of unique partition values of the destination.

5   Evaluation

We validated that by batch shuffling tuples between DQE instances we would save bandwidth, improving execution time of the shuffling stage. We considered a synthetic data set and shuffled rows between distinct DQE instances. The data set used was extracted from the TPC-DS [22], a benchmark suite tailored for data analytics. We extracted a single relation (web_sales) which is composed of 35 distinct attributes, configuring TPC-DS with a scale factor of 50 GB. This resulted in a relation with 9.4 GB corresponding to 36 million rows.

The outcome of the mechanism we propose is directly related with the data distribution considered. In order to bound the outcome of our contribution in terms of the lower and upper performance bounds, we statistically analyzed the considered relation. The lower bound is set by not using the *similarity* mechanism. The upper bound is set by considering the relation attributes that would favor data distribution. This was achieved by identifying the placement key attribute, but also a candidate attribute to be the partitioning clause or shuffling key (PBK) of the WF. The placement key attribute will define the data distribution in each DQE Storage Node through the use of an Hash function, and the PBK will define the runtime partitioning within the WF environment.

The results are depicted in Fig. 6. The top plot presents the number of partitions in each single attribute in the considered relation. That is, the number of unique values in each attribute. The bottom plot depicts the average cardinality of each partition. That is, the average number of elements in each group of unique values in each attribute. The ideal candidate attribute to become the relation placement key is the attribute that displays the highest partition number and at the same time holds the smallest cardinality, ensuring an even data distribution and reduced data skew. Observing both plots leads us to consider attribute with index 17 (ws_order_number), displaying the highest number of

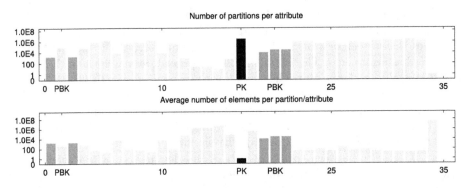

Fig. 6. Number of partitions per attribute (top) and the average number of elements per partition/attribute (bottom). The horizontal axis represents the attribute index. The vertical axis quantifies each measure in logarithmic scale. The attribute considered for placement key (PK) is shown in black and the candidates for WF Partition By key (PBK) are shown in dark gray.

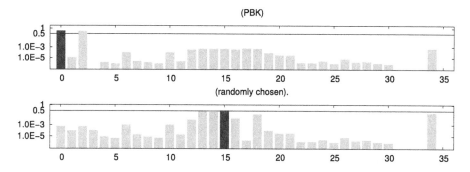

Fig. 7. Similarity between attributes in two data nodes. Horizontal axis represents the attribute index. Vertical axis represents the *Similarity measure* in logarithmic scale.

partitions, each one with a single element. On the other hand, the candidate attributes to be selected as WF PBK are the attributes that would hold at the same time a high number of partitions and high partition cardinality. These are good PBK candidates since they will induce a number of logical partitions that is above the configured DOP. The observation of the plots leads to identify as candidates the attribute indexes depicted in dark gray, from which we select attribute 0 (ws_sold_date_sk) as PBK.

After the election for the PK and PBK keys, we conducted a second experiment to verify the computed *similarity measure*. Figure 7 depicts the results of applying the metric in two scenarios. In both cases, we consider our scenario to be built from several DQE instances and corresponding Storage Nodes. On all experiments, we considered only the communication layer of the DQE where our contribution is, thus avoiding the SQL parsing and optimization stages. Each data partition was computed by applying an Hash function with the elected PK dividing the data into as many partitions as configured DQE instances. We first considered the configuration with 2 instances A and B. In the experiment in the top plot we computed the *similarity measure* between the PBK of location A and each distinct attribute in location B. It is possible to observe that attribute 0 in location B presents the highest similarity, followed by attribute two. These are also the only attributes that are above the set up threshold of 0.5 denoted by the horizontal line. The remaining attributes have a residual similarity measure. The bottom plot depicts a different configuration where attribute 15 was randomly chosen among all non candidate attributes. The similarity measure in this attribute is lower than our threshold, even though it seems to be equal given the logarithmic scale required to observe the remainder attributes. Therefore, the results achieved during the first configuration would induce the shuffler to use batching mechanisms to forward partitions among DQE instances, instead of hash forwarding. The latter would culminate in sending a single row at a time.

In order to verify the impact of our contribution regarding network usage, we conducted an experiment to assess the magnitude of the network savings promoted. Namely, we considered configurations with 2, 4 and 8 DQE and Storage instances. The computing nodes were only set up with the communication layer responsible for the shuffling in the WF environment. Each node is comprised of commodity hardware, with an Intel i3-2100-3.1 GHz 64 bit CPU with 2 physical cores (4 virtual), 8 GB of RAM memory and one SATA II (3.0 Gbit/s) hard drive, running Ubuntu 12.04 LTS as the operating system and interconnected by a switched Gigabit Ethernet network. During execution, each computing node acts as a DQE instance shuffler, forwarding data to the remainder instances. In a distributed deployment, the DQE instance will be co-located with other services (e.g., storage node) which will typically restrict the available memory to the DQE instance.

We evaluated two configurations where the first represents a baseline comparison, forwarding all data by hash shuffling, and a second where data is forwarded according to our *similarity* mechanism.

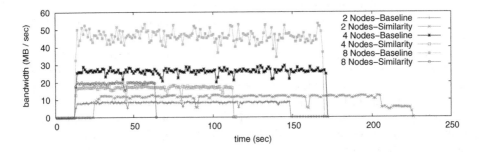

Fig. 8. Bandwidth (outbound) registered during shuffling between instances.

The results depicted in Fig. 8 are twofold. The *similarity measure* registered both a decrease in bandwidth and it also promoted a shorter execution period for the shuffling technique. This is the result of pairing the batch shuffling mechanism together with the proposed *similarity measure*. The savings induced come at a residual cost, since the statistical information is not collected for the single purpose of this improvement, nor it has to be updated in each query execution. The *similarity measure* technique only proved effective from the configuration with 4 instances onward, since it is only from that configuration that both bandwidth and execution time are lower than the baseline. For the configuration with only two nodes, the baseline technique proved to be better by both shortening the shuffling time and registered bandwidth. However, in the configurations with 4 and 8 nodes, the *similarity measure* was able to reduce the bandwidth and execution time when compared with the baseline approach. As the number of partitions in the system increase, each single partition becomes responsible for a shorter set of data, promoting bandwidth savings up to 7.30 times for the 8 node configuration.

The previous experiment evaluated the shuffling mechanism by considering an attribute with ideal *similarity measure* and partitioning on the storage layer.

Table 1. Total Bandwidth (sent) and execution time registered for each configuration.

	2 nodes	4 nodes	8 nodes
Baseline (MB)	1,132.45	4,172.59	7,237.56
Similarity (MB)	2,365.34	1,695.24	991.72
Bandwidth Gain (x)	−0.48	2.46	7.30
Shuffle time			
Baseline (sec)	149	172	170
Similarity (sec)	226	114	65
Speed up (x)	−0.48	1.55	2.61

In order to demonstrate the impact of selecting an attribute that do not favor an uniform distribution of data among data partitions, we conducted a second experiment that considered an attribute with poor partitioning properties (i.e., reduced number of partitions). The results consider the same component configuration, but selected attribute 15 (`ws_warehouse_sk`) for the partitioning. When selecting an attribute that lacks the desirable distribution, the logical partitions will present an imbalance, thus promoting a low *similarity measure*. Therefore, the shuffling mechanism will not be able to maximize network usage and will end up having to consider the `HASHSHUFFLING` mechanism to forward data. The results are not thoroughly presented due to space constraints. However, we point out that they are in line with the considered baseline results presented in Table 1, registering a bandwidth variance of ±4%. Moreover, even though we do not consider it, the use of compression techniques may further increase the observed savings.

6   Related Work

Window Functions were introduced in the 2003 SQL standard. Despite its relevance, parallel implementations and optimizations considering this operator are almost non existing. Works such as [4] or [23] fit in the first category, respectively tackling optimization challenges related with having multiple window functions in the same query, and showing that it is possible to use them as a way to avoid sub-queries and lowering quadratic complexity. However, such approaches do not offer parallel implementations of this operator. A vast array of correlation mechanisms have been so far deeply studied in the literature. Nonetheless, most of the conducted studies focus on efficient ways to discover and exploit soft and hard correlations [15], allowing to find different types of functional dependencies. Works like [18] introduced mechanisms to improve the performance of the WF environment when many-core architectures are used. Distinct approaches and algorithm improvements are introduced, enabling to parallelize the distinct stages of the operator.

When addressing WFs, a common misconception generally brings a comparison between SQL WF (in which our contribution focuses) and CEP windowing.

Differences are both semantical and syntactical. On the one hand, the CEP environment is characterized by an incoming and infinite stream of events. From there, a configurable, but constant sample (e.g., window) builds a sketch [10] where aggregations are derived. On the other hand, SQL WF are computed over finite sets built from SQL relations. While the former windows are fixed and the data moves through, in the latter, the data is fixed and the window performs the movement. Moreover each approach considers distinct SQL keywords (e.g., `OVER`, `RETAIN`) and subsequent syntax.

7 Conclusion

WF with ranking analytical functions are required to have full disclosure of a given logical partition. Data partitioning is required to enable systems to scale, but harms data locality, which poses added difficulties when trying to parallelize these functions.

In this paper we motivate and validate how similarity between partitions can be used to promote efficient data forwarding among instances of a DQE. We introduced an algorithm to choose whether to batch or to hash forward rows between such instances by understanding how the *similarity measure* between distinct partitions of a DQE can be used towards the effectiveness of the WF environment.

The WF environment changes how analytical functions are computed, requiring specific implementation details for each functions. We therefore plan to leverage such parallelization opportunities to other analytical functions.

Acknowledgments. The research leading to these results was part-funded by (1) the European Union's Horizon 2020 - The EU Framework Programme for Research and Innovation 2014–2020, under grant agreement No. 732051; (1) Project TEC4Growth - Pervasive Intelligence, Enhancers and Proofs of Concept with Industrial Impact/NORTE-01-0145-FEDER-000020 is financed by the North Portugal Regional Operational Programme (NORTE 2020), under the PORTUGAL 2020 Partnership Agreement, and through the European Regional Development Fund (ERDF) and by (1) the ERDF – European Regional Development Fund through the Operational Programme for Competitiveness and Internationalisation - COMPETE 2020 Programme within project POCI-01-0145-FEDER-006961, and by National Funds through the FCT – Fundação para a Ciência e a Tecnologia (Portuguese Foundation for Science and Technology) as part of project UID/EEA/50014/2013.

References

1. ANSI: Information technology - database languages - SQL multimedia and application packages. Technical report, ANSI (2003). http://webstore.ansi.org/RecordDetail.aspx?sku=ISO%2fIEC+13249-2%3a2003
2. Apache: The apache derby project. Technical report, Apache Foundation (2016). https://db.apache.org/derby/derby_charter.html

3. Brown, P.G., Hass, P.J.: BHUNT: automatic discovery of fuzzy algebraic constraints in relational data. In: Proceedings of the 29th International Conference on Very Large Data Bases, vol. 29, pp. 668–679. VLDB Endowment (2003)
4. Cao, Y., Chan, C.Y., Li, J., Tan, K.L.: Optimization of analytic window functions. Proc. VLDB Endowment **5**(11), 1244–1255 (2012)
5. Coelho, F., Pereira, J., Vilaça, R., Oliveira, R.: Holistic shuffler for the parallel processing of SQL window functions. In: Jelasity, M., Kalyvianaki, E. (eds.) DAIS 2016. LNCS, vol. 9687, pp. 75–81. Springer, Cham (2016). doi:10.1007/978-3-319-39577-7_6
6. Microsoft Corporation: Transact-SQL. Technical report, Microsoft Corporation (2013). https://msdn.microsoft.com/library/ms189461(SQL.130).aspx
7. Oracle Corporation: SQL analysis and reporting. Technical report, Oracle Corporation (2015). http://docs.oracle.com/database/121/DWHSG/analysis.htm#DWHSG8659
8. Cruz, F., Maia, F., Oliveira, R., Vilaça, R.: Workload-aware table splitting for NoSQL. In: Proceedings of the 29th Annual ACM Symposium on Applied Computing, SAC 2014, pp. 399–404. ACM, New York (2014). http://doi.acm.org/10.1145/2554850.2555027
9. Fan, W., Geerts, F., Jia, X., Kementsietsidis, A.: Conditional functional dependencies for capturing data inconsistencies. ACM Trans. Database Syst. (TODS) **33**(2), 6 (2008)
10. Garofalakis, M., Keren, D., Samoladas, V.: Sketch-based geometric monitoring of distributed stream queries. Proc. VLDB Endowment **6**(10), 937–948 (2013). http://dx.doi.org/10.14778/2536206.2536220
11. George, L.: HBase: The Definitive Guide: Random Access to Your Planet-Size Data. O'Reilly Media, Inc., USA (2011)
12. Gonçalves, R.C., Pereira, J., Jiménez-Peris, R.: An RDMA middleware for asynchronous multi-stage shuffling in analytical processing. In: Jelasity, M., Kalyvianaki, E. (eds.) DAIS 2016. LNCS, vol. 9687, pp. 61–74. Springer, Cham (2016). doi:10.1007/978-3-319-39577-7_5
13. Hadoop Apache: Hadoop (2009)
14. IBM: OLAP specification. Technical report, IBM (2013). http://www.ibm.com/support/knowledgecenter/SSEPGG_10.5.0/com.ibm.db2.luw.sql.ref.doc/doc/r0023461.html
15. Ilyas, I.F., Markl, V., Haas, P., Brown, P., Aboulnaga, A.: CORDS: automatic discovery of correlations and soft functional dependencies. In: Proceedings of the 2004 ACM SIGMOD International Conference on Management of Data, pp. 647–658. ACM (2004)
16. Jimenez-Peris, R., Patiño-Martinez, M., Magoutis, K., Bilas, A., Brondino, I.: Cumulonimbo: a highly-scalable transaction processing platform as a service. ERCIM News **89**(null), 34–35 (2012)
17. Kornacker, M., Behm, A., Bittorf, V., Bobrovytsky, T., Ching, C., Choi, A., Erickson, J., Grund, M., Hecht, D., Jacobs, M., et al.: Impala: a modern, open-source SQL engine for hadoop. In: CIDR, vol. 1, p. 9 (2015)
18. Leis, V., Kundhikanjana, K., Kemper, A., Neumann, T.: Efficient processing of window functions in analytical SQL queries. Proc. VLDB Endowment **8**(10), 1058–1069 (2015). http://dx.doi.org/10.14778/2794367.2794375
19. Liu, H., Xiao, D., Didwania, P., Eltabakh, M.Y.: Exploiting soft and hard correlations in big data query optimization. Proc. VLDB Endowment **9**(12), 1005–1016 (2016). http://dx.doi.org/10.14778/2994509.2994519

20. Postgresql: Advanced features - window functions. Technical report, Postgresql (2015). https://www.postgresql.org/docs/9.4/static/tutorial-window.html
21. SAP: SAP HANA SQL reference (2014). https://help.sap.com/hana/SAP_HANA_SQL_and_System_Views_Reference_en.pdf?original_fqdn=help.sap.de
22. Transaction Processing Performance Council: TPC Benchmark DS (2012). http://www.tpc.org/tpcds/spec/tpcds_1.1.0.pdf
23. Zuzarte, C., Pirahesh, H., Ma, W., Cheng, Q., Liu, L., Wong, K.: Winmagic: subquery elimination using window aggregation. In: Proceedings of the 2003 ACM SIGMOD International Conference on Management of Data, pp. 652–656. ACM (2003)

DIsCO: DynamIc Data COmpression in Distributed Stream Processing Systems

Nikos Zacheilas$^{(\boxtimes)}$ and Vana Kalogeraki

Athens University of Economics and Business, Athens, Greece
{zacheilas,vana}@aueb.gr

Abstract. Supporting high throughput in Distributed Stream Processing Systems (DSPSs) has been an important goal in recent years. Current works either focus on automatically increasing the system resources whenever the current setup is inadequate or apply load shedding techniques discarding some of the incoming data. However, both approaches have significant shortcomings as they require on the fly application reconfiguration where the application needs to be stopped and re-uploaded in the cluster with the new configurations, and can lead to significant information loss. One approach that has not yet been considered for improving the throughput of DSPSs is exploiting compression algorithms to minimize the communication overhead between components especially in cases where we have large-sized data like live CCTV camera reports. This work is the first that provides a novel framework, built on top of Apache Storm, which enables dynamic compression of incoming streaming data. Our approach uses a profiling algorithm to automatically determine the compression algorithm that should be applied and supports both lossless and lossy compression techniques. Furthermore, we propose a novel algorithm for determining when profiling should be applied. Finally, our detailed experimental evaluation with commonly used stream processing applications, indicates a clear improvement on the applications' throughput when our proposed techniques are applied.

1 Introduction

In recent years we observe a growing need for supporting complex real-time processing of "big data". Many systems need to process large volumes of live data to detect events of interest in real-time. For example, in a traffic monitoring application it is necessary to inform the city's authorities for events like traffic congestion or accidents [19] as they occur. Similarly, healthcare applications [11] receive input from multiple sensors to detect unusual behavior in the patients' conditions. In order to be able to analyze such a high volume of data, novel distributed systems such as Storm [14], Spark [21] and Flink [4] have been proposed that enable us to perform scalable and low latency complex event detection.

One important challenge in such systems is to support high throughput during the applications' execution despite changes in the data size or the input rate.

© IFIP International Federation for Information Processing 2017
Published by Springer International Publishing AG 2017. All Rights Reserved
L.Y. Chen and H.P. Reiser (Eds.): DAIS 2017, LNCS 10320, pp. 19–33, 2017.
DOI: 10.1007/978-3-319-59665-5_2

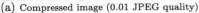

(a) Compressed image (0.01 JPEG quality)   (b) Original Image

Fig. 1. Image degradation due to *JPEG* compression.

In the literature, diverse techniques such as elasticity [9] and load shedding [16] have been proposed for solving this problem. Elasticity schemes like [9,19], automatically increase the amount of system resources (*i.e.*, stream processing operators or components) in order to adapt to sudden load spikes. Such techniques have significant shortcomings: (a) often DSPSs do not support this feature so applications need to be stopped and re-uploaded in the cluster with the new configurations, and (b) approaches such as load shedding [8,16], automatically drop incoming data when load spikes occur; this penalizes the results' accuracy as many tuples will not be processed and thus important events of interest may be lost.

A technique that has not been fully exploited in these settings is the use of data compression. Data compression can reduce the impact of large-sized data in the components' communication time and thus enables the system to process data faster, increasing the system's throughput. However, applying compression is not always beneficial as it creates additional processing overhead as tuples need to be compressed/decompressed before the operator processes them. In recent years, we observe a plethora of novel compression algorithms [2] or commonly used compression libraries such as LZ4 [13], Zip [22] and Snappy [15] which are applied in the distributed system's domain [5]. However, in current systems the compression algorithm must be manually provided by the users and cannot change during the application's lifetime. Furthermore, it is not trivial for the end-user to determine how useful a compression technique is, when it should be applied, and which compression algorithm is most appropriate to maximize the system throughput. In general, compression techniques can be divided in two major categories, *lossless* and *lossy*. The main difference is that *lossless* techniques enable the perfect reconstruction of the input data and therefore the decompressed data will be the same as the initial data. In contrast, *lossy* techniques include the class of data encoding methods that use inexact approximations and partial data discarding, in order to represent the content. So these techniques lead to data degradation and possibly to inaccurate results if they are applied in event detection applications.

In the following application example we demonstrate that the compression ratio of *lossy* techniques needs to be carefully chosen, taking into account the impact of the compression on the results' accuracy. Our application (described in

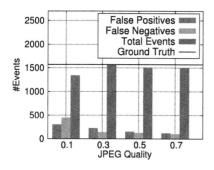

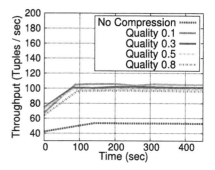

Fig. 2. JPEG's quality metric impact on the results' accuracy.

Fig. 3. Throughput using *JPEG* with varying quality.

more details in Sect. 4) receives as input CCTV camera images streamed in real-time in Dublin city and utilizes a simple image similarity algorithm [12] against historical images which depict normal and abnormal traffic conditions. More specifically, for each incoming image we find the most similar historical image and based on the characterization of the latter (*i.e.*, whether it depicts normal or abnormal traffic conditions) we alert the traffic authorities. In Figs. 1(a), (b) we illustrate how the *JPEG quality* metric affects the image in terms of visibility. As it can observed when we use very low *JPEG* quality the image is not visible (*i.e.*, in Fig. 1(a) the obstacle that fell on the road is blurred) and therefore the application is not able to detect the actual accident that happened (*i.e.*, depicted in Fig. 1(b)).

So the *JPEG* quality affects the accuracy of the results and this can be clearly shown in Fig. 2 where we illustrate the number of detected events and how many of them are false positives and false negatives. As it is shown in the figure, when we use low compression quality the false positives and negatives events increase due to the degradation of the images. However, when low compression quality is applied it increases the system's throughput due to the smaller image sizes. This is clearly illustrated in Fig. 3 where we display the application's throughput using varying *JPEG* quality.

This trade-off between the applications' *accuracy* and the system's *throughput* needs to be taken into account when we determine whether a lossy compression technique like *JPEG* should be applied. Furthermore, it is not trivial for the end-user to understand when compression is beneficial and how different compression algorithms can affect these two metrics. So our aim in this work is to provide a framework that is able to provide answers to the following questions:

1. When is it beneficial to compress the incoming data of a DSPS?
2. Which algorithm should be used for the compression?
3. How the chosen algorithm will be applied efficiently in a distributed streaming environment where the overhead of compression should be minimal?

We propose a novel framework, *DIsCO*, that executes on top of Apache Storm and enables the automatic compression of incoming streaming data for the users' applications. Our approach monitors the application's performance and automatically adjusts the compression algorithm that should be applied taking into account the impact of the compression on the observed throughput and the results' accuracy. The key contributions of this work are as follows:

- We apply a profiling technique that aims to determine when compression is beneficial for Storm applications and which algorithm should be applied. In our framework we consider well-known compression algorithms like *Zip*, *LZ4*, *Snappy* and *JPEG*. Our technique has as goal to find the compression algorithm that balances the trade-off between the application's throughput and the results' accuracy. Our approach works adaptively, where the profiling algorithm is re-invoked when the performance of the application in terms of throughput and results' accuracy has significantly decreased.
- We enhance the Storm system by adding special threads that are part of the Storm's components (*i.e.*, spouts/bolts) and perform the compression/decompression procedure in parallel. This way we minimize the compression/decompression overhead (*i.e.*, due to the time required for compressing and decompressing the tuples) on the application's throughput.
- We conduct an extensive experimental evaluation in our local cluster using different applications that process both text and image data. More specifically, we used a traffic monitoring application that performs image similarity on Dublin's CCTV camera reports, an application that periodically crawls 5 major news sites and searches for traffic incidents and a Twitter First Detection application [20] which processes the Twitter stream and detects first story events. Our experimental results indicate the benefits of our approach and illustrate that we can automatically determine the compression technique that should be applied during the applications' execution.

2   Preliminaries and System Model

In this section we provide a brief description of Apache Storm and provide the key parameters of our approach.

2.1   Preliminaries

Storm is one of the most widely used DSPS mainly because it provides low end-to-end tuples' latency and is widely used in a wide range of application domains including traffic monitoring [19] and Twitter analysis [20]. In Storm, the logic of a stream processing application is packaged into a Storm *topology*; a graph whose nodes are operators that encapsulate the processing logic and edges model data flows among operators. Storm uses a Master-workers architecture where the Master node (*i.e.*, Nimbus) orchestrates the execution of topologies in the available workers. In the Storm terminology nodes are called *components* and the unit of information that is transferred between components is referred to as a *tuple*. Users can define two types of components: (i) *spouts* which are the input sources of the topology, and (ii) *bolts* that encapsulate the processing logic, performing operations such as filtering, correlating and transforming tuples.

In general, there are two main approaches for processing streaming data either on a per tuple basis or in *mini-batches*. The first approach has the lowest per tuple latency, as tuples are immediately forwarded to the downstream components. However, this approach can increase the communication cost and thus affects the system's throughput [6]. On the other hand, when mini-batches are used, tuples are stalled until the mini-batch is considered ready for further processing [21]. Usually, time (*i.e.,* 1 s has elapsed since the creation of the mini-batch) or size (*e.g.,* emit the mini-batch when it comprises 50 tuples) based criteria are applied for determining when the mini-batch should be forwarded.

Mini-batches are expected to improve the system's throughput but they add overhead on the per tuple's latency as tuples need to wait until the mini-batch is considered ready for processing. We have enhanced the Storm API to support the processing of mini-batches for two main reasons: (1) mini-batches improve the topology's throughput [7], and (2) they enable us to parallelize the compression/decompression procedure and thus minimize its overhead on the application's throughput (*i.e.,* see Sect. 3.2 for more details). Finally, we did not consider frameworks like Apache Spark [21] and Apache Flink [4] that use only mini-batches for the data processing as we wanted to be able to support the per tuple processing offered by Storm to support applications with very strict time requirements like stock market applications.

2.2 System Model

In this section we define the parameters of our approach. For each Storm topology the user provides the set of *Spouts* that comprise the topology's input sources and the set of *Bolts* which are the topology's processing components. Furthermore, the user provides *CompressAlgos* which is the set of different compression algorithms that can be applied for compressing the streaming data that are exchanged between the topology's components. In our framework, we support some well-known algorithms (*e.g., Snappy*) but the user can provide also custom implementations. Finally, the user defines the *batchThr* parameter which controls the frequency with which monitor reports will be sent to Nimbus. For example, if this parameter is set to 10 then every 10 processed mini-batches the tasks will send a monitor report to Nimbus.

When the topology processes *batchThr* mini-batches, Nimbus receives a monitor report regarding the performance of the compression algorithm c that is currently utilized. More specifically, it receives the $throughput_c$ metric which depicts the number of processed tuples per second when c is applied. Based on the compression algorithm that is utilized we end up with different values for this metric as each algorithm has different effect on the communication cost and also on the time required for the compression/decompression procedure.

Furthermore, lossy techniques penalize the accuracy of the application as they modify the input data. For example, when JPG compression with low quality is applied, the image degrades and some of its characteristics are not visible. In order to take into account this fact, we also measure the number of false positive (*i.e.*, $falsePos_c$) and false negative (*i.e.*, $falseNeg_c$) events when $batchThr$ mini-batches have been processed by a lossy compression algorithm c. Moreover, we compute the number of true positive (*i.e.*, $truePos_c$) and true negative events (*i.e.*, $trueNeg_c$). In our traffic monitoring application (*i.e.*, described in Sect. 1), false positive events occur when we mistakenly report that we have traffic congestion. This happens because the image resolution has degraded and the similarity algorithm points out a historical image without traffic congestion as the most similar one. The inverse problem occurs with the false negative events. For lossless techniques, the $falsePos_c$ and $falseNeg_c$ metrics are equal to zero as these techniques guarantee the perfect reconstruction of the input data and thus when they are applied we detect the exact same events as with the case of no compression.

3   Methodology

In this section we describe the basic components of our framework.

3.1   Profiling

The first component of our approach is the use of profiling for determining if compression should be applied and which algorithm to use. Profiling techniques are commonly used for determining the appropriate configuration parameters to be utilized in distributed processing systems [7]. For example profiling has been efficiently applied in the context of Spark applications to determine the appropriate number of nodes that should be allocated to the applications [17]. The benefit is that they can capture the system conditions (*e.g.*, throughput) which can be extremely useful in streaming environments like the one we consider where conditions vary over time.

Our technique receives as input a list of the possible compression algorithms and a threshold on the number of mini-batches that will be processed by each algorithm. In this work we consider three well-known lossless compression techniques (*i.e, Zip, Snappy* and *LZ4*) and one lossy compression algorithm (*i.e, JPEG*). The *JPEG* algorithm is examined only when we have image data to be processed while the other techniques are used mainly in case of text data. Moreover, *JPEG* compression depends on the quality metric that determines the compression ratio, so when this compression algorithm is considered the profiling algorithm receives as input the quality metrics that need to be examined. For example, if we want to evaluate three possible values for the quality metric (*i.e.*, 0.1, 0.5, 0.9) then the profiling algorithm will consider three different variations of the *JPEG* algorithm, one for each quality metric.

The basic idea of our algorithm is to execute for a fixed number of mini-batches each possible configuration (*i.e.*, compression algorithm), compute the throughput and the results' accuracy for each compression technique, and then choose the most appropriate technique. Moreover, the profiling technique also examines these two metrics when no compression algorithm is utilized in order to determine whether compression is beneficial. For the results' accuracy we take into account the fact that lossy compression algorithms can lead to false positive and false negative events (as we indicated in Sect. 1). More formally, we compute the results' accuracy via the following Formula:

$$acc_c = \frac{truePos_c + trueNeg_c}{truePos_c + trueNeg_c + falsePos_c + falseNeg_c}, \forall c \in CompressAlgos \quad (1)$$

The acc_c metric captures the percentage of false positives and false negatives produced when c is utilized. When lossless techniques are applied those two metrics are equal to zero therefore we have accurate results as acc_c equals 1. However, when lossy compression algorithms are considered we expect a decrease in the accuracy as more false positives and false negatives events will be reported and thus the denominator in Eq. 1 will increase. In contrast, we expect better throughput when lossy techniques are applied as smaller-size data are transferred between the components. To balance the throughput with the results' accuracy, we introduce a utility score function as follows:

$$utility_c = throughput_c * w + acc_c * (1 - w), \forall c \in CompressAlgos \quad (2)$$

where $w \in [0, 1]$ is a weight given by the user based on where he wants to put more emphasis, *i.e.*, the application's throughput or the accuracy of the results. Furthermore, $throughput_c$ is normalized so that it is in the same range as acc_c.

The goal of our profiling algorithm is to identify the compression algorithm that maximizes Eq. 2. The algorithm runs in the Nimbus node as it requires information from all the topology's components. More specifically, our technique consists of the following steps:

1. Initially the profiling algorithm sends to the topology's spouts all the compression algorithms that need to be examined and a threshold on the number of mini-batches to emit for each compression algorithm.
2. The algorithm waits for the monitor reports (*i.e.*, described in Sect. 2.2) from the bolts that receive and process the data.
3. Upon receiving all reports, the profiling algorithm computes the utility scores of the different compression algorithms using Formula 2. Then it detects the compression algorithm that has the largest utility score (*i.e.*, this indicates that the compression algorithm balances better the trade-off between throughput and accuracy) and informs the spouts that they should use this compression technique from now on.

Algorithm 1. Trigger Algorithm

1: **Input:** $prevTan$: the previous tan that we have computed, $prevReport$: the previous utility score, $monitorReports$: the monitor reports that will be checked for a significant decrease in their utility scores, θ: the threshold used for determining when we have a significant decrease.

2: **Output:** $applyAlgorithm$: a Boolean variable that will determine if the profiling algorithm should be re-applied.

3: $applyAlgorithm \leftarrow true$

4: **for** $(report \in monitorReports)$ **do**

5:     $tan \leftarrow \frac{report.getUtility() - prevReport.getUtility()}{report.getTime() - prevReport.getTime()}$

6:     **if** $(tan > 0 \ || \ |\frac{tan - prevTan}{prevTan}| < \theta)$ **then**

7:         $applyAlgorithm \leftarrow false$

8:         $prevReport \leftarrow report$

9:         $prevTan \leftarrow tan$

10:         **return** $applyAlgorithm$

11: $prevTan \leftarrow tan$

12: $prevReport \leftarrow monitorReports.getLast()$

13: **return** $applyAlgorithm$

In order to take into account dynamic changes in the system's condition, we keep monitoring the utility score and if we observe that its value drops significantly we re-apply our profiling algorithm. The technique we used for determining when the profiling algorithm should be re-applied is described in Algorithm 1. Nimbus continues to receive monitor reports and computes their utility scores. When a certain number of reports have been gathered, we compare them with a previous report in terms of utility scores. More specifically, we compute the tan of the line that is drawn between the utility scores of the new and the previous report (*i.e.,* Line 5 in Algorithm 1). We use the tan metric because it provides an indication of how much the utility score has changed (decreased or increased) from the previous report [3]. If the computed tan is positive we have an increase in the utility score and thus we stop the search as there is no point to re-apply the profiling algorithm. However, if it is negative (*i.e.,* the utility score has decreased) we must examine whether the difference between the computed tan and the previous one (*i.e.,* $prevTan$) exceeds a user-determined threshold θ. More formally, we examine whether the following condition is true:

$$|\frac{tan - prevTan}{prevTan}| > \theta \tag{3}$$

If the condition is true for all the reports that Nimbus has received, then we re-apply the profiling algorithm. Essentially, the tan difference helps us identify whether the utility score has decreased from its previous value significantly (*i.e.,* based on the θ parameter).

The performance of the algorithm depends on the θ threshold and the number of monitor reports that we consider. Using a large threshold we expect fewer re-invocations of the profiling algorithm as it will be harder to satisfy the

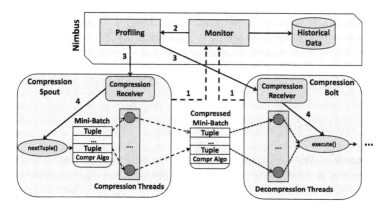

Fig. 4. Implementation details.

re-invocation condition (*i.e.*, Eq. 3). Furthermore, the number of reports that we use in Algorithm 1 also affects the re-invocations as when we use multiple reports it will be harder to satisfy the condition in all of them so we expect less re-invocations of the profiling algorithm. We evaluated how these two parameters affect the re-invocations in our experimental evaluation (*i.e.*, see Sect. 4). In general, we observed that we need at least three reports to be sure that we have a significant change in the utility score and thus re-applying the profiling technique is beneficial. In contrast, using only one report leads to multiple invocations of the profiling algorithm due to short-term fluctuations of the utility score and this can penalize the application's throughput as when the profiling algorithm is re-applied we have to examine again all the compression algorithms.

3.2   Parallel Data Compression/Decompression

In Fig. 4 we illustrate how the compression algorithms are applied on the mini-batches to be processed. The benefit of utilizing mini-batches is that they enable us to parallelize the compression/decompression procedure. We use multiple threads that run in parallel to perform the decompression whenever the processing component receives a mini-batch. The decompressed data are kept in a mini-batch which will be used for feeding the component with the input tuples. A similar procedure is followed when we compress the data after the output mini-batch is complete (*i.e.*, reached the required batch size) and needs to be emitted to downstream components. In this case the mini-batch is forwarded to multiple concurrently running threads for the compression.

The number of compression/decompression threads can be provided by the user. In most cases the number of threads will be fewer than the number of tuples in the mini-batch so we have to distribute the tuples that comprise it to the available threads. In order to balance the work among the threads we follow a round-robin approach for assigning the tuples to the compression/decompression threads. More formally, assuming that we have N threads, T tuples in the mini-batch and each tuple t in the mini-batch has an id $id_t \in [0, T - 1]$ then the thread that will compress tuple t is computed as: $thrId = id_t \% N$, where $thrId$ will be the id of the thread that will be responsible for compressing (or decompressing) tuple t. This simple technique balances the load between the threads and minimizes the compression/decompression overhead.

4   Implementation and Evaluation

Implementation. We have implemented our framework[1] as a module of Apache Storm and in Fig. 4 we illustrate the components we have added in order to support dynamic data compression. More specifically, we have added two extra components on Nimbus that are responsible for auto-tuning the compression algorithm that is used by the topology's processing components. The $Profiling$ component is responsible for invoking the profiling algorithm described in Sect. 3.1 and for adjusting the compression algorithm of the Storm components' (spouts or bolts). The second component (*i.e.*, $Monitor$ in Fig. 4) monitors the performance of all the topology's components. More specifically, $Monitor$ receives reports from the bolts' tasks whenever the threshold of processed mini-batches has been reached (*i.e.*, $batchThr$ parameter in Sect. 2.2), computes the utility score (*i.e.*, Eq. 2) and informs the $Profiling$ component about the new value.

In order to be able to exploit the auto-compression features we offer, users must extend two abstract classes. More specifically, the $CompressionSpout$ class must be extended by the users' spouts while the $CompressionBolt$ class must be extended by the users' bolts. Each instance of these classes uses a special thread for receiving the compression algorithm that should be applied. Furthermore, these classes create the compression/decompression threads (*i.e.*, see Sect. 3.2) that are used for minimizing the computation overhead. Users still have to provide the implementation of $nextTuple$ (*i.e.*, for spouts) and $execute$ (*i.e.*, for bolts) methods in order to be able to utilize their processing components in their topologies.

Evaluation Setup. We have evaluated our approach in our local 8 nodes cluster. Each node had attached 8 CPU processors and 16 GB RAM. All nodes were connected to the same LAN and their clocks were synchronized using the NTP protocol. We implemented our proposals on top of Storm 0.10.2 and used a dedicated Nimbus node to avoid overloading one of the nodes. We considered the following applications for examining the performance of our approach:

- **Traffic Monitoring Application:** This application receives as input live CCTV data from Dublin city and detects events by invoking a simple image similarity algorithm (supplied by LIRE framework [12]) against historical images depicting normal and abnormal traffic conditions. More specifically, for each incoming image we find the most similar historical image and based on the characterization of the latter we inform the traffic authorities.

---

[1] http://rtds.aueb.gr/index.php/software/.

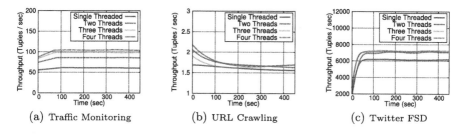

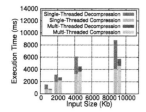

(a) Traffic Monitoring

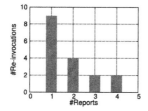

(b) URL Crawling

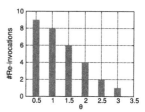

(c) Twitter FSD

Fig. 5. Parallel compression results.

Fig. 6. Impact of data size on compression/decompression time.

Fig. 7. Impact of reports on the number of profiling algorithm's invocations.

Fig. 8. Impact of θ on the number of profiling algorithm's invocations.

- **URL Crawling:** The application crawls web pages and detects keywords in them. More specifically, we crawl well-known sites (*e.g.*, https://news.google.ie/) and try to detect events like accidents in Dublin city.
- **Twitter First Story Detection (Twitter FSD)** [20]: This application retrieves data from the Twitter Streaming API and detects tweets that correspond to new events (*e.g.*, a traffic accident in Dublin city).

Our goal was to consider applications that process both image and text data. The difference between the two text processing applications is the size of the data. For the URL crawling application we have larger input data (*i.e.*, approximately 600 kB) therefore compression may be beneficial while for the Twitter application the tweets are usually small-sized (*i.e.*, less than 200 bytes) so compression may penalize the application's performance.

Performance of parallel compression/decompression. In the first set of experiments we illustrate the benefits of performing the parallel compression/decompression procedure. More specifically, we compare our multi-threaded compression technique varying the number of threads. For the traffic monitoring application we used *JPEG* compression with quality 0.1 while for the other two applications we used *Zip* compression (similar results were observed with the other compression algorithms but we do not display them due to lack of space). As can be observed in Figs. 5(a), (b) and (c) using more threads improves

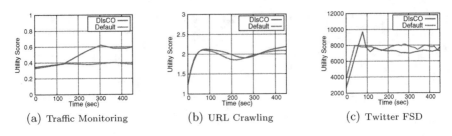

Fig. 9. Utility scores comparison.

throughput as long as we do not exceed the available CPU cores on the nodes. We argue that using at maximum four threads for the compression/decompression procedure is a valid choice when we have 8 core nodes in the cluster. Furthermore, we wanted to evaluate how the compression overhead (*i.e.*, in terms of execution time) is affected by the size of the data that we want to compress/decompress. We used synthetic test data for this experiment and we applied the *Zip* compression algorithm. As we illustrate in Fig. 6, our multi-threaded technique (using 4 compression/decompression threads) is able to keep the overhead low (*i.e.*, less than 6 s) even when we consider data larger than 8 MB.

Profiling re-invocation. In the second set of experiments (*i.e.*, Figs. 7 and 8) we perform a sensitivity analysis on the two parameters that affect the performance of our proposed re-triggering mechanism (*i.e.*, Algorithm 1 in Sect. 3.1). We considered as input the utility scores of the Twitter FSD application when no compression algorithm is applied (see the *Default* approach in Fig. 9(c)) and we examined how the number of monitor reports and the θ parameter affect the number of times that the profiling algorithm will be re-applied.

As we illustrate in Figs. 7 and 8 both parameters influence the number of times we re-invoke the profiling algorithm with the one that affects the most being the number of monitor reports to consider for the evaluation. In Fig. 7 we set θ to 0.5 while in Fig. 8 we used 2 reports. As it can be observed in Fig. 7, if we use more than 4 reports the number of re-invocations is minimized. In contrast, when we use only one monitor report for the comparison, we end up invoking constantly the profiling algorithm. For the rest of the experiments we set θ to 0.5 and use 3 previous reports.

Dynamic compression evaluation. In the last set of experiments we evaluated the applicability of our framework to detect the correct compression algorithm that should be utilized. In Figs. 9(a), (b) and (c) we illustrate the utility score when our framework is applied against the default approach (*i.e.*, *Default* in the Figures) that does not apply any compression algorithm. The weight of the utility score was set to 0.5. As it can be observed, *DIsCO* is able to maximize the utility score in all applications. For example, in case of the traffic monitoring application our framework exploits *JPEG* compression and it is able to guarantee that the impact on the results' accuracy will be minimal. *DIsCO* decides to compress the images using the *JPEG* compression algorithm with quality 0.3. So we have less than 200 false positives and negative events as it can be observed in Fig. 2 in Sect. 1.

For the other two applications the utility score depends solely on the throughput metric as we considered only lossless compression techniques (*i.e.*, for this reason the utility score in Figs. 9(b) and (c) is not scaled between 0 and 1). The URL crawling application exploits the *Snappy* compression algorithm which is able to achieve better throughput than the *Default* approach. In contrast, in the Twitter FSD application, *DIsCO* detects that it is not beneficial to use a compression algorithm as the improvements in the communication cost are negligible compared to the time required for compressing/decompressing the tweets. However, because *DIsCO* samples all the possible compression algorithms, in this case the *Default* approach has better throughput.

5   Related Work

In recent years we have observed a plethora of stream processing frameworks including Spark [21] and Flink [4]. Despite their popularity, there has been little work in exploiting data compression. One recent proposal comes from the Spark community with the implementation of a novel distributed filesystem called Succint [1] which keeps the data in a compressed form using Arrays of Suffixes (AoS) and enables the processing of the data in this form. However, the wide adoption of such system requires time as the majority of the data are stored in either HDFS or distributed databases like MongoDB or Cassandra. So an approach like ours that performs on-the-fly compression on the data streams is beneficial to the system's performance.

Previous work exploiting compression for improving the energy efficiency in Hadoop clusters was done in [5]. Our work differs in, that, we examine the problem in a distributed stream processing setting trying to maximize the observed system throughput. Authors in [8] propose the use of an unsupervised learning technique for detecting patterns in the incoming data flow and minimize the amount of emitted tuples by not transmitting tuples that will not contribute on the query's results. In our approach we decided to avoid such load shedding techniques to minimize the information loss. Novel frameworks like [10,18] have been proposed for performing analysis on streaming data using a compressed representation of the input dataset. Authors in [18] propose the use of dictionaries for keeping the incoming data and process them in this compressed form while in [10] the authors describe the use of compressed buffer trees (CBTs) for keeping the in-memory data. We could exploit such techniques in *DIsCO* as users can easily plugin their custom compression algorithms.

6   Conclusions

In this paper we present *DIsCO*, a novel auto-tuning framework on top of the Apache Storm whose goal is to balance the trade-off between application's throughput and results' accuracy by dynamically deciding whether data compression would be useful in the streaming applications and which compression algorithm would be the most appropriate. Our approach is able to efficiently adjust the compression algorithm to be utilized during the application's execution, and by exploiting the use of mini-batches it can further maximize the system's throughput and minimize the compression/decompression overhead. In our experimental evaluation on our local cluster using well-known stream processing applications, we demonstrate the benefits of our approach and illustrate a clear improvement on the applications' performance.

Acknowledgment. This research has been financed by the European Union through the FP7 ERC IDEAS 308019 NGHCS project and the Horizon2020 688380 VaVeL project.

References

1. Agarwal, R., Khandelwal, A., Stoica, I.: Succinct: enabling queries on compressed data. In: NSDI, Oakland, CA, pp. 337–350 (2015)
2. Bicer, T., Yin, J., Chiu, D., Agrawal, G., Schuchardt, K.: Integrating online compression to accelerate large-scale data analytics applications. In: IPDPS, Cambridge, MA, USA, pp. 1205–1216 (2013)
3. Boutsis, I., Kalogeraki, V.: Location privacy for crowdsourcing applications. In: UbiComp, Heidelberg, Germany, pp. 694–705 (2016)
4. Carbone, P., Ewen, S., Haridi, S., Katsifodimos, A., Markl, V., Tzoumas, K.: Apache flink: stream and batch processing in a single engine. Data Engineering, p. 28 (2015)
5. Chen, Y., Ganapathi, A., Katz, R.H.: To compress or not to compress-compute vs. io tradeoffs for mapreduce energy efficiency. In: ACM SIGCOMM Workshop on Green Networking, New Delhi, India, pp. 23–28 (2010)
6. Chintapalli, S., Dagit, D., Evans, B., Farivar, R., Graves, T., Holderbaugh, M., Liu, Z., Nusbaum, K., Patil, K., Peng, B.J., et al.: Benchmarking streaming computation engines: storm, flink and spark streaming. In: Parallel and Distributed Processing Symposium Workshops, Chicago, IL, USA, pp. 1789–1792 (2016)
7. Das, T., Zhong, Y., Stoica, I., Shenker, S.: Adaptive stream processing using dynamic batch sizing. In: SoCC, Seattle, WA, USA, pp. 1–13 (2014)
8. Eberle, J., Wijaya, T.K., Aberer, K.: Online unsupervised state recognition in sensor data. In: PerCom, St. Louis, MO, USA, pp. 29–36 (2015)
9. Gedik, B., Schneider, S., Hirzel, M., Wu, K.L.: Elastic scaling for data stream processing. IEEE Trans. Parallel Distrib. Syst. **25**(6), 1447–1463 (2014)
10. Hu, L., Schwan, K., Amur, H., Chen, X.: Elf: efficient lightweight fast stream processing at scale. In: Usenix ATC, Philadelphia, PA, USA, pp. 25–36 (2014)
11. Liu, M., Ray, M., Zhang, D., Rundensteiner, E.A., Dougherty, D.J., Gupta, C., Wang, S., Ari, I.: Realtime healthcare services via nested complex event processing technology. EDBT, Berlin, Germany, pp. 622–625 (2012)
12. Lux, M., Chatzichristofis, S.A.: LIRe: lucene image retrieval: an extensible Java CBIR library. In: ACM International Conference on Multimedia, Vancouver, British Columbia, Canada, pp. 1085–1088 (2008)
13. LZ4. https://github.com/jpountz/lz4-java

14. Nathan Marz's Storm. https://github.com/nathanmarz/storm
15. Snappy. https://github.com/xerial/snappy-java
16. Tatbul, N., Çetintemel, U., Zdonik, S.: Staying fit: efficient load shedding techniques for distributed stream processing. In: VLDB, pp. 159–170 (2007)
17. Venkataraman, S., Yang, Z., Franklin, M., Recht, B., Stoica, I.: Ernest: efficient performance prediction for large-scale advanced analytics. In: NSDI, Santa Clara, CA, USA, pp. 363–378 (2016)
18. Yang, F., Tschetter, E., Léauté, X., Ray, N., Merlino, G., Ganguli, D.: Druid: a real-time analytical data store. In: SIGMOD, Snowbird, UT, USA, pp. 157–168 (2014)
19. Zacheilas, N., Kalogeraki, V., Zygouras, N., Panagiotou, N., Gunopulos, D.: Elastic Complex Event Processing exploiting Prediction. Big Data, Santa Clara, CA, USA, pp. 213–222 (2015)
20. Zacheilas, N., Zygouras, N., Panagiotou, N., Kalogeraki, V., Gunopulos, D.: Dynamic load balancing techniques for distributed complex event processing systems. In: Jelasity, M., Kalyvianaki, E. (eds.) DAIS 2016. LNCS, vol. 9687, pp. 174–188. Springer, Cham (2016). doi:10.1007/978-3-319-39577-7_14
21. Zaharia, M., Das, T., Li, H., Shenker, S., Stoica, I.: Discretized Streams: Fault Tolerant Streaming Computation at Scale, pp. 423–438. SOSP, Farmington, PA, USA (2013)
22. Zip. https://docs.oracle.com/javase/7/docs/api/java/util/zip/package-summary.html

Distributed Random Process for a Large-Scale Peer-to-Peer Lottery

Stéphane Grumbach and Robert Riemann[(✉)]

Inria, Lyon, France
{stephane.grumbach,robert.riemann}@inria.fr

Abstract. Most online lotteries today fail to ensure the verifiability of the random process and rely on a trusted third party. This issue has received little attention since the emergence of distributed protocols like Bitcoin that demonstrated the potential of protocols with no trusted third party. We argue that the security requirements of online lotteries are similar to those of online voting, and propose a novel distributed online lottery protocol that applies techniques developed for voting applications to an existing lottery protocol. As a result, the protocol is scalable, provides efficient verification of the random process and does not rely on a trusted third party nor on assumptions of bounded computational resources. An early prototype confirms the feasibility of our approach.

Keywords: Distributed aggregation · Online lottery · DHT · Trust · Scalability

1 Introduction

Lottery is a multi-billion dollar industry [1]. In general, players buy lottery tickets from an authority. Using a random process, e.g. the drawing of lots, the winning tickets are determined and the corresponding ticket owners receive a reward.

In some lotteries, the reward may be considerable, and so is the incentive to cheat. The potential of fraud gained attention due to the *Hot Lotto* fraud scandal. In 2015, the former security director of the Multi-State Lottery Association in the US was convicted of rigging a 14.3 million USD drawing by the unauthorised deployment of a self-destructing malware manipulating the random process [2].

In order to ensure fair play and ultimately the trust of players, lotteries are subject to strict legal regulations and employ a technical procedure, the *lottery protocol*, to prevent fraud and convince players of the correctness. Ideally, players should not be required to trust the authority. Verifiable lottery protocols provide therefore evidence of the correctness of the random process.

In a simple paper-based lottery protocol, tickets are randomly drawn under public supervision of all players from an urn with all sold tickets to determine the winners. Afterwards, all tickets left over in the urn are also drawn to confirm their

L.Y. Chen and H.P. Reiser (Eds.): DAIS 2017, LNCS 10320, pp. 34–48, 2017.
DOI: 10.1007/978-3-319-59665-5_3

presence and convince the losers of the correctness. Without public supervision, the random process can be repeated until by chance a predefined result occurred. Further, the process can be replaced entirely by a deterministic process.

In practice, the public supervision limits the number of lottery players and is further very inconvenient, because players are required to respect the time and locality of the drawing procedure. With the advent of public broadcasting channels, first newspapers, then radio and television broadcasting, protocols were employed that replaced the public supervision by a public announcement. Only few players and notaries verify here the correctness of the random process. In consequence, the majority of non-present players are required to trust the few present individuals for the sake of scalability. With the increasing availability of phones and later the internet, protocols have been adapted to allow also the remote purchase of lottery tickets, e.g. from home or a retail store.

The technical evolution lead to a gradual change of how people play lottery, but in many cases, the drawing procedure has not been adapted and resembles more a legacy that prevails for nostalgic reasons than to provide security. In the simple paper-based lottery protocol, the chain of custody establishes trust. All operations may be inspected by eye-sight.

This technique cannot be directly adapted for an online lottery. Thus, most verifiable online lottery protocols [3–5] rely on a concept based on two elements. All players can actively contribute to the random process. Nobody can compute the random process result or its estimation as long as it is possible to contribute or buy new tickets. The latter is required to prevent educated contributions to circumvent the uniform distribution of the random process. It is the lottery protocol that must ensure the order in time of the contribution and the actual determination of winners.

A protocol consisting of equipotent players contributing each to the randomness of the publicly verifiable random process is promising for its similarity with the simple paper-based lottery protocol. Again, all players participate in the execution and supervision of the random process. The feasibility to construct such protocols with no trusted third parties has been demonstrated by the crypto-currency Bitcoin [6] that is a distributed protocol for remote financial transactions, while previously online banking based on trusted financial authorities, the bank institutes and central banks, has been without alternative [7]. Lottery protocols based on Bitcoin have been already considered [8], c.f. Sect. 2.

Although different, the security requirements of lotteries share common concerns with those of voting systems [9]. Both lottery and voting protocols have to assure trust in an environment of mutual distrust among players, respectively voters, and the potentially biased authorities. The literature on voting protocols and online voting protocols is extensive and comprises flexible protocols that may be adapted to different voting systems beyond the general case of majority voting. Of particular interest for a lottery are online voting protocols that allow for a random choice. Already the paper-based voting common for general elections provides a solution to improve the scalability of the simple paper-based lottery protocol: the introduction of multiple offices run in parallel. We focus on online voting protocols that do not rely on trusted parties and aim to provide security properties that we adopt for lottery applications as follows:

Correctness of the random process. All numbers are equally likely to win. Nobody can predict the random process better than guessing.

Verifiability of the random process. Players can be convinced that the random process has not been manipulated.

Privacy of the player. Players do not learn the identity of other players to prevent blackmailing or begging.

Eligibility of the ticket. Tickets cannot be forged. Especially, it is impossible to create a winning ticket after the outcome of the random process is known.

Confidentiality of the number. Numbers are confidential to ensure fairness. Tickets of other players cannot be copied to reduce their potential reward.

Completeness of the reward. Players can verify the number of sold tickets that may determine the reward.

Our contribution is a novel protocol for verifiable large-scale online lotteries with no trusted authority to carry out the random process, for which we use concepts originating from online voting.

The paper is organized as follows. In the next section, we review related work addressing both lottery and voting protocols. Our protocol is based on an existing online lottery protocol and the distributed hash table Kademlia that are presented in Sect. 3. Then, we introduce our protocol in Sect. 4 and discuss its properties in Sect. 5.

2   Related Work

Different protocols have been proposed that allow players to contribute to the publicly verifiable random process and take measures to prevent early estimations of the result while it is still possible to contribute.

A trivial solution in the context of secure parameters for cryptography is recalled in [10]. In a first round, all players choose secretly a number and publish on a public broadcasting channel a commitment on their number, e.g. using a hash. In a second round, all secret numbers are revealed and verified using the commitment. Finally, all values are concatenated using the XOR operation to form the result. The protocol owes its correctness due to the clear separation in two rounds of player's contributions. However, the authors stress that the protocol is neither robust nor scalable. A termination is not possible if one player does not reveal its secret number and for the verification, all players have to run as many XOR operations and send as many messages as there are players.

Subsequently, a random process protocol with only one round is proposed [10]. A delay between player contribution and winner identification by the authority is imposed, so that estimations would be available only after contributions are no longer allowed. Players or any other third party can engage before a deadline in the collection of arbitrary data, e.g. using social networks like Twitter, to generate a seed, an essentially random bit string. Right after the deadline, the authority publishes a commitment on an additional, secretly chosen seed. Both seeds provide the input for a *proof of work*. A proof of work is computationally expensive to generate and thus time-consuming. A delay is inevitable. However, due to its asymmetry, the proof allows for efficient verification. Once the proof is found, the winners are derived from it. The additional seed prevents dishonest players to predict the results for different potential last-minute contributions. One has to assume that the last honest contribution is made sufficiently late to prevent the same attack from the authority.

Chow's online lottery protocol [5] published prior to [10] relies on a technique called *delaying function* [3] that is similar to a proof of work, but is not asymmetric and does not provide efficient verification. The authority commits here on the concatenation of the players' commitments on their secretly chosen number and derives then the winners. Players can claim the reward by publishing the input data of their commitment. Similar to [10], a late honest player commitment is assumed to prevent a prediction by the authority. Then, all security measures from the introduction are provided. The protocol requires players to process the commitment of all other players and recompute the delaying function in order to verify the random process, which is impractical for large-scale lotteries.

Solutions for a scalable probabilistic verification of online lotteries [11] or online voting [12] have been presented based on a concatenation/aggregation over a tree structure. In order to verify the result at the root of the tree, players or voters can repeat the computation of intermediate results for a predefined or random subset of all tree nodes. With increasing number of verified nodes, the probability of a manipulated result at the root node diminishes.

Other online lottery protocols introduce mutually distrusting, non-colluding authorities to allow for a *separation of powers*. In [13], a distinct auditor ensures secrecy and immutability of the player's tickets and prevents the lottery authority from adding illegitimately tickets. For this, blind signatures and public-key encryption are employed. The protocol does not cover the random process and its verification. Authorities are assumed not to collude.

In [14], the secrecy of online lottery and voting protocols is addressed at the same time. A mechanism based on homomorphic encryption, distributed key generation and threshold decryption is proposed. A set of mutually distrusting authorities have to cooperate to decrypt the result of the random process or the voting. A colluding set of dishonest authorities below the threshold cannot reveal prematurely the result, i.e. to add a winning ticket in the lottery case. Players or voters are entitled to trust that the set of dishonest, colluding authorities does not meet the threshold. Ideally, the power to decrypt would be shared among all players or voters. Practically, this is often not feasible due to scalability issues.

The *Scalable and Secure Aggregation* (SPP) online voting protocol [15] builds also on distributed decryption and employs a tree overlay network to improve the scalability. A small set of authorities is randomly chosen among all voters. If too many of those chosen voters are absent after the aggregation, the decryption threshold cannot be reached and, consequently, a protocol termination is impossible.

The potential of the Bitcoin blockchain [6] for a distributed random process has been examined. However, it has been shown that the manipulation of presumably random bits is realistic even with limited computational capacity and financial resources [8]. An integration of the proof of work from [10] and an alternative crypto-currency Ethereum [16] has been proposed[1] with no practical solution yet for a verification due to the limitation imposed by the blockchain.

3   Preliminaries

The starting point for the proposed protocol is the centralised online lottery protocol of [5], recalled hereafter with an alternative verification based on hash trees [11]. For the proposed lottery protocol, we choose to distribute the random process to all players. The overlay network comprising all players is provided by the distributed hash table (DHT) Kademlia [17] that is described in Sect. 3.2. The integration of these building blocks is shown in Sect. 4.

3.1   Centralised Online Lottery Protocol

The following presentation of Chow's protocol [5,11] is reduced to aspects required for our proposition. We use the following notation:

A	authority (Dealer in [5])
P_i	player, i-th out of n
n_i	number in the set $\mathbb{L}$ chosen by player P_i
r_i	random bit string of given length chosen by player P_i
$\eta(\cdot)$	cryptographic hash function, e.g. SHA-3
$\eta_0(\cdot)$	cryptographic hash function mapping any r_i to $\mathbb{L}$
$\sigma_A(\cdot)$	authority's signature scheme using key-pair (pk_A, sk_A)

Chow's protocol implements a lottery in which every player P_i has to choose a number $n_i \in \mathbb{L}$ and send a commitment on it to the authority A. A aggregates all commitments to a value h. That means, every P_i contributes to h. The aggregate h is used as an input parameter for a *delaying function* (DF) preventing A from early result estimations. The outcome of DF is used to compute the winning number n_R with a *verifiable random function* and the secret key of A. Players do not have the secret key required to compute n_R, but can verify n_R using the public key of A.

During the *ticket purchase* phase, P_i acquires from A a personal sequence number s_i. P_i has to choose its number n_i and a random bit string r_i to compute its commitment ticket$_i$ with bit string concatenation $||$ and XOR operation $\veebar$. P_i sends ticket$_i$ to A and receives in return the signature $\sigma_A(\text{ticket}_i)$ as a receipt.

$$\text{ticket}_i = s_i||(n_i \veebar \eta_0(r_i))||\eta(n_i||s_i||r_i)$$

[1] http://www.quanta.im, https://kiboplatform.net (accessed 02/02/2017).

The DF cannot be evaluated before h depending on all commitments is given, which is ideally only after the purchase phase. In [5], the DF input parameter h is recursively computed from all n commitments with $h = \eta(\text{chain}_n)$ and $\text{chain}_i = \eta(\text{chain}_{i-1}\|\text{ticket}_i)$ with an empty initial chain chain_0. An alternative introduced in [11] consists of a computation of h using a T-ary Merkle tree [18] with ticket_i assigned to the leaf tree nodes. In both cases, all ticket_i are published to allow the verification of h by the players requiring memory and computational resources of respectively $\mathcal{O}(n)$ and $\mathcal{O}(\log_T(n))$.

Once the authority has published the verifiable winning number n_R, the *reward claiming* phase begins in which players P_i with $n_i = n_R$ provide their sequence number s_i and their secret random value r_i to A via a secure channel. Upon verification of the commitment ticket_i by A, the reward is granted. P_j with $n_j \neq n_R$ may verify that their commitment ticket_j has been used to compute h and are assumed to have trust in the infeasibility of A to compute DF more than once between the latest honest ticket contribution and the publication of n_R.

3.2   Distributed Hash Table Kademlia

The distributed hash table (DHT) Kademlia [17] provides efficient discovery of lottery players and routing which is a precondition for the aggregation protocol in Sect. 4.1. Therefore, a binary overlay network is established in which each player P_i is assigned to a leaf node x_i, that is a bit string of size B. The notation is as follows:

x	a Kademlia leaf node ID (KID) of size B
B	size of a KID in bits, e.g. 160
x_i	KID of player P_i
d	node depth, i.e. number of edges from the node to the tree root
$\widehat{\mathbb{S}}(x,d)$	subtree whose root is at depth d which contains leaf node x
$\mathbb{S}(x,d)$	*sibling subtree* of which the root is the sibling of the root of $\widehat{\mathbb{S}}(x,d)$
k	maximum number of contacts per Kademlia subtree

The leaf node identifiers $x \in \{0,1\}^B$ (B bits) span the Kademlia binary tree of height B and are denoted KID. Each player P_i joins the Kademlia overlay network using its KID defined as $x_i = \eta(t_i)$ with an authorization token t_i and the hashing function $\eta(\cdot)$. The value t_i is generated as part of the ticket purchase. B is chosen sufficiently large, so that hash collisions leading to identical KIDs for distinct players are very unlikely. Consequently, the occupation of the binary tree is very sparse.

A node in the tree is identified by its depth $d \in \{0,\ldots,B\}$ and any of its descendant leaf nodes with KID x. A *subtree* $\widehat{\mathbb{S}}(x,d)$ is identified by the depth d of its root node and any of its leaf nodes x. We overload the subtree notation to designate as well the set of players assigned to leaves of the corresponding

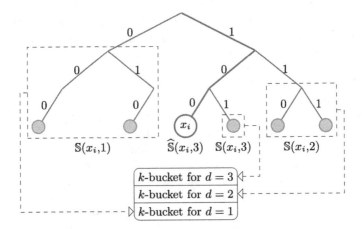

Fig. 1. Example of Kademlia k-buckets for KID $x_i = 100$ assuming $B = 3$. The sparse tree is partitioned into subtrees $\mathbb{S}(x_i, d)$ with their root node depth d. The k-buckets for each d contain at most k players $P_j \in \mathbb{S}(x_i, d)$.

subtree. Further, we introduce $\mathbb{S}(x, d)$ for the sibling subtree of $\widehat{\mathbb{S}}(x, d)$, so that $\widehat{\mathbb{S}}(x, d) = \widehat{\mathbb{S}}(x, d+1) \cup \mathbb{S}(x, d+1)$. The entire tree is denoted $\widehat{\mathbb{S}}(x, 0)$. We observe that $\forall d : P_i \in \widehat{\mathbb{S}}(x_i, d)$ and $\forall d : P_i \notin \mathbb{S}(x_i, d)$.

Kademlia defines the distance $d(x_i, x_j)$ between two KIDs as their bit-wise XOR interpreted as an integer. In general, a player P_i with KID x_i stores information on players with x_j that are close to x_i, i.e. for small $d(x_i, x_j)$. For this purpose, P_i disposes of a set denoted k-bucket of at most k players $P_j \in \mathbb{S}(x_i, d_j)$ for some $d_j > 0$.[2] See Fig. 1 for an example. The size of subtrees decreases exponentially for growing depth d. Hence, the density of known players of corresponding k-buckets grows exponentially.

Kademlia ensures that the routing table, that is the set of all k-buckets, is populated by player lookup requests for random KIDs to the closest already known players. Requests are responded with a set of closest, known players from the routing table. One lookup might require multiple, consecutive request-response cycles. Further, Kademlia provides requests to lookup and store values. All operations scale with $\mathcal{O}(\log n)$ [19]. Kademlia is used by many BitTorrent clients and as such well tested.

4   Distributed Lottery

We introduce now the lottery protocol. It is run by an authority that handles the ticket purchase and carries out the distribution of the reward upon winner verification, but not the random process itself. The random process is distributed

---

[2] Note that originally [17] the common prefix length b is used to index k-buckets/sibling subtrees while we use the depth $d = b + 1$ of the root of the subtree.

to all players using the protocol described below. The description of the lottery protocol is given in Sect. 4.2.

4.1 Distributed Aggregation Protocol

We present a distributed aggregation protocol based on Kademlia. It relies on ADVOKAT [20], whose aggregation algebra, distributed aggregation algorithm, and measures to increase its Byzantine fault tolerance are briefly recalled.

Aggregation Algebra. *Aggregates* are values to be aggregated, whether *initial aggregates*, constituting inputs from players, or *intermediate aggregates* obtained during the computation. The aggregation operation, $\oplus$, combines two *child aggregates* to a *parent aggregate* in $\mathbb{A}$, the set of aggregates. We assume $\oplus$ to be commutative. For the lottery, $\oplus$ maps pairwise bit strings provided by all players to one final bit string used to determine the winners. The algebra is sufficiently flexible to cover a broad range of aggregation-based applications and has been devised initially for distributed online voting [20].

Aggregates are manipulated through *aggregate containers*, i.e. a data structure that contains next to the aggregate itself the context of the ongoing computation. The aggregate container of àn aggregate a associates a to a Kademlia subtree $\widehat{\mathbb{S}}(x, d)$ and ensures integrity and verifiability of the aggregation. It has the following attributes:

h	hash $\eta(\cdot)$ of the entire aggregate container, but h
a	aggregate, $a = a_1 \oplus a_2$
c	counter of initial aggregates in a, $c = c_1 + c_2$
c_1, c_2	counter of initial aggregates of child aggregates
h_1, h_2	container hashes of child aggregates
$\widehat{\mathbb{S}}(x, d)$	identifier of subtree whose initial aggregates are aggregated in a

Similar to the aggregation of aggregates, one or two aggregate containers of a_1, a_2 can be aggregated to a parent aggregate container. To inherit the commutativity of the aggregation of aggregates $\oplus$, (h_1, c_1) and (h_2, c_2) must be sorted in e.g. ascending order of the child hashes h_1 and h_2.

Distributed Aggregation Algorithm. Using the aggregation operator $\oplus$, every player P_i computes the intermediate aggregate for all the parent nodes from its corresponding leaf node x_i up to the root node of the Kademlia overlay tree. The aggregates used to compute any intermediate aggregate of a given subtree $\widehat{\mathbb{S}}(x_i, d)$ are given by its child nodes' aggregates of $\widehat{\mathbb{S}}(x_i, d+1)$ and $\mathbb{S}(x_i, d+1)$. Hence, aggregates have to be exchanged between players of the sibling subtrees and Kademlia's k-buckets provide the required contact information.

The aggregation is carried out in B epochs, one tree level at a time. Epochs are loosely synchronized, because players may have to wait for intermediate aggregates to be computed in order to continue. First, every player P_i computes a container for its initial aggregate a_i. The container is assigned to represent the subtree $\widehat{\mathbb{S}}(x_i, B)$ with only P_i. In each epoch for $d = B, \ldots, 1$, every player P_i requests from a random $P_j \in \mathbb{S}(x_i, d)$ the aggregate container of subtree $\mathbb{S}(x_i, d)$. With the received container of $\mathbb{S}(x_i, d)$ and the previously obtained of $\widehat{\mathbb{S}}(x_i, d)$, player P_i computes the parent aggregate container, that is then assigned to the parent subtree $\widehat{\mathbb{S}}(x_i, d-1)$. If $\mathbb{S}(x, d) = \emptyset$ for any d, the container of $\widehat{\mathbb{S}}(x, d-1)$ is computed only with the aggregate container of $\widehat{\mathbb{S}}(x, d)$ from the previous epoch.

After B consecutive epochs, player P_i has computed the root aggregate a_R of the entire tree $\widehat{\mathbb{S}}(x_i, 0)$ that contains the initial aggregates of all players. If all players are honest, the root aggregate is complete and correct. Due to the commutativity of the container computation, all players find the same hash h_R for the container of the root aggregate a_R. An individual verification is implicitly given, because every player computes a_R starting with its a_i.

Byzantine Fault-Tolerance. The distributed aggregation is very vulnerable to aggregate corruptions leading to erroneous root aggregates containers. We present intermediate results to safeguard the aggregation. Please refer to [20] for a more in-depth discussion. For the attack model, we assume a minority of dishonest (Byzantine) players controlled by one adversary that aims to interrupt the aggregation, and manipulate root aggregates. Dishonest players can behave arbitrarily. Like in Kademlia, time-outs are used to counter unresponsive players.

To prevent Sybil attacks, it must be ensured that a player (a) cannot choose on its own discretion its tree position given by the leaf node x_i but (b) can proof its attribution to x_i [21]. Every player P_i generates a key pair (pk_i, sk_i) which must be signed by A. Hence, P_i sends pk_i to A during the ticket purchase and receives the signature of A to be used as the authorization token $t_i = \sigma_A(pk_i)$. The KID $x_i = \eta(t_i)$ is derived from t_i and is neither chosen unilaterally by A nor by P_i. Eventually, players provide for every message m exchanged among players the signature of the sender $\sigma_i(m)$, its public key pk_i to verify $\sigma_i(m)$, and the authorization token t_i to verify pk_i.

Moreover, a dishonest authority shall be prevented to add new players after the aggregation has started and dishonest players to delay their contributions after predefined, global deadlines. In order to suppress both, signatures of those players are considered invalid, who are at the start of the aggregation not in the corresponding k-bucket even though the bucket contains less than k players and should be exhaustive.

Further, player signatures are employed to detect deviations from the protocol. For every computed aggregate container of $\widehat{\mathbb{S}}(x_i, d)$ with hash h and counter c, player P_i produces an aggregate container signature $\sigma_i(h, d, c)$. Other players can verify the signature using pk_i and verify using $x_i = \eta(t_i)$ that $P_i \in \widehat{\mathbb{S}}(x_i, d)$. Hence, pk_i and t_i must be provided along every signature $\sigma_i(h, d, c)$.

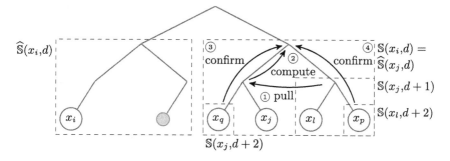

Fig. 2. P_j with x_j produces a confirmed aggregate container of $\mathbb{S}(x_i, b)$. This scheme applies to all tree levels with possibly large subtrees to request from. If the subtrees $\mathbb{S}(x_j, d+2), \mathbb{S}(x_l, d+2)$ are empty, the depth is further increased until a non-empty subtree may be found.

The impact of dishonest players is limited by redundant requests to confirm a computed so-called *candidate container* using signatures of other players on the same container hash as depicted in Fig. 2. Next to the proper signature (②) on h and h_1, a signature on h from a player in each child subtree (③ and ④) and one on h_2 (①) must be provided for a confirmation if the respective subtree is non-empty which can be determined using Kademlia lookup requests. The number of distinct signatures on h, here 3, is a security parameter denoted l.

Only the *confirmed container* including the signatures is used to respond to requests from players in the sibling subtree. If a confirmation is not possible, e.g. due to non-cooperating dishonest players, the confirmed child containers are provided instead, so that the receiver can compute the aggregation on its own.

If confirmation requests reveal diverging containers, a majority vote using the number of distinct signatures for every container hash is used. If another container than the previously computed is selected and if h_2 differs, then the request for the sibling aggregate container (①) is repeated, otherwise, the previous epoch is repeated allowing for a recursive correction.

The majority vote confirms for subtrees with many players with great probability the aggregate container of the honest players. The attribution of KIDs x_i to players P_i is random, so that a global minority of dishonest players is uniformly distributed over all subtrees and a honest majority can be assumed for most local subtrees.

Though, dishonest players may have a local majority in subtrees with only few players. Here, an analysis of the signatures of confirmed containers allows honest players to detect dishonest behaviour in the following cases with certainty. Given two signatures $\sigma_i(h, d, c)$ and $\sigma_i(h', d, c)$ from the same player P_i with different hashes $h \neq h'$, P_i deviated from the protocol with certainty if $c \leq l$. Either P_i signed two distinct initial aggregate containers or accepted a non-confirmed container. For $c > l$, there is a non-zero probability that P_i is honest, but may have been tricked. A manipulation may not be detected or only later during the recursive correction. The number of distinct signatures l can be increased to detect manipulations with certainty for higher c, and may depend on the player configuration in the respective subtree.

At last, the root aggregate container a_R shall be confirmed more often, i.e. more signatures on its hash h are gathered from different players, to increase the confidence that it has been adopted by the majority of honest players.

4.2　Lottery Protocol

The proposed protocol allows for a lottery with playing mode CL or LO [13]:

Classic Lottery (CL)
Rewards are distributed with respect to a randomly ordered list of all players.
Lotto (LO)
Rewards are distributed based on the secret, prior choice of each player.

The protocol has six phases of which *ticket purchase*, *reward claiming* and *winner verification* follow closely Chow's protocol [5]. Its model provides for an authority A, a tracker and players P_i. For CL, $\eta_0(\cdot)$ is identical to $\eta(\cdot)$, so that the root aggregate a_R of the distributed aggregation is in the domain of the KIDs x.

Setup

1. A generates a key-pair (pk_A, sk_A) and chooses a random bit string r_A.
2. A publishes the ticket purchase deadline, pk_A, $\eta(\cdot)$, $\eta_0(\cdot)$ and $\eta(\eta(r_A))$. Further, A specifies the duration of the aggregation epoch for each tree level.

Ticket Purchase

1. P_i picks a random string r_i, and for CL its number n_i. It generates (pk_i, sk_i).
2. P_i sends pk_i to the authority and obtains in return a sequence number s_i and its authorization token $t_i = \sigma_A(pk_i)$.
3. P_i computes $x_i = \eta(t_i)$ and connects to the Kademlia DHT using an already connected contact provided by the authority or a separate tracker.
4. P_i prepares its initial aggregate $a_i = \eta(\text{ticket}_i)$. For CL, $\text{ticket}_i = s_i \| r_i$ and for LO, $\text{ticket}_i = s_i \| (n_i \overset{\vee}{} \eta_0(r_i)) \| \eta(n_i \| s_i \| r_i)$, c.f. Sect. 3.1.

Distributed Random Process

1. After the ticket purchase deadline, A publishes the number of sold tickets n.
2. All P_i compute jointly the root aggregate a_R. The $\oplus$-operation is given by $a_i \oplus a_j = \eta(a_{ij})$ with $a_{ij} = a_i \| a_j$, if $a_i < a_j$, otherwise $a_{ij} = a_j \| a_i$. It is a commutative variant of the binary Merkle tree scheme proposed in [11].
3. Proofs of protocol deviation in form of pairs of signatures are sent to A that can reveal the corresponding players and revoke their right to claim a reward.

Winner Identification

1. A requests the root aggregate of multiple random P_i until a considerably large majority of the sample confirmed one a_R.

2. A publishes a_R, r_A and the winning number $n_w = \eta_0(a_R) \veebar \eta_0(r_A)$.
3. For CL, A computes all $x_i = \eta(t_i)$, orders all P_i by their Kademlia XOR distance $d(n_w, x_i) = n_w \veebar x_i$ and players on a par by $n_w \veebar s_i$, and publishes as many ordered x_i as there are rewards. For LO, winners P_i have $n_i = n_w$.

Reward Claiming

1. The winner P_i sends all its confirmed aggregate containers to A to proof their participation. For LO, P_i must also provide its ticket$_i$ and (s_i, r_i).
2. Proofs are published for verification by other players.

Winner Verification

1. $\eta(\eta(r_A))$ is computed for comparison with the previously published value and n_w is verified.
2. Players verify that winner P_i participated in the aggregation by comparing its published containers with their computed containers.
3. For CL, player verify the order of the published winners and compare it to their own positioning. For LO, ticket$_i$ is reproduced for the given (s_i, r_i) and its hash must equal a_i found in the published confirmed aggregate containers.
4. If the rewards depend on the number of sold tickets n, n is compared to the counter c of the root aggregate container.

5 Evaluation

We analyse the protocol with respect to the security properties introduced in Sect. 1 under the adversary model from Sect. 4.1 of an adversary D controlling a fraction $b < 0.5$ of dishonest players of n players in total. The performance of the protocol depends upon b, the security parameter l and the distribution of honest and dishonest players over the tree. We assume that D and A collude.

Most Likely Scenario. Due to the uniform player distribution and for a reasonably sized b, D has most likely a dishonest majority only in subtrees with large depth $d > 1$ containing only a small number n' of players. l can be adjusted to detect container manipulations of subtrees with $n' \leq l$ using signatures. Most likely, all dishonest players have to provide a container with their signature to at least one honest player, which corresponds to a commitment to their ticket$_i$, before D can learn all containers for a given depth d.

1. The *correctness* of the random process and its implicit *verification* [11] due to the distributed computation is with great probability ensured, because D cannot change or add tickets after a prediction becomes possible.
2. The *privacy* of players is ensured. Other players cannot learn the identity of each other from the exchanged messages.[3]

---

[3] The leak of the identity due to the communication channel, e.g. by the IP address, may be solved using privacy networks like Tor and is out of the scope of this paper.

3. The authorization token t_i ensures *eligibility*. A participation after the aggregation has started even with a valid t_i is unlikely, because honest players close in the tree deny belated players and do not confirm their containers.
4. The commitment scheme for LO provides *confidentiality*, because number n_i of P_i cannot be revealed without knowledge of the secret r_i [5].
5. The counter c of the root aggregate container allows to examine the *completeness* of the reward.

Worst Case Scenario. The distribution of honest and dishonest players is highly unbalanced. We assume a majority of dishonest players in a subtree $\mathbb{S}(x_e, d)$ for some d with $n' > l$. Neither the majority nor the confirmation criterion prevent a manipulation with certainty. The local minority of honest players may be excluded from the aggregation unable to proof their participation. As the manipulation is bounded locally, correctness and eligibility are only locally violated.

If D has further in all other non-sibling subtrees $\widehat{\mathbb{S}}(\cdot, d)$ at least one dishonest player to provide the local aggregate container, D can compute with the secret r_A from A the winning number n_w while the container for $\widehat{\mathbb{S}}(x_e, d)$ is not yet known to honest players and may be altered to change n_w. A proof of work is required to choose a particular n_w. The correctness is not ensured.

The distribution of n' honest or dishonest players to $\widehat{\mathbb{S}}(x_e, d)$ and its sibling subtree $\mathbb{S}(x_e, d)$ follows the Binomial distribution $B(n', p)$ with $p = 0.5$ and a variance of the ratio of players in $\widehat{\mathbb{S}}(x_e, d)$ of p^2/n'. As a result, the probability of a local dishonest majority decreases reciprocally in n'. n' decreases for increasing d, but for large d, it is unlikely to have a dishonest player in all non-sibling subtrees for the limited number of dishonest players.

Scalability. Kademlia's communication and memory resources are $\mathcal{O}(\log n)$ [19]. The same applies to the distributed aggregation and its verification [20] if upper bounds are defined for the number of attempts and stored container candidates of the confirmation and correction mechanism of the distributed aggregation.

6   Conclusion

We have presented a novel online lottery protocol that relies on a distributed random process carried out by all players in a peer-to-peer manner. Players are assumed to participate throughout the random process. Unlike Chow's protocol [5], it allows for both classic lottery and lotto. It provides correctness and verification of the random process based on the assumption of a well-distributed minority of dishonest players. In the most likely scenario, the correctness of the random process is based on an information theoretical secure sharing scheme instead of assumptions on the communication or computational capacities of the authority or the adversary. Further, cryptography has been reduced to asymmetric encryption and signatures. As in many distributed protocols [6,15], the provided security is probabilistic, which may be acceptable for a lottery. We leave for future work a quantitative analysis of the impact of the adversary.

A basic demonstrator has been implemented to carry out a classical lottery. The authority has been omitted in favour of free participation. Redundant requests for Byzantine fault-tolerance are not covered yet. Based on HTML5, it runs in the browser. The implementation of ADAVOKAT is based on the Kademlia library kad[4] and was tested previously with up to 1000 simulated nodes [20]. Message passing among players relies on WebRTC allowing for browser-to-browser communication. Tests have been run with few players at this stage.

Acknowledgments. The authors would like to thank Pascal Lafourcade and Matthieu Giraud for fruitful discussions concerning the security of the lottery protocol and the underlying distributed aggregation algorithm.

References

1. Isidore, C.: Americans spend more on the lottery than on ... (2015). http://money.cnn.com/2015/02/11/news/companies/lottery-spending/. Accessed 16 Feb 2017
2. Rodgers, G.: Guilty verdict in Hot Lotto scam, but game safe, official says (2015). http://dmreg.co/1JbGgRN. Accessed 23 Jan 2017
3. Goldschlag, D.M., Stubblebine, S.G.: Publicly verifiable lotteries: applications of delaying functions. In: Proceedings of the Financial Cryptology 1998, pp. 214–226. Springer (1998). doi:10.1007/BFb0055485
4. Zhou, J., Tan, C.: Playing lottery on the internet. In: Qing, S., Okamoto, T., Zhou, J. (eds.) ICICS 2001. LNCS, vol. 2229, pp. 189–201. Springer, Heidelberg (2001). doi:10.1007/3-540-45600-7_22
5. Chow, S.S.M., Hui, L.C.K., Yiu, S.M., Chow, K.P.: An e-Lottery scheme using verifiable random function. In: Gervasi, O., Gavrilova, M.L., Kumar, V., Laganà, A., Lee, H.P., Mun, Y., Taniar, D., Tan, C.J.K. (eds.) ICCSA 2005. LNCS, vol. 3482, pp. 651–660. Springer, Heidelberg (2005). doi:10.1007/11424857_72
6. Nakamoto, S.: Bitcoin: A Peer-to-Peer Electronic Cash System (2008). https://bitcoin.org/bitcoin.pdf
7. Perez-Marco, R.: Bitcoin and Decentralized Trust Protocols (2016)
8. Pierrot, C., Wesolowski, B.: Malleability of the blockchain's entropy. In: ArcticCrypt 2016, pp. 1–20 (2016)
9. Lambrinoudakis, C., Gritzalis, D., Tsoumas, V., Karyda, M., Ikonomopoulos, S.: Secure electronic voting: the current landscape. In: Gritzalis, D.A. (ed.) Secure Electronic Voting, pp. 101–122. Springer, USA (2003)
10. Lenstra, A.K., Wesolowski, B.: A random zoo: sloth, unicorn, and trx. In: NIST Workshop on Elliptic Curve Cryptography Standards 3 (2015)
11. Liu, Y., Hu, L., Liu, H.: Using an efficient hash chain and delaying function to improve an e-Lottery scheme. Int. J. Comput. Math. **84**(7), 967–970 (2007). doi:10.1080/00207160701294426
12. Markowitch, O., Dossogne, J.: E-voting: Individual verifiability of public boards made more achievable. In: 31st Symposium on Information Theory in the Benelux, pp. 5–10. Werkgemeenschap voor Informatie en Communicatietheorie (2010)

---

[4] http://kadtools.github.io/, v1.6.2 released on November 29, 2016.

13. Kuacharoen, P.: Design and implementation of a secure online lottery system. In: Papasratorn, B., Charoenkitkarn, N., Lavangnananda, K., Chutimaskul, W., Vanijja, V. (eds.) IAIT 2012. CCIS, vol. 344, pp. 94–105. Springer, Heidelberg (2012). doi:10.1007/978-3-642-35076-4_9

14. Fouque, P.-A., Poupard, G., Stern, J.: Sharing decryption in the context of voting or lotteries. In: Frankel, Y. (ed.) FC 2000. LNCS, vol. 1962, pp. 90–104. Springer, Heidelberg (2001). doi:10.1007/3-540-45472-1_7

15. Gambs, S., Guerraoui, R., Harkous, H., Huc, F., Kermarrec, A.-M.: Scalable and secure aggregation in distributed networks. arXiv e-prints (2011)

16. Wood, G.: Ethereum: a secure decentralised generalised transaction ledger (2014). http://gavwood.com/paper.pdf

17. Maymounkov, P., Mazieres, D.: Kademlia: A Peer-to-Peer Information System Based on the XOR Metric. Springer, Heidelberg (2002)

18. Merkle, R.C.: A digital signature based on a conventional encryption function. In: Pomerance, C. (ed.) CRYPTO 1987. LNCS, vol. 293, pp. 369–378. Springer, Heidelberg (1988). doi:10.1007/3-540-48184-2_32

19. Cai, X.S., Devroye, L.: A probabilistic analysis of kademlia networks. In: Cai, L., Cheng, S.-W., Lam, T.-W. (eds.) ISAAC 2013. LNCS, vol. 8283, pp. 711–721. Springer, Heidelberg (2013). doi:10.1007/978-3-642-45030-3_66

20. Riemann, R., Grumbach, S.: Secure and trustable distributed aggregation based on kademlia. In: Proceedings of the 32nd IFIP SEC. Springer, Rome (2017)

21. Baumgart, I., Mies, S.: S/Kademlia: a practicable approach towards secure key-based routing. In: Proceedings of the ICPADS 2007, pp. 1–8. ICS, USA (2007)

Storing Data Smartly (Data storage)

DDFLASKS: Deduplicated Very Large Scale Data Store

Francisco Maia[✉], João Paulo, Fábio Coelho, Francisco Neves, José Pereira, and Rui Oliveira

HASLab, INESC TEC, University of Minho, Braga, Portugal
{fmaia,jtpaulo,jop,rco}@di.uminho.pt,
{fabio.a.coelho,francisco.t.neves}@inesctec.pt

Abstract. With the increasing number of connected devices, it becomes essential to find novel data management solutions that can leverage their computational and storage capabilities. However, developing very large scale data management systems requires tackling a number of interesting distributed systems challenges, namely continuous failures and high levels of node churn. In this context, epidemic-based protocols proved suitable and effective and have been successfully used to build DATAFLASKS, an epidemic data store for massive scale systems. Ensuring resiliency in this data store comes with a significant cost in storage resources and network bandwidth consumption. Deduplication has proven to be an efficient technique to reduce both costs but, applying it to a large-scale distributed storage system is not a trivial task. In fact, achieving significant space-savings without compromising the resiliency and decentralized design of these storage systems is a relevant research challenge.

In this paper, we extend DATAFLASKS with deduplication to design DDFLASKS. This system is evaluated in a real world scenario using Wikipedia snapshots, and the results are twofold. We show that deduplication is able to decrease storage consumption up to 63% and decrease network bandwidth consumption by up to 20%, while maintaining a fully-decentralized and resilient design.

1 Introduction

For many years now we hear promises of the emergence of the Internet of Things (IoT) and of Edge Computing. Still, the world of interconnected things has remained more an idea than a concrete reality. Recent predictions from the International Data Corporation (IDC) studies, however, point to significant developments in this area and it is expected that by 2020 there will be an extraordinary number of 32 billion things connected to the Internet [14]. Moreover, the amount of digital data will grow from 4.4 ZB in 2013 to 44 ZB in 2020.

Naturally, an explosion in the number of connected devices and in the amount of data being produced and exchanged demands for novel approaches to data management. Massive scale systems, composed of thousands to millions of devices, exhibit specific characteristics that are specially challenging and need to be

L.Y. Chen and H.P. Reiser (Eds.): DAIS 2017, LNCS 10320, pp. 51–66, 2017.
DOI: 10.1007/978-3-319-59665-5_4

addressed. Namely, the increase in scale is necessarily accompanied by an increase in system dynamism. Such dynamism arises both from failures that, in these environments, become the rule instead of the exception and by the natural constant entrance and departure of devices, which we will call nodes from now on.

Alongside, real world applications start to struggle to find affordable systems to manage and store massive amounts of data. As an example, the Wikimedia Foundation is currently requesting help to users that have spare storage and bandwidth capabilities to store and host Wikipedia snapshots[1]. These snapshots contain the entire history of Wikipedia across distinct periods of time and are valuable for a wide variety of users including researchers. However, they are not easily accessible due to limited storage capabilities. Thus, offering a massive scale storage system able to accommodate the entire Wikipedia and its history relying only on commodity hardware becomes of significant interest. Moreover, serving all these snapshots from an unified storage service, instead of scattering the snapshots across independent storage systems, is key for users to have an efficient way of accessing the full history of Wikipedia.

Recent research work proposed a data store entirely built with epidemic protocols, tailored precisely for large scale environments [18]. The success of DATAFLASKS, with respect to coping with high levels of system dynamism, lies in its autonomous and unstructured approach to node organization and in its pro-active approach to fault tolerance. In DATAFLASKS, nodes autonomously organize themselves into groups that are responsible for a subset/partition of the data. Then, the number of nodes in a group determines the data replication factor for the data being stored. The effectiveness of a pro-active approach to data replication comes, unfortunately, with an increase in storage and network resource usage. In fact, bandwidth is actually a bottleneck for scalability in this type of systems and, even though DATAFLASKS autonomous data partitioning alleviates the problem, this still weakens its applicability in real world scenarios [2]. Alongside, as all nodes belonging to the same group are fully-replicated, the available storage space provided by the group is limited to the size manageable by the single node with the lesser storage capabilities. This restriction is of special importance if we consider each node to be commodity hardware or even smaller edge devices where storage space available is limited.

Data deduplication has proven to be an efficient technique for finding and eliminating duplicate content in large volumes of data [21]. Moreover, it was used in the past to reduce the network bandwidth consumption of distributed storage systems. However, leveraging deduplication in a massive-scale data store such as DATAFLASKS is not a trivial task. One approach is to apply local deduplication only for the data stored in each node. As this approach does not eliminate duplicates stored across distinct nodes, it requires an efficient content-aware policy for distributing data to nodes that maximizes the obtainable space-savings. Other approach is to perform global deduplication across data stored in all nodes, thus finding redundancy across the entire storage system. However, finding duplicates across all nodes requires global metadata and coordination, which not

---

[1] https://dumps.wikimedia.org.

only increases the complexity of the system but may also compromise the decentralization, fault-tolerance, and performance of systems such as DATAFLASKS.

Contributions. We propose DDFLASKS, a massive scale deduplicated data store. It shows the applicability of integrating DATAFLASKS, a massive scale data store, with deduplication, without loosing any of its design guarantees, such as decentralization and high churn tolerance. Additionally, we evaluate its effectiveness using a real workload, specifically storing and serving simultaneously both the most recent versions of Wikipedia [10] articles and their older historical versions. In fact, using real data from Wikipedia, we show that our system is able to store and serve articles across several nodes with high levels of storage savings up to 63% and network savings up to 20%.

Roadmap. The rest of the paper is organized as follows. In Sect. 2 we describe the architecture and design of DATAFLASKS, the baseline system used to build our novel approach. Next, in Sect. 3 we describe the Wikipedia use case and present some preliminary results that motivate the usage of deduplication. In Sect. 4 we introduce DDFLASKS. We then proceed to DDFLASKS evaluation in Sect. 5 and present related work in Sect. 6. The paper is concluded in Sect. 7.

2 DATAFLASKS: Epidemic Store for Massive Scale Systems

The pivotal idea guiding the design of DATAFLASKS is decentralization, where each node is autonomous and all nodes play the same role [18]. A node progresses relying solely on local decisions without depending on any other node and on any kind of hierarchy. When a client issues a request, such request is disseminated throughout the system and each node decides how to handle it. Store requests are composed by an identifier of the object to be stored that must be unique, by the version of the object to be stored, and by the object's data. Storing several versions of the same object is important for many applications that resort to data versioning.

Briefly, the API is composed by a *get* and *put* operation. When a *get* is received, if the node holds the corresponding triple (key, version, object) it replies to the client. Otherwise, it ignores the request. In the case of a *put* operation, the node locally decides to store the corresponding triple (key, version, object) or to discard it. The decision to store or not the data is used to implement data distribution and replication. DATAFLASKS ensures that a sufficient number of nodes actually decides to store each data object in order to guarantee data replication, and thus, to tolerate node failures.

The set of nodes that takes the same decisions on whether to store data objects or not is viewed as a group. Accordingly, the decision of which data to store is reduced to the decision of which group a node belongs to. Once that decision is made, each node is responsible for a subset of the data according to a deterministic mapping between the pair (key, version) of an object and the group it belongs to.

Data is thus distributed by groups, providing load balancing, and replicated a number of times equal to the size of the group. Strikingly, each node is able to decide to which group it belongs without requiring any kind of coordination.

In order to achieve this, the system is entirely built with unstructured and pro-active epidemic protocols. They are characterized by their independence from any kind of structure or hierarchy among nodes and by the fact that they rely on pro-active mechanisms for fault tolerance that are able to antecipate system repair. The result is a completely decentralized and coordination-free data store. Characteristics that make DATAFLASKS inherently scalable and able to cope with unprecedented levels of system dynamism, may it be caused by membership instability or by failures.

In the system's architecture, each node runs five components: *Membership*, *Group Construction*, *Storage*, *Replica Maintenance* and *Interface*. In order to provide some background and context to the design of the system proposed in this paper, we briefly describe how each component works in the original setting.

The *Membership* component is responsible for providing each node with a list of available nodes in the system. It does so guaranteeing that such list represents a random sample of nodes from the entire system and that it is periodically refreshed. It is important to notice that each membership list is always a small subset of nodes with respect to the system size, which allows the system to scale.

The *Group Construction* This component is responsible for determining to which group the node belongs. As described previously, the group determines which data to locally store or to discard. Without going into much detail, this component works by leveraging information being propagated at the membership level to estimate the number of groups needed to satisfy a desired, user defined, replication factor. Then, the node places himself on one of those groups guaranteeing that system nodes are uniformly distributed across the different groups. For a detailed description of the protocol please refer to [18]. Once in a group, each time a *put* operation is issued for a certain key, that key is mapped deterministically to a group by using an hash function. As described further on, this mapping allows different versions of the same key to be placed in the same replication group. This will allow maximizing deduplication effectiveness.

The *Storage* component abstracts the actual medium to which the data is persisted. Currently, this component can be configured to be a in-memory store or a disk-based one. This paper introduces a new storage component to support data deduplication.

In order to maintain the replication level in the presence of churn, the *Replica Maintenance* component periodically publishes to other nodes in the group the set of keys it currently holds locally. Within a group, all nodes store the same set of data objects. Upon receiving a maintenance message, each node checks if it is storing all keys correspondent to the group. If not, it requests the missing data from the nodes in its group. In this paper we provide a new replica maintenance component which allows to optimize this process by avoiding to transmit duplicate data through the network.

Finally, the *Interface* component is responsible for handling the incoming connections from other nodes and managing the request workflow in the system. In order to issue *put* or *get* requests the client only needs to be able to contact a single node in the system. The request is then forward appropriately to the correct nodes that can fulfill it.

3 Duplicates in the Real World

Many large information systems tend to exhibit a significant amount of duplicate data [19]. This is particularly true for storage systems that evolve incrementally with time. A paradigmatic example is Wikipedia, also known as the Internet encyclopedia [10]. The Wikipedia allows users to create and complement articles about virtually any subject. Articles evolve through time and periodic snapshots of the entire Wikipedia are stored for future reference. Because Wikipedia serves a very high volume of requests and stores a growing large volume of data, it is a suitable use case for DATAFLASKS that can leverage its highly scalable infrastructure to serve Wikipedia's high demand.

Naturally, different versions of the same article share significant portions of the text, which is redundant when stored. This means that a storage system holding the full history of Wikipedia is expected to have a considerable amount of duplicate content [11]. A possible approach to eliminate this redundancy would be to use a traditional compression technique such as gzip. However, compression techniques are ideally designed to eliminate intra-file redundancy or redundancy over a small group of files, typically stored together in the same operation. In the Wikipedia use-case, new versions of the same article are created over time and must be retrieved efficiently if requested. This means compressing and decompressing data several times which results in a significant penalty on storage requests performance. Another possible approach to eliminate such redundancy and to spare storage space is to use incremental backup techniques such as delta-encoding. With this technique new versions of a previously stored article are stored as deltas or *diffs* that only contain the content that was actually modified. These deltas can then be applied to the original (base) article to rebuild a specific version of the article. Although this technique is efficient in terms of storage space savings, it requires additional computational power and it is slower than deduplication, specially when articles have a large number of versions and several deltas must be applied to the base article to retrieve latest versions. For this reason, this paper proposes the use of block-based deduplication, which allows users to query any article version in the past and get the response without the need to rebuild a set of deltas or decompress data [21].

To validate that deduplication is, in fact, suitable and effective for a deployment where DATAFLASKS is serving Wikipedia articles, we performed the following experiment. We used 15 monthly Wikipedia snapshots taken for the period between November of 2014 and January of 2016 (See footnote 1). Each snapshot has the latest full version of all articles belonging to the English version of Wikipedia. The snapshots were processed by the order they were taken and the corresponding articles were stored in a way that mimics the distributed storage approach taken by DATAFLASKS in a real deployment *i.e.*, articles were divided into groups and stored accordingly. Each group of articles represents the data partition that would be assigned to a specific set of DATAFLASKS nodes. We then focus our analysis on each one of the partitions. It is important to notice that deduplication will be applied locally by each node. Consequently, nodes in the same group, that replicate the same data partition, will store the same content, which makes it sufficient to analyze a single node per group. Additionally, across consecutive snapshots there are some repeated articles that remained unmodified and were not stored in our experiment.

On the other hand, new versions of previously stored articles were routed to the same data group, where their ancestors were persisted, and were stored as new objects (files) with distinct version identifiers. This way, the experiments stored the full content for each article version which is in conformity with the rationale explained previously where our very large data store is used to serve several articles and their distinct versions without requiring the usage of incremental backup techniques.

Table 1. Analysis of duplicates results with 1024, 2048 and 4096 bytes Rabin fingerprints for a single group of the DataFlasks configuration with 40 groups.

Fingerprint Avg size	# articles	Total space (GB)	Total # blocks	# unique blocks	# duplicate blocks	Avg # copies/duplicated block	Space saved (GB)	Duplicate space %
1024	1,393,130	7.63	7,046,744	4,226,205	2,820,539	3.20	3.27	42.88
2048	1,393,130	7.63	3,995,416	2,870,780	1,124,636	2.59	2.59	33.99
4096	1,393,130	7.63	2,550,938	2,132,849	418,089	2.65	1.89	24.81

After populating the distinct data groups with the Wikipedia dataset the global storage space in use was ≈305 GB, corresponding to 55,745,648 articles. In order to check the percentage of redundancy in the stored dataset, we resort to the DUPSANALYSER tool an open-source project (https://github.com/jtpaulo/dupsanalyzer) that processes the content of files and extracts statistics for the duplicate content found. Duplicates can be found either by searching for duplicate blocks with a fixed or variable size. The latter resorts to an implementation of the Rabin Fingerprint scheme for calculating variable-sized blocks and their corresponding content hashes efficiently [20]. As Wikipedia articles are text articles, using variable sized blocks is a better choice for finding duplicates [11,21]. Briefly, lets consider two versions of the same article where version *A* only differs from version *B* by a single character that was added to the beginning of the latter version. If the two articles are scanned with a fixed size partitioning scheme, no blocks from version *A* will match blocks from version *B*. In contrast, the Rabin fingerprint scheme uses a sliding window that moves through the data until a fixed content pattern defining the block boundary is found. This approach generates variable-sized blocks and solves the issue of inserting a single byte in the beginning of version B. More precisely, only the first block from version B will differ from the first block of version A due to the byte addition, while the remaining blocks will still be duplicate. Finally, the Rabin scheme is configurable with target average, maximum and minimum block size, which allows avoiding the generation of very small or large blocks while still keeping their sizes variable. In the results discussed next, we used DUPSANALYSER to process the articles, and corresponding versions, stored at each data group. Individually, for each data group, our analysis tool processed all stored files to find intra and inter-file duplicates.

Distinct Group Sizes Results. Our first experiment was designed to check the amount of duplicates found per group node when dividing articles into 10, 20 and 40 groups for different block sizes: 1024, 2048 and 4096 bytes. With 10 groups each group node holds ≈30 GB, with 20 groups ≈15 GB and with 40 groups ≈7.5 GB. We noticed that the percentage of duplicates found does not increase significantly if a group holds more data, because most redundancy is originated by storing distinct versions of the same article in the same group, which happens identically for the three group sizes.

Single Group Analysis for the 40 Groups Scenario. Since the percentage of duplicates does not change significantly when considering different number of groups, we show in Table 1 a more detailed analysis of the stored content in a single group for the experiment with 40 groups. The analyzed group holds 7.63 GB of data corresponding to more than one million articles. For each Rabin fingerprint size, the total number of generated blocks diverges and, as expected, with a smaller size it is possible to find more duplicates and have significantly higher space savings. However, reducing the block size increases the size of the metadata used to index all stored blocks and to find duplicates.

To conclude, these results show that single-node deduplication with a variable 1024 bytes fingerprinting scheme allows reducing 45% of the storage space occupied by 15 snapshots of the English Wikipedia version.

4 DDFLASKS

Recalling Sect. 2, data distribution and replication in DATAFLASKS is achieved by dividing nodes into groups. Each group is responsible for a set of data and, accordingly, each node belonging to that group will have to store that specific set of data in its local storage. The Wikipedia study discussed in the previous section shows that a significant percentage of duplicates exists in each node when all the versions of a specific article are grouped together. In DDFLASKS, this insight is leveraged by ensuring that data objects identified by a key are always assigned to the same group independently of their version. With this approach, all the versions of an article are stored in the same group while clients can still retrieve specific versions of an article by specifying the article's key and the desired version. This is achieved by taking into advantage the load balancing mechanism from the original DATAFLASKS, which deterministically routes a certain key to

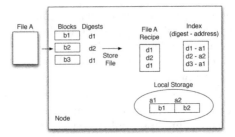

Fig. 1. Deduplication in DDFLASKS

a group. DDFLASKS inherits characteristics from DATAFLASKS, such as fully-decentralization. In particular, it resorts to node-local deduplication that does not require any global index or coordination mechanisms that would impact high-churn tolerance and the performance of storage requests[21].

In comparison with the baseline architecture discussed in Sect. 2, DDFLASKS is extended with storage and network deduplication mechanisms. The resulting open-source system is available at http://github.com/fmaia/dataflasks.

First, a new storage component is provided with integrated in-line local storage deduplication, which works as follows. In each node, duplicates are identified and eliminated before actually being stored persistently. In the literature this approach is known as in-line deduplication[21]. Duplicates are found by resorting to an *index* that maps blocks with unique content to their respective storage addresses. When a block is being written, a digest of the block's content is calculated and the index is searched for a possible duplicate. If a duplicate exists, then the new block does not need to be stored, otherwise, the block is stored and the index is updated with a new entry for that block. A Rabin Fingerprint scheme identical to the one described in Sect. 3 is used to divide files into variable-size blocks and to calculate small digests of their content[20]. This way, the index does not store the actual block but a smaller digest identifying the content of that block. Fingerprints are deterministically calculated per-file. Thus, at each node, storing files in different orders does not affect the correctness of the approach. In order to retrieve files from the storage system, an additional metadata structure, that we refer to as *file recipe* is used. Each file recipe identifies a single file stored on DDFLASKS and tracks the digests of the blocks that belong to that specific file. The actual storage address of these digests can be consulted at the index. Deduplication is thus achieved because file recipes with duplicate content share digests that are mapped to the same storage block. Figure 1 shows an example of the proposed single-node deduplication mechanism. As the first step, File A is routed to the correct group of nodes. Then, in each node storing the file, the file is divided into variable-sized blocks and a digest for the content of each block is calculated. In the example, block1 and block3 have the same content. Each digest is checked at the index and if not found, a new entry is added while the corresponding block is stored in a append-only storage. In the figure blocks $b1$ and $b3$ are duplicates, so only block $b1$ and $b2$ are stored. Finally, the file recipe for File A is also kept at the node in order to fetch all the necessary blocks when a client asks for that file. The index keeps the digests and corresponding location for all blocks at the local storage which enables both intra- and inter-file deduplication for all files stored in the same node. In Sect. 5 we show that our approach is still able to achieve significant storage space savings even when metadata space is accounted for.

In this paper we do not address data deletion functionalities. This is motivated by the fact that DDFLASKS is a large-scale system intended to store large amounts of archival data. For use-cases such as the Wikipedia one used in the paper, this is a practical assumption since the main goal is to keep all versions of wikipedia articles without ever deleting them. As described in the previous section, for this use case, single-node deduplication proves to be an efficient technique to spare redundant storage space and avoids scalability issues found in large-scale in-line deduplication systems that must maintain a global index for finding duplicates across remote storage nodes [7,8].

The second deduplication mechanism proposed in the paper aims at optimizing the network bandwidth used by DDFLASKS data replication techniques. In order to cope with high levels of node churn and to maintain desirable data replication levels, each system node proactively and periodically contacts other nodes in the same group to announce the set of files it is currently storing. If one node receives this set and verifies that its local storage is currently missing some files, it must contact other nodes in the same group to ask for those files. Naturally, when churn levels become significantly high, the volume of data traversing the network increases as more files are being exchanged. We propose to mitigate this problem by employing deduplication to the data being exchanged between nodes. In detail, nodes periodically announce to the group not only the set of files that they currently hold but also the digests that compose those files. When a node receives this list and verifies that a set of files is missing, it checks first what digests from those files are already stored locally. This can be done by leveraging the index metadata used for local storage deduplication. Then, the node only requests the blocks that are actually missing in its local storage. After receiving these blocks the node updates the index and creates the corresponding file recipes. A key advantage of this mechanism is that it relies on the metadata already used for performing in-line deduplication, which is an idea that has proven successful in previous proposals for backing up data across peer-to-peer networks [5,20]. Although this strategy requires sending the list of digests when announcing the files that nodes currently hold, we show in Sect. 5 that it still spares significant network bandwidth. Note that although single-node deduplication is already provided in several storage appliances, it is not trivial to incorporate these solutions with DDFLASKS and take advantage of the deduplication metadata, that is in most cases is protected within the appliance, to implement the previous network optimizations.

Implementation Details. The two deduplication mechanisms were implemented on top of the current implementation of the system described in Sect. 2. The deduplication index is an in-memory HashMap that maps blocks digests (8 bytes) to storage addresses (8 bytes)[2]. Similarly, file recipes are stored in an in-memory HashMap that maps the identifier of a file (16 bytes, 8 bytes for the file key and 8 bytes for the version) to its file recipe whose size depends on the number of block digests composing that file. DDFLASKS is mainly thought for running in commodity hardware nodes and the amount of data hold by each node is not expected to be very large (tens to hundreds of GBs). So, the amount of metadata held by each node is also expected not grow to large values. Additionally, in the context of this paper we assume that, even in the presence of high levels of churn, for each group there is always a set of live nodes. This way metadata for freshly booted nodes can always be reconstructed from live nodes.

5   Evaluation

DDFLASKS was evaluated in a real deployment to validate two main claims. First, that deduplication allows sparing significant storage space for each node. Second, that the network bandwidth used by nodes when exchanging messages is also reduced.

To this end, we have performed a set of experiments that demonstrate the effectiveness of the deduplication mechanism implemented. Each experiment was run both in the original DATAFLASKS, non-deduplicated system (used as the baseline) and in DDFLASKS. The experiment set up consists of a cluster of commodity hardware nodes equipped either with a 3.1 GHz Dual-Core Intel i3 Processor, 8 GB of RAM and a 7200 RPMs SATA disk or a 3.7 GHz Dual-Core Intel i3 Processor, 8 GB of RAM and a SSD disk. All nodes are connected through a gigabit ethernet switch. It is important to notice that hardware heterogeneity does not impact the results of our experiments. In fact, it is out of the scope of the present paper the evaluation of system performance metrics. These metrics will mostly be affected by the deduplication approach being used *i.e.,* fingerprinting scheme, index scheme, etc. As discussed in previous work, each scheme adds different tradeoffs in terms of storage performance, deduplication performance and resources (RAM, CPU, Disk) consumption [21].

Instead, we focus on analyzing storage and network savings achievable by our system. Similarly, the validation of DDFLASKS scalability to thousands of nodes and resiliency to high churn rations is already addressed in previous work [18].

Leveraging the results obtained in Sect. 3 and aiming at real world assessment of DDFLASKS, all the experiments presented next resort to actual Wikipedia data.

5.1   Storage Savings

In order to evaluate the storage behavior of DDFLASKS we have considered 15 Wikipedia monthly snapshots. Each one of these snapshots contains a set of

---

[2] For each entry at the index, 4 extra bytes must be stored because variable sized blocks are being used and their size must also be kept.

articles from the English version of the Wikipedia. From snapshot to snapshot each article may change reflecting its evolution through time. In the real world deployment of Wikipedia, users see only a single (latest) snapshot. However, in our scenario we want to go a step forward and it is our goal to simultaneously store and serve several Wikipedia snapshots.

The 15 snapshots used amount to ≈115 GB corresponding to ≈6.3 million articles. Each article is stored as a single data object in the storage system and each new article snapshot corresponds to a new version of such object. Moreover, article versions are treated as new articles thus identified with the same key as the original article but with a different version number. This information is used by DDFLASKS to collocate articles with their subsequent versions in the same node group.

We configured both DATAFLASKS and DDFLASKS to arrange nodes into 16 groups. Each group is responsible for storing a subset of the articles written to the store. As described previously, all nodes belonging to a certain group store the same data and deduplication is applied locally to each node. Consequently, in order to observe the system's behavior it is sufficient to analyze the behavior of a single node per group. Other nodes in the same group will exhibit exactly the same results as the ones presented next.

The experiment consisted on loading both DATAFLASKS and DDFLASKS with the 15 data snapshots writing each article and subsequent versions in chronological order (from the oldest snapshot to the latest one). After the load was completed we analyzed the storage usage of a node per group.

Table 2. Storage and metadata space occupied for DDFLASKS and the DATAFLASKS storage systems

	DATAFLASKS	DDFLASKS
Global storage space (GB)	115.5	42.4
Average storage space/node (GB)	7.2 (± 0.08)	2.65 (± 0.05)
Global deduplication savings (GB)	-	73.1
Average deduplication Savings/node (GB)	-	4.55
Global metadata space (GB)	1.32	12.04
Metadata space/node (GB)	0.08 (± 0.003)	0.75 (± 0.05)

In Table 2 we present the results of this experiment. It is observable that DDFLASKS is significantly more frugal than DATAFLASKS with respect to storage space usage. The former requires 42.4 GB to store all the articles while the latter, without deduplication, requires 115.5 GB. In detail, 73.1 GB are saved by using deduplication which corresponds to a space saving of 63% when compared to the baseline approach. Please note that, when compared with the motivation tests described in Sect. 3, there is an improvement in the storage savings results. This improvement is explained by the fact that, in this real deployment, we used

Table 3. Space occupied by DDFLASKS index and file recipe

Metadata	Global space (GB)	Space/node (GB)
Index	5.35	0.33 ($\pm$0.002)
File recipe	6.69	0.42 ($\pm$0.003)

a sample of the articles (and corresponding versions) used in the motivation experiments, which happen to exhibit slightly higher redundancy between them. Additionally, we can observe that the local storage space required by nodes in different groups is similar and that the deduplication savings in each node are identical to the one observed globally for the whole storage by considering a load balancing strategy that routes articles uniformly across distinct groups.

Going into some detail, we also show in the table the space used by metadata structures. In both systems, more than 390,000 articles were stored in each node. As expected, deduplication requires additional metadata space for storing and indexing articles' blocks, while in the baseline system it is only required a simpler file recipe that points a specific file to its storage address. Nevertheless, the space savings achieved clearly compensate the overhead introduced by the extra metadata structures used in DDFLASKS. In fact, less than 17% of the space spared by deduplication is needed for fulfilling the extra metadata space overhead. Finally, Table 3 shows the exact space occupied by the index and file recipe metadata in our system. Again, the space occupied by each metadata structure across different nodes does not change significantly.

5.2   Network Savings

Replication is achieved in our system resorting to periodic message exchanges between nodes with information about the data objects they are storing. Each time, following a message exchange, a node detects it is missing some object it requests it from other nodes in the same group. Naturally, if the system is stable, it is expected that nodes store all correspondent data objects and that these message exchanges do not yield missing data requests. However, when nodes fail or enter the system data objects need to be requested to maintain the desirable replication levels.

In this experiment, we show that deduplication can reduce network consumption of the data exchange mechanism between nodes. We focus on two nodes belonging to the same group and observe their behavior when one of them keeps failing and re-entering the system while the system is continuously being loaded with new data. Naturally, it is expected that each time the node re-enters the system it will request missing data from its peer that runs continuously. The test ran for 2 h and after the first 30 min one of the nodes was stopped in intervals of 20 min. In detail, after being stopped the node remains offline for 20 min and then it is rebooted again and it is kept online for additional 20 min. This cycle was repeated until the last 30 min of the test when the two nodes were kept online. The node being stopped saved its metadata to disk periodically to ensure that when rebooted the index and file recipe metadata were holding previously stored information. Again, 15 Wikipedia monthly snapshots were used, and both systems (DDFLASKS and baseline) stored more than 400,000 articles, which corresponds to ≈8.3 GB. Please recall that the two nodes were configured to be in the same group so these were fully-replicated, each holding the same amount of articles mentioned previously. In terms of storage space savings the DDFLASKS nodes stored 4.3 GB while the baseline system nodes stored 8.3 GB. This corresponds to a space saving of ≈49%, which is in conformity with the results discussed previously and in Sect. 3. The metadata space required by each node is also compensated by the space savings as in the previous results.

The baseline approach, without network deduplication, sends more than 22 GB through the network while the deduplication approach only sends 17.71 GB. Note that these bandwidth consumption results consider all network traffic. In fact, while most of this traffic is due to the data replication mechanism, system control traffic and client requests are also accounted for in the total value. Moreover, both systems rely on the UDP protocol that requires resending messages that are lost due to failures of the protocol, which also increases network bandwidth usage. Nevertheless, these results show that only by using deduplication for the data replication mechanism it is possible to spare ≈20% of all the data exchanged across replicated peers.

The previous results show that significant storage space and network bandwidth can be spared with DDFLASKS. We expect these savings to be similar for other backup workloads with periodic snapshots. In fact, as presented in [19], some of these backup workloads will have higher duplication ratios than Wikipedia, meaning that the network and storage savings achievable should also be higher.

6 Related Work

In the pursuit for large scale data management, traditional relational database systems have been, for certain domains and applications, largely replaced by new approaches to data management. Commonly know as NoSQL data stores, these data management systems offer relaxed consistency guarantees when compared with traditional relational database management systems. Examples are Dynamo, PNuts, Bigtable, Cassandra and Riak [3,4,6,15,16]. One of the key features of these data stores is how they implement data distribution and discovery. Leveraging scalability properties of peer-to-peer protocols, all these data stores rely on a distributed hash table (DHT) such as Chord or variants to distribute and locate data objects [24]. The exceptions are Bigtable and PNUTS, which are centrally managed instead and typically use a specific DHT variation called 'one-hop' DHT [13]. This variation allows faster lookups but requires complete membership knowledge, *i.e.*, each node knows about all other nodes in the system. Moreover, DHTs are know to struggle in the presence of high levels of churn [23]. As a result, even if the distributed and peer-to-peer nature of these data stores is closely related to DATAFLASKS, this system presents an unique unstructured and pro-active approach to node organization and data replication.

To our best knowledge, applying deduplication to epidemic massive scale systems for improving the usable storage space of peers and to improve the network bandwidth usage of gossip protocols and pro-active replication mechanisms is a novel contribution of this paper. To achieve these goals, we leverage ideas of previous work on deduplication for distributed storage systems [21]. In more detail, for achieving both storage and network savings, in-line local deduplication is applied so that duplicates are eliminated before being stored persistently [8, 22]. In fact, for sparing network bandwidth, duplicates are eliminated before even being sent through the network [20].

Peer-to-peer in-line deduplication, where backups are made cooperatively with remote nodes, was introduced in Pastiche [5]. In this system, nodes backup their data to other remote nodes that are chosen by their network proximity and data similarity. Only non-duplicate data is sent through the network and since nodes with similar datasets are chosen, the amount of data that must be sent through the network and stored in each peer is reduced significantly. Other distributed deduplication systems propose novel load balancing designs that route similar data to the same node in order to optimize the amount of duplicates found and, consequently, maximize storage space savings. These proposals rely on centralized indexes that have global knowledge of the content stored in all nodes, on distributed indexes that scale better than the centralized ones, on statefull and stateless routing algorithms, and on probabilistic routing algorithms that do not need a global knowledge of the content of each node in the system [1,7–9,11,12,17,25].

Although DDFLASKS could benefit from some of the ideas and optimizations discussed in previous deduplication systems, our current design uses the original load balancing algorithm proposed by DATAFLASKS. Our approach collocates different versions of the same data objects, which are expected to have duplicated content. Deduplication is thus performed locally on each node *i.e.*, each node manages its own index and only eliminates duplicates that are stored on its local storage. Strikingly, as shown in the paper, for realistic use-cases such as the Wikipedia one, ensuring that the same versions of articles are routed to the same DDFLASKS group is enough to achieve significant storage space savings while keeping metadata overhead acceptable. Additionally, our deduplication design can be leveraged to spare not only storage space but also network bandwidth usage across nodes. For epidemic data stores such as DDFLASKS this is a novel contribution that reduces significantly the number of messages exchanged across nodes, thus improving the efficiency of current gossip protocols, which is of particular importance since bandwidth consumption is critical in these systems [2]. Furthermore, our approach does not impact the decentralization and high-churn tolerance assumptions of the original DATAFLASKS system.

7 Conclusion

This paper describes a deduplicated massive scale data store, which can handle high volumes of data while minimizing storage resource usage. DDFLASKS is built resorting to a stack of proactive and completely decentralized gossip-based protocols.

The core idea driving this store is effective data dissemination and independent, local decisions of what to do with the data at each node. In-line deduplication is employed at each node and we show, resorting to a real world scenario, that the system is able to save up to 63% of storage space, in comparison with a non deduplicated one.

Additionally, DDFLASKS design is completely decentralized and is able to cope with unprecedented amounts of churn, while saving up to 20% in network bandwidth consumption when compared with the original DATAFLASKS non deduplicated system.

Acknowledgments. The research leading to these results was part-funded by (1) Project TEC4Growth - Pervasive Intelligence, Enhancers and Proofs of Concept with Industrial Impact/NORTE-01-0145-FEDER-000020 is financed by the North Portugal Regional Operational Programme (NORTE 2020), under the PORTUGAL 2020 Partnership Agreement, and through the European Regional Development Fund (ERDF); (2) the ERDF European Regional Development Fund through the Operational Programme for Competitiveness and Internationalisation - COMPETE 2020 Programme within project POCI-01-0145-FEDER-006961, and by National Funds through the FCT Portuguese Foundation for Science and Technology as part of project UID/EEA/50014/2013 and by (3) the European Union's Horizon 2020 - The EU Framework Programme for Research and Innovation 2014–2020, under grant agreement No. 732051.

References

1. Bhagwat, D., Eshghi, K., Long, D.D.E., Lillibridge, M.: Extreme binning: scalable, parallel deduplication for chunk-based file backup. In: International Symposium on Modelling, Analysis, and Simulation of Computer and Telecommunication Systems, pp. 1–9 (2009)
2. Blake, C., Rodrigues, R.: High availability, scalable storage, dynamic peer networks: pick two. In: Conference on Hot Topics in Operating Systems, vol. 9, p. 1 (2003)
3. Chang, F., Dean, J., Ghemawat, S., Hsieh, W.C., Wallach, D.A., Burrows, M., Chandra, T., Fikes, A., Gruber, R.E.: Bigtable: a distributed storage system for structured data. ACM Trans. Comput. Syst. (TOCS) **26**(2), 4 (2008)
4. Cooper, B.F., Ramakrishnan, R., Srivastava, U., Silberstein, A., Bohannon, P., Jacobsen, H.A., Puz, N., Weaver, D., Yerneni, R.: Pnuts: Yahoo!'s hosted data serving platform. VLDB Endowment **1**(2), 1277–1288 (2008)
5. Cox, L.P., Murray, C.D., Noble, B.D.: Pastiche: making backup cheap and easy. In: Symposium on Operating Systems Design and Implementation, pp. 1–13 (2002)
6. DeCandia, G., Hastorun, D., Jampani, M., Kakulapati, G., Lakshman, A., Pilchin, A., Sivasubramanian, S., Vosshall, P., Vogels, W.: Dynamo: amazon's highly available key-value store. ACM SIGOPS Oper. Syst. Rev. **41**(6), 205–220 (2007)

7. Dong, W., Douglis, F., Li, K., Patterson, H., Reddy, S., Shilane, P.: Tradeoffs in scalable data routing for deduplication clusters. In: USENIX Conference on File and Storage Technologies, pp. 15–29 (2011)
8. Douceur, J.R., Adya, A., Bolosky, W.J., Simon, D., Theimer, M.: Reclaiming space from duplicate files in a serverless distributed file system. Technical report MSR-TR-2002-30, Microsoft Research, July 2002
9. Dubnicki, C., Gryz, L., Heldt, L., Kaczmarczyk, M., Kilian, W., Strzelczak, P., Szczepkowski, J., Ungureanu, C., Welnicki, M.: HYDRAstor: a scalable secondary storage. In: USENIX Conference on File and Storage Technologies, pp. 197–210 (2009)
10. Wikimedia Foundation: Wikipedia web page (2016). https://www.wikipedia.org
11. Frey, D., Kermarrec, A.M., Kloudas, K.: Probabilistic deduplication for cluster-based storage systems. In: ACM Symposium on Cloud Computing, pp. 1–14 (2012)
12. Fu, Y., Jiang, H., Xiao, N.: A scalable inline cluster deduplication framework for big data protection. In: International Middleware Conference, pp. 354–373 (2012)
13. Gupta, A., Liskov, B., Rodrigues, R.: Efficient routing for peer-to-peer overlays. In: USENIX Symposium on Networked Systems Design and Implementation (2004)
14. IDC: the digital universe of opportunities: rich data and the increasing value of the internet of things, April 2014. http://www.emc.com/leadership/digital-universe/2014iview/executive-summary.htm
15. Klophaus, R.: Riak core: building distributed applications without shared state. In: ACM SIGPLAN Commercial Users Functional Programming, p. 14 (2010)
16. Lakshman, A., Malik, P.: Cassandra: a decentralized structured storage system. ACM SIGOPS Oper. Syst. Rev. **44**(2), 35–40 (2010)
17. Lillibridge, M., Eshghi, K., Bhagwat, D., Deolalikar, V., Trezise, G., Camble, P.: Sparse indexing: large scale, inline deduplication using sampling and locality. In: USENIX Conference on File and Storage Technologies, pp. 111–123 (2009)
18. Maia, F., Matos, M., Vilaça, R., Pereira, J., Oliveira, R., Rivire, E.: Dataflasks: epidemic store for massive scale systems. In: International Symposium on Reliable Distributed Systems, pp. 79–88 (2014)
19. Meyer, D.T., Bolosky, W.J.: A study of practical deduplication. ACM Trans. Storage **7**(4) (2012). Article No. 14
20. Muthitacharoen, A., Chen, B., Mazières, D.: A low-bandwidth network file system. In: Symposium on Operating Systems Principles, pp. 174–187 (2001)
21. Paulo, J., Pereira, J.: A survey and classification of storage deduplication systems. ACM Comput. Surv. **47**(1), 11: 1–11: 30 (2014)
22. Quinlan, S., Dorward, S.: Venti: a new approach to archival storage. In: USENIX Conference on File and Storage Technologies, pp. 1–13 (2002)
23. Rhea, S., Geels, D., Roscoe, T., Kubiatowicz, J.: Handling churn in a DHT. In: Proceedings of the USENIX Annual Technical Conference (2004)
24. Stoica, I., Morris, R., Liben-Nowell, D., Karger, D.R., Kaashoek, M.F., Dabek, F., Balakrishnan, H.: Chord: a scalable peer-to-peer lookup protocol for internet applications. Netw. IEEE/ACM Trans. **11**(1), 17–32 (2003)
25. Xia, W., Jiang, H., Feng, D., Hua, Y.: Silo: a similarity-locality based near-exact deduplication scheme with low RAM overhead and high throughput. In: USENIX Annual Technical Conference, pp. 26–30 (2011)

Block Placement Strategies
for Fault-Resilient Distributed Tuple Spaces:
An Experimental Study
(Practical Experience Report)

Roberta Barbi[1], Vitaly Buravlev[2], Claudio Antares Mezzina[2(✉)],
and Valerio Schiavoni[1(✉)]

[1] Université de Neuchâtel, Neuchâtel, Switzerland
{roberta.barbi,valerio.schiavoni}@unine.ch
[2] IMT School for Advanced Studies Lucca, Lucca, Italy
{vitaly.buravlel,claudio.mezzina}@imtlucca.it

Abstract. The tuple space abstraction provides an easy-to-use programming paradigm for distributed applications. Intuitively, it behaves like a distributed shared memory, where applications write and read entries (tuples). When deployed over a wide area network, the tuple space needs to efficiently cope with faults of links and nodes. Erasure coding techniques are increasingly popular to deal with such catastrophic events, in particular due to their storage efficiency with respect to replication. When a client writes a tuple into the system, this is first striped into k blocks and encoded into $n > k$ blocks, in a fault-redundant manner. Then, any k out of the n blocks are sufficient to reconstruct and read the tuple. This paper presents several strategies to place those blocks across the set of nodes of a wide area network, that all together form the tuple space. We present the performance trade-offs of different placement strategies by means of simulations and a Python implementation of a distributed tuple space. Our results reveal important differences in the efficiency of the different strategies, for example in terms of block fetching latency, and that having some knowledge of the underlying network graph topology is highly beneficial.

1 Introduction

We are currently observing a deluge of data originated by our personal devices. Distributed applications must be able to efficiently collect, store, process and expose data. When dealing with such applications, developers need to settle on a specific programming model, to (i) facilitate the implementation of such systems and (ii) retain user-friendliness and ability to scale, both horizontally and geographically. Distributed storage systems are one prominent example of such applications. They are typically operated across wide area networks, such

© IFIP International Federation for Information Processing 2017
Published by Springer International Publishing AG 2017. All Rights Reserved
L.Y. Chen and H.P. Reiser (Eds.): DAIS 2017, LNCS 10320, pp. 67–82, 2017.
DOI: 10.1007/978-3-319-59665-5_5

as Amazon AWS, which currently spans across 15 geographical regions.[1] In such deployment scenarios, applications must transparently tolerate faults, a common threat for distributed systems.

A trivial strategy to tolerate faults is to rely on replication. Block replication obviously entails a huge storage overhead. A state-of-the-art solution to decrease such overhead while providing the same level of fault-tolerance is to use erasure coding techniques [15]. With a systematic (n, k) linear code, each codeword (an element of the linear code) consists of n blocks: k source blocks for the original data, and $n - k$ redundant blocks. The storage overhead is $\frac{n-k}{k}$, and if the code is Maximum Distance Separable (MDS) [15], any k of the n blocks are necessary and sufficient to recover the original data.

From a fault tolerance point of view, it is optimal to place the n blocks of a codeword on different logical units (with respect to failures), so that the MDS code can tolerate up to $n - k$ failures. A logical unit can be a single node (in this case for the optimum it is sufficient to place different blocks of a codeword on different nodes), but it can also be a cluster of nodes (e.g. a set of machines physically hosted in a single room can go down at the same moment if the cooling system of the room fails). In this second scenario, one is tempted to spread different blocks of a codeword into separate and faraway clusters. Although being optimal with respect to fault tolerance, this solution affects negatively the latency to fetch the required blocks.

The case of distributed tuple spaces. A programming model can be made of two separate pieces: the *computation* model and the *coordination* model. The computation model allows programmer to build a single computational unit, while the coordination model is the glue that binds separate activities into an ensemble [10]. The tuple space paradigm, based on this idea, offers a flexible technique to program parallel and distributed systems, by providing the abstraction of a shared space where all the processes can access. In this model, communication between processes is *indirect* and *anonymous* as it is done through the shared (distributed) space. Moreover, data exists in a tuple space and do not belongs to any process. Despite the simplicity of the model, very few implementations of tuple spaces offer fault tolerant facilities usually in the form of data replication ([4,16]), with the drawbacks of space overhead and consistency maintenance. In this paper, we consider an extended, distributed tuple space system with erasure-coding capabilities. A tuple to be inserted in the tuple space is *erasure-coded* and its blocks are placed across the nodes joining the tuple space group.

Contributions. First, we study how to distribute the encoded blocks of single codewords over a large-scale network, in order to decrease the fetch latency. We do so by designing and evaluating several different block placement heuristics, over synthetic and real-world network topologies. Second, we evaluate how the proposed heuristics behave with respect to data loss when injecting faults into

---

[1] http://docs.aws.amazon.com/AWSEC2/latest/UserGuide/
using-regions-availability-zones.html.

the topology. Third, we leverage the results of our simulations to identify two suitable placement strategies that we deploy atop a simple distributed tuple space system with the aim of evaluating their performance in a practical setting.

This paper is organized as follows. First, we present the related work (Sect. 2). Next, Sect. 3 introduces the tuple space paradigm. In Sect. 4 we describe the block placement heuristics. Section 5 presents some modeling results that we leverage to drive the prototype implementation. Section 6 presents its implementation details and the extensions done to support both erasure-coding techniques and a pluggable mechanism to choose among the different placement strategies. We present the evaluation of the complete prototype in Sect. 7. We conclude in Sect. 8.

2   Related Work

The tuple space coordination model is very appealing for distributed systems thanks to its space and time decoupling and its synchronization power. As a consequence, researchers have tried to add fault-tolerance and security to tuple spaces.

One recent result is DEPSPACE [3], a Byzantine fault-tolerant coordination service, which employs process replication for handling crashes and providing fault tolerance.

An alternative to process replication is block replication which entails the problem of block placement.

Block placement policies have been mainly studied in MapReduce contexts such as Hadoop [18]. The main purpose of Hadoop's data placement policy is to provide good balance between reliability, write bandwidth, read performance and load balancing [19]. Placing all replicas on a single node incurs the lowest write bandwidth penalty but it lacks redundancy: if the node fails, data is lost. On the other hand, placing replicas in different data centers maximize redundancy, but at the cost of bandwidth.

Hadoop's default strategy is to place the first replica on the same node as the client (for clients running outside the cluster, a node is chosen at random, although the system tries not to pick nodes that are too full or too busy). The second replica is placed on a different rack from the first, chosen at random. The third replica goes to the same rack as the second, but on a different node. Further replicas are placed on random nodes on the cluster, although Hadoop's block scheduler avoids placing too many replicas on the same rack. Our *cluster-aware* and *distance-aware* strategies share some similarity with this approach, in that they take into account zones of the system that are more sensitive to simultaneous failures. Several enhancement were introduced in Hadoop with respect to block placement policies, such as pluggable policies (since v0.21) or guarantees of even distributions across the cluster (since v0.17). We envision a similar technique to rebalance blocks of the tuple space according to the announced load ratio.

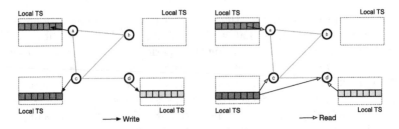

Fig. 1. Example of distributed tuple space: each node writes tuples in its own local tuple space (left) and read tuples from local and remote nodes (right).

CoHADOOP [7] is a lightweight Hadoop extension that gives applications a fine-grain control of data location. Similarly, our scheduling policies allow deployers to choose the destination of the blocks according to different performance criteria.

ADAPT [13] introduced a strategy to mitigate availability heterogeneity issues in non-dedicated distributed computing environments. ADAPT dynamically dispatches data blocks according to hosts' storage capacities. Through simulations, this strategy is shown to reduce the application runtime by more than 30%, increasing data locality and reducing data migration cost, even though the improvement of performances is less significant for environment with higher network connectivity.

3   Tuple Spaces in a Nutshell

The tuple space paradigm, made popular by Linda [9], is an abstraction of shared associative memory for parallel and distributed computing. A tuple space is a repository of tuples that processes can concurrently access via *pattern-matching*. Processes create new tuples (`out` or `write` operation), test the existence of a tuple (`read`) and consume a tuple (via the `in` operation). The simplicity of this coordination model makes this model intuitive and easy to use, also for distributed applications. In fact, some synchronization primitives (e.g. semaphores, synchronization barriers) can be easily implemented [6] leveraging this coordination model. Tuple space interaction model provides time and space decoupling, in that tuple producers and consumers remain anonymous with respect to each other [8]. Moreover a tuple has to survive its producer's termination, which can be caused by a node crash or due to the ending of the normal execution. In a distributed tuple space, each node writes tuples in its own local space, but it can read tuples also from remote ones. For example, in Fig. 1 node **D** reads also the tuple produced by node **C**.

Despite the wide development of tuple space implementations [5], very few of them offer support for distribution. While some systems use replication to guarantee data availability [16] or to be resilient to Byzantine faults [4], no existing system handle link or node faults to guarantee availability of data via erasure-coding. The extensions presented in Sect. 6 fill this gap.

4 Block Placement Strategies

In this section we describe several heuristics for block placement. Data is stored in the nodes of a graph representing a distributed storage system adding redundancy via standard [10,14] Reed-Solomon code. The aim of the code is to map 10-blocks-inputs into 14-blocks-codewords in such a way that any 10 encoded blocks are sufficient to recover the original 10. In other words, this linear code can withstand loss of any 4 blocks of a codeword. Then the code provides the same level of fault-tolerance as 5 times replication while entailing a storage overhead of 40% only.

In this configuration, from a fault-tolerance point of view, it is optimal to place the 14 blocks of a codeword on units failing independently, such as geographically remote nodes. In reality, nodes hosted in the same data center have a higher likelihood to fail or being unreachable at the same time. Indeed there are several threats that can lead a data center to a power outage. We can mention cyber attacks, UPS system failures, air conditioner failures or human errors [11].

The proposed strategies must consider a trade-off between:

– *Latency efficiency:* placing blocks apart from each other negatively affects the fetch latencies;
– *Failure resiliency:* if related blocks are placed geographically close to each other, a failure affecting a wide geographical area will affect several blocks at once.

With the aim of understanding experimentally this trade-off, we study 5 different placement heuristics. They take into account several structural graph properties (e.g. the clustering degree) with the objective of minimizing the latency for fetching blocks.

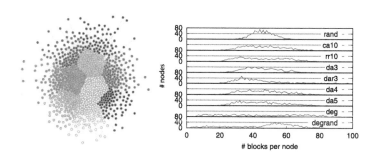

Fig. 2. Left: random graph used in this experiment. Center and right: blocks distribution induced by the placement strategies under study.

Round-robin (rr). The graph is divided into $\mathcal{K}$ clusters $C_1, \ldots, C_{\mathcal{K}}$ using $\mathcal{K}$-means algorithm [12]. We place the first block in a random node inside cluster C_1, the second block in a random node in cluster C_2 and so on. We proceed until all blocks are placed.

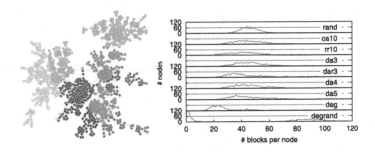

Fig. 3. Left: scale-free graph used in this experiment. Center and right: blocks distribution induced by the placement strategies under study.

Degree proportional (deg). This strategy places more blocks in nodes with higher degree. Intuitively, it let nodes with higher network capacity serve more blocks, irrespectively of their geographical location.

Cluster-aware (ca). This strategy assumes knowledge of the clustering of the network and places blocks in the cluster hosting the emitting node and two neighboring clusters. Using $\mathcal{K}$-means, we divide the graph in $\mathcal{K}$ cluster $C_1, \ldots, C_{\mathcal{K}}$. We say that cluster C_i is at distance 1 from cluster C_j if there is an edge of the graph with source/target in C_i and target/source in C_j. For each C_i, we compute all clusters being at distance 1 from C_i.

We say that clusters C_i and C_j are at distance δ from each other if we must cross $\delta - 1$ clusters to go from C_i to C_j and this is the smallest number possible. For each C_i, we compute all clusters being at distance 2 from C_i.

In our simulations, we statically precompute the distances between clusters. We select a first cluster C at random for each codeword. Then, we extract at random 8 nodes from C, 4 different ones from a cluster at distance 1 from C, and finally 2 more from a cluster at distance 2. The chosen nodes receive the 14 blocks of the codeword. Notice that this heuristic needs at least 3 clusters to work.

Distance-aware (da). This strategy takes into account the distance between the node emitting the block and the other nodes in the graph. It assumes the knowledge of the diameter of the graph (d_max), and proceeds as follows. First, 3 ranges of node-to-node distances (3 being a parameter of the algorithm) must be fixed: *short* (from the minimum to the 33rd percentile of d_max), *mid* (from the 33rd to the 66th percentile of d_max), and *long* from the 66th to d_max. Then, for each codeword the algorithm picks a node N at random, and respectively 7 short-range nodes, 4 at mid-range and 2 from long-range nodes, for a total of 14 target nodes. Finally it places the 14 blocks of the codeword in such nodes. We report results for 3 ranges (da3), for 4 ranges (da4, for which the percentiles are 25th, 50th, 70th and the number of blocks are 6, 4, 2, 1 for each range,

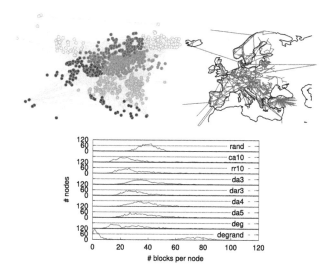

Fig. 4. NREN topology and its blocks distribution.

respectively) and finally for 5 ranges (da5, using the percentiles 20th, 40th, 60th, 80th and the number of blocks are 5, 5, 1, 1, 1 for each range respectively).[2]

Random-Degree (drnd). This strategy combines a naive random strategy with deg. Each strategy contributes for the placement of half of the blocks.

5 Simulation Results

This section presents the results of our simulations with the aim of evaluating how the different placement strategies perform with respect to fetch-latency and data loss.

Load Balancing. We begin by studying how the strategies spread blocks on 4 different graph topologies. First, we consider a random graph of 1000 nodes, as depicted in Fig. 2 on the left, where we highlight the 10 clusters computed by $\mathcal{K}$-means using the Euclidean distance between nodes. The distribution of blocks among nodes is presented in Fig. 2 (right). As expected, the rnd strategy produces a Gaussian distribution, while the other approaches tend to flatten and/or shift the bell.

Figure 3 shows topology and block distribution for a scale-free graph of 1000 nodes built using the preferential attachment method [2]. This topology closely maps a real Internet topology, yet is simple to study and analyze. We observe that deg and drnd produce a long-tail block distribution: several nodes have few

---

[2] The number of blocks assigned to each class of range nodes (da3, da4, da5) has been experimentally proved to work better in practice.

blocks (right side of the figure), while few nodes store plenty of blocks (left side of the figure).

Finally, we consider two real-world topologies. The first is the Full European NREN network [14]. This graph has 1157 nodes and 1465 edges. When computing 10 clusters, we observe 1170 inter-cluster edges (i.e. source and destination nodes belong to different clusters). Topology and block distributions are presented in Fig. 4. As an empirical confirmation that scale-free graphs are well-suited for representing Internet topologies, we underline the similarity between the two block distributions.

The second real-world topology, depicted in Fig. 5, is the Cogent network [14]. It is smaller than the NREN topology (197 nodes, 245 edges) nevertheless it extends across Europe and US. This topology presents trans-oceanic links, with 13 edges to connect nodes across the Europe and North America. Different ranges in the block distribution with respect to other graphs are due to the much smaller number of nodes (while we distribute the same amount of data blocks).

Overall, block distributions generated by the da and rr strategies tend to be bell-shaped, while dar and deg entail left-sided pick and long tail corresponding to few blocks in many nodes and few nodes hosting many blocks respectively.

For NREN and Cogent, we know the geographical coordinates of the nodes. To take into account of the curvature of the Earth and place more precisely the centroids of the clusters, we use the Haversine distance [17] as $\mathcal{K}$-means distance function.

We fix the number of cluster $\mathcal{K} = 10$ in our simulations except for Cogent topology which is split in $\mathcal{K} = 2$ clusters corresponding to USA and Europe. For the same reason, results of ca are not available for Cogent, since the heuristic requires at least 3 clusters.

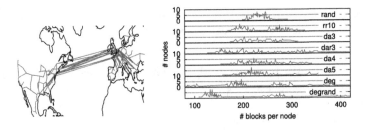

Fig. 5. Cogent topology and its blocks distribution.

Fetching latency. We continue by evaluating how the proposed strategies differ in terms of block recovery latency, as observed by the clients wishing to reconstruct matching tuples. We assume that the fetch-latency is proportional to the distance between nodes. Hence, we measure the length of the minimum paths between the node hosting the target block and the client.

We observe that a node storing a lot of blocks we necessarily need to fetch only few ones to reconstruct tuples. Hence, for each topology and each placement

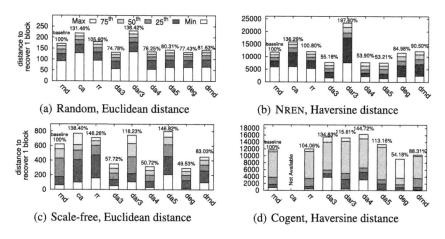

Fig. 6. Distance for fetching blocks *(lucky node)*.

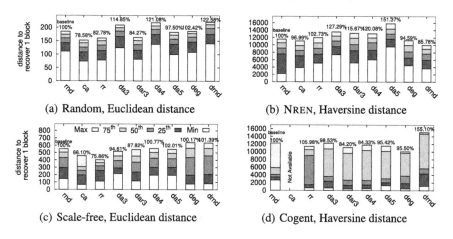

Fig. 7. Distance for fetching blocks *(unlucky node)*.

heuristic, we distinguish 3 types of clients based on the number of blocks they store. The *lucky* and the *unlucky* node stores the greatest and the smallest amount of blocks respectively.

We use a representation based on stacked percentiles throughout the reminder of this section. The white bar at the bottom represents the minimum value, the pale gray on top the maximal value. Intermediate shades of gray represent the 25th, 50th –the median– and 75th percentiles. We compare the results against a baseline `rnd` strategy that randomly places blocks across the graph. Figures 6 and 7 presents the case of the *lucky* and *unlucky* node respectively.

These results validate the intuition that the number of blocks the client is storing greatly affects the observed fetch-latency. For instance, `da3` performs better than other heuristics in 3 out of 4 topologies when the client is *lucky*.

However, this is not the case for the *unlucky* case, where `deg` and `rr` perform better instead. These observations suggest that no strategy wins in all possible topologies, and that deployers need to carefully consider the different trade-offs for their applications and workloads.

Fetching latency under faults. Next, we perform a set of experiments that faults into the graph. For each graph, we select the most populated among the 10 clusters and we crash 1% of its nodes. This setting simulates a catastrophic event occurring to nodes geographically close to each other. Once the faults are injected, we use the *lucky* nodes (Fig. 8) and *unlucky* nodes (Fig. 9) to try to reconstruct all data stored.

During these simulations, we did not observe any data loss. Hence, the heuristics are spreading blocks sufficiently apart from each other to tolerate crashes within the same cluster.

However, when injecting faults the fetch-latency highly depends on the particular failing nodes. In the case of the Cogent topology, the `deg` strategy greatly improves the results produced by the `rnd` placement, while on the scale-free graph performance degrades for the unlucky client. The `da3` strategy outperforms the other heuristics in the NREN topology. More in general, distance-aware heuristics seem to be well-suited for the random graph.

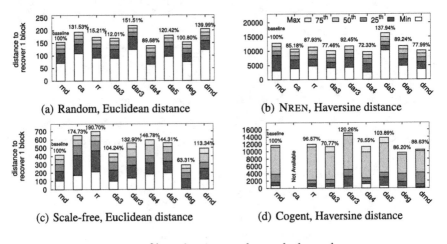

(a) Random, Euclidean distance   (b) NREN, Haversine distance

(c) Scale-free, Euclidean distance   (d) Cogent, Haversine distance

Fig. 8. 1% crashes in one cluster, lucky node.

Statistical analysis. Finally, to evaluate the statistical significance of the differences recorded by the simulations between the various heuristics, we perform two sets of *t-tests* [12] on fault-free graphs. First, we build the dataset with one entry for every node. In this entry we compute the cumulative distance, that is, the sum of the length of all minimum paths covered to retrieve all data in the system from that particular client. We fix a topology and compare different heuristics against each other. We find the following p-values:

	scale-free graph	random graph	NREN	Cogent
t.test(rnd,deg)	0.2486	0.03055	0.00761	0.7828
t.test(rnd,da3)	0.4805	0.3242	0.3774	0.2203

These p-values answer the question: "what is the probability that the means of the cumulative distances covered by the two heuristics are equal?". For every graph we found an heuristic between da3 and deg such that the probability is less the 25%. We consider this a low evidence that the two means are the same but still such a value does not provide a decisive response.

For this reason, instead of using cumulative distances, we create a dataset of the distances covered to fetch every block by each node in the graph (e.g. in the case of the scale-free graph the dataset has 1000 entries times the number of blocks fetched, *i.e.* 3276000 entries). We run t-tests on random 1000-entries-samples from this dataset to compare different heuristics against each other. We find the following p-values:

	scale-free graph	random graph	NREN	Cogent
t.test(rnd,deg)	0.1661	$6 \cdot 10^{-6}$	0.0004	0.6475
t.test(rnd,da3)	0.4215	0.0406	0.2936	0.1042

So for every topology we can find a heuristic between deg and da3 with support less than 16% for the hypothesis that the distance covered is the same as the one covered by rand. We take into account the modeling and statistical results to implement deg and da3 into in a real tuple space and evaluate how they perform in a practical setting.

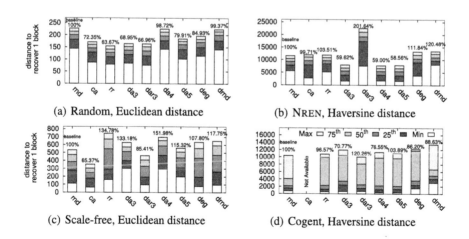

(a) Random, Euclidean distance   (b) NREN, Haversine distance

(c) Scale-free, Euclidean distance   (d) Cogent, Haversine distance

Fig. 9. 1% crashes in one cluster, unlucky node.

6   Implementation

We implement and deploy three of the described blocks placement strategies (da3, deg and rnd) atop SIMPLETS,[3] a tuple-space implemented in Python (v3.4.0). The original implementation of SIMPLETS did not support remote tuple space nodes. Therefore, we first extended it to support a distributed scenario, leveraging PYRO (v4.0),[4] a remoting library for Python. Overall, our modifications to the SIMPLETS source code consist of only 250 additional lines of code.

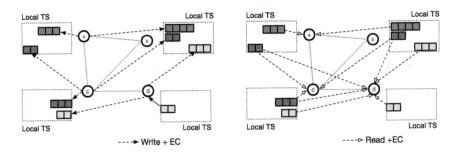

Fig. 10. Distributed tuple space with erasure code: write ops. spread blocks apart driven by a specific strategy; read ops. fetch blocks from remote nodes.

To add erasure coding and block placement techniques, we extend the tuple space APIs with additional operations to properly handle writing, reading, and deletion of encoded tuples. For example, using a [10, 14] Reed-Solomon code, the out(t) operation that emits the tuple t in the tuple space, becomes out_ec(t). This version encodes the tuple, splits it into 14 blocks and, according to the chosen strategy, distributes these blocks among the other nodes. To this end, from the original tuple a list of tuples of the following form is created: <tupleUID, blocksAndIndicesList, nodeList> where tupleUID is a unique identifier of the original tuple t, blocksAndIndicesList is a list of pairs (b_i, i) indicating that b_i is the i-th block of the codeword and nodeList is a list of nodes containing the remaining blocks. Figure 10 shows the extended version of SIMPLETS with erasure coding abilities.

In this configuration, reading a tuple only require to fetch 10 out of the 14 existing blocks. The tuple space programming paradigm requires the reading operations to operate via pattern-matching [9]. In the case of encoded tuples, the tuple space needs to decode the tuple. Therefore, this operation sequentially reads a tuple with blocks from the tuple space. Specifically, it leverages the nodeList index to discover and retrieve the missing blocks from other nodes in order to reconstruct the tuple. Then it checks whether the reconstructed tuples matches the template. Clearly, in the worst case to find a matching tuple the

---

[3] https://github.com/jmbjorndalen/SimpleTS.
[4] https://pythonhosted.org/Pyro4/.

system has to decode the entire tuple space. We assume the existence of an up-to-date indexing service that serves the purpose of speeding up the process of discovering the location of the required blocks. In our evaluation, we assume to know the location of the nodes storing the blocks required to decode the tuple. It is out of the scope of this work how to efficiently maintain this index.

We implement both `da3` and `deg` strategies on our tuple space and test them on a *scale-free* network made of 100 nodes. We emulate a large-scale network deployment using Docker (v1.13.1). We map each SIMPLETS node (with its local tuple space) to a standalone container. The latency between two nodes, say i and j, is proportional to their minimum distance on the graph. Latency (by mean of a `sleep` system call) is then interposed by the proxy interface of the Pyro service exposed by each tuple space process. In practice, when node i contacts node j to read (or write) a tuple, node j sleeps $latency_{i,j}$ milliseconds before replying. An alternative method is be to add latency at the OS level, e.g. by implementing a software router.[5]

7 Prototype Evaluation

This section presents our evaluation with the extended SIMPLETS system. Due to the lack of hardware resources, we are limited to a cluster of 100 node mimicking a *scale-free* network. Each node is executed by a SIMPLETS Docker container. In this evaluation, only communication delays among nodes are emulated.

Erasure-coding overhead. To evaluate the overhead of erasure coding, we execute an initial set of microbenchmarks for reading times. In this experiment, we vary the size of data stored in each tuple, from 1 byte to 512 KB. At the beginning, we randomly distribute 1000 tuples across 100 nodes. Then, 10 random nodes read all the 1000 tuples. We measure the time for reading each tuple, and we report them as Cumulative Distribution Function (CDF). As shown in Fig. 11 (left), the size of the tuple only modestly affects the reading time from the tuple space without encoding.

When erasure coding is enabled, Fig. 11 (right), the reading time is more sensitive to the tuple size: it grows from milliseconds for the tuples containing 1 byte to several seconds for the size of 512 KB. For bigger tuples, the time for encoding and decoding is significantly higher. We believe that a highly optimized erasure-code library, such as Intel ISA-L [1], would greatly reduce the overhead and make it more practical.

Experiments with different strategies. This experiment evaluates the performances of the tuple space using different block placement strategies. At the beginning, each of the 100 nodes writes 10 tuples. The tuples are encoded and

---

[5] We report on our failed attempt in using Linux `tc`'s traffic shaping (using *delay.sh* https://gist.github.com/arr2036/6598137) to emulate network latencies. In particular, the current Docker networking layer does not cope well with this approach, where all nodes in a given network class (such as all the Docker containers running in the same host) apply the same delay, preventing the emulation of more complex graph topologies.

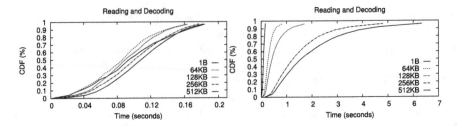

Fig. 11. Distribution (CDF) of tuple's reading performance for increasing tuple size. Left: without erasure-coding. Right: with erasure-coding.

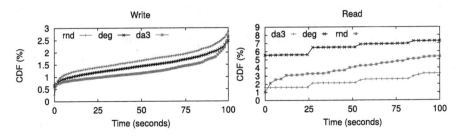

Fig. 12. Writing and the reading times for different strategies of blocks placement

split into blocks. Those are dispatched to remote nodes according to the given strategy. Finally, a node is chosen to fetch and reads the blocks of its own tuples.

Figure 12 presents our results for write and read operations.[6] The plot shows the CDF of the timings to write/read the tuples into/from the tuple space. The da3 strategy achieves the best performances for writes, because the writing time depends on the number of nodes used to spread each tuple's blocks. Random placement offers the worst performance as it involves a high number of nodes. The reading time depends on the distribution of the blocks among the nodes. The distributions obtained reflect the ones shown in Fig. 3 and we do not report them here due to lack of space. For the distance-aware and random strategies, distributions are more uniform and the times are low. For the degree-aware strategy, nodes with the higher degree have considerably more blocks and the reading time vary significantly. As consequence, the reading time depends also on the order in which tuples are written. In the case of SIMPLETS, the tuple space is implemented as a list, hence the reading time will be greater for the tuples which were written toward the end.

8   Conclusion

The problem of data block placement in a wide-area network setting is of paramount importance. Several distributed applications rely on a random strategy.

---

[6] We omit the results for withdrawing operations. They show similar trends to read results plus a small overhead due to the fetching of all the 14 blocks.

In this paper we considered a scenario where distributed applications are implemented via the tuple space paradigm. These systems need to efficiently cope with network faults to avoid losing tuples, while at the same time being storage efficient and allow fast fetching time. We extended an open-source Python-based tuple-space implementation with distribution capabilities and erasure-coding features. We presented a study of several block placement strategies to dispatch blocks over the nodes of a distributed tuple space. We considered synthetic and real-world graph topologies, up to thousands of nodes. Our modeling, statistical analysis and system performance results, also based the evaluation of our full working prototype, shed some light on the trade-offs that one need to accept when deploying such systems. Our results reinforce the believe that it is important to gather structural informations about the underlying network topology to wisely choose the appropriate block placement heuristic.

In this work we considered the distributed tuple space as practical use-case. We stress that our strategies are general purpose and can be deployed in other distributed systems such as distributed key-value stores.

Acknowledgments. The authors are grateful to Hugues Mercier and Pascal Felber for invaluable discussions during the preliminary phases of this work. We are grateful to Rocco De Nicola for fruitful discussions around tuple spaces. This research was partially supported by the European Union's Horizon 2020 - The EU Framework Programme for Research and Innovation 2014–2020, under grant agreement No. 653884.

References

1. Intel's ISA-L. https://github.com/01org/isa-l
2. Barabási, A.-L., Albert, R.: Emergence of scaling in random networks. Science **286**(5439), 509–512 (1999)
3. Bessani, A.N., Alchieri, E.P., Correia, M., Fraga, J.S.: Depspace: a byzantine fault-tolerant coordination service. In: ACM SIGOPS Operating Systems Review, vol. 42, pp. 163–176. ACM (2008)
4. Bessani, A.N., Correia, M., da Silva Fraga, J., Lung, L.C.: An efficient byzantine-resilient tuple space. IEEE Trans. Comput. **58**(8), 1080–1094 (2009)
5. Buravlev, V., De Nicola, R., Mezzina, C.A.: Tuple spaces implementations and their efficiency. In: Lluch Lafuente, A., Proença, J. (eds.) COORDINATION 2016. LNCS, vol. 9686, pp. 51–66. Springer, Cham (2016). doi:10.1007/978-3-319-39519-7_4
6. Carriero, N., Gelernter, D.: How to Write Parallel Programs: A First Course. MIT Press, Cambridge (1990)
7. Eltabakh, M.Y., Tian, Y., Özcan, F., Gemulla, R., Krettek, A., McPherson, J.: CoHadoop: flexible data placement and its exploitation in Hadoop. Proc. VLDB Endowment **4**(9), 575–585 (2011)
8. Eugster, P.T., Felber, P.A., Guerraoui, R., Kermarrec, A.-M.: The many faces of publish/subscribe. ACM Comput. Surv. **35**(2), 114–131 (2003)
9. Gelernter, D.: Generative communication in Linda. ACM Trans. Programm. Lang. Syst. (TOPLAS), **7**(1), 80–112 (1985)
10. Gelernter, D., Carriero, N.: Coordination languages and their significance. Commun. ACM **35**(2), 97–107 (1992)

11. Ponemon Institute: 2013 cost of data center outages (2013)
12. James, G., Witten, D., Hastie, T., Tibshirani, R.: An Introduction to Statistical Learning, vol. 6. Springer, New York (2013)
13. Jin, H., Yang, X., Sun, X.-H., Raicu, I.: Adapt: availability-aware mapreduce data placement for non-dedicated distributed computing. In: 2012 IEEE 32nd International Conference on Distributed Computing Systems (ICDCS), pp. 516–525. IEEE (2012)
14. Knight, S., Nguyen, H., Falkner, N., Bowden, R., Roughan, M.: The internet topology zoo. IEEE J. Sel. Areas Commun. **29**(9), 1765–1775 (2011)
15. MacWilliams, F.J., Sloane, N.J.A.: The Theory of Error-Correcting Codes. Elsevier, New York (1977)
16. Patterson, L.I., Turner, R.S., Hyatt, R.M.: Construction of a fault-tolerant distributed tuple-space. In: SAC 1993, pp. 279–285. ACM, New York (1993)
17. Robusto, C.C.: The Cosine-Haversine formula. Am. Math. Mon. **64**(1), 38–40 (1957)
18. Shvachko, K., Kuang, H., Radia, S., Chansler, R.: The Hadoop distributed file system. In: 2010 IEEE 26th Symposium on Mass Storage Systems and Technologies (MSST), pp. 1–10. IEEE (2010)
19. White, T.: Hadoop: The Definitive Guide. O'Reilly Media, Inc., Sebastopol (2012)

Private Data System Enabling Self-Sovereign Storage Managed by Executable Choreographies

Sinică Alboaie[1,2] and Doina Cosovan[1(✉)]

[1] Alexandru Ioan Cuza University of Iasi, Iaşi, Romania
salboaie@gmail.com, doina.cosovan@info.uaic.ro
[2] Technical University of Cluj-Napoca, Iaşi, Romania

Abstract. With the increased use of Internet, governments and large companies store and share massive amounts of personal data in such a way that leaves no space for transparency. When a user needs to achieve a simple task like applying for college or a driving license, he needs to visit a lot of institutions and organizations, thus leaving a lot of private data in many places. The same happens when using the Internet. These privacy issues raised by the centralized architectures along with the recent developments in the area of serverless applications demand a decentralized private data layer under user control.

We introduce the Private Data System (PDS), a distributed approach which enables self-sovereign storage and sharing of private data. The system is composed of nodes spread across the entire Internet managing local key-value databases. The communication between nodes is achieved through executable choreographies, which are capable of preventing information leakage when executing across different organizations with different regulations in place.

The user has full control over his private data and is able to share and revoke access to organizations at any time. Even more, the updates are propagated instantly to all the parties which have access to the data thanks to the system design. Specifically, the processing organizations may retrieve and process the shared information, but are not allowed under any circumstances to store it on long term.

PDS offers an alternative to systems that aim to ensure self-sovereignty of specific types of data through blockchain inspired techniques but face various problems, such as low performance. Both approaches propose a distributed database, but with different characteristics. While the blockchain-based systems are built to solve consensus problems, PDS's purpose is to solve the self-sovereignty aspects raised by the privacy laws, rules and principles.

Keywords: Privacy Enhancing Technique · Privacy by Design · Privacy by Default · Data self-sovereignty · Privacy · Private data · Distributed storage · Executable choreography

© IFIP International Federation for Information Processing 2017
Published by Springer International Publishing AG 2017. All Rights Reserved
L.Y. Chen and H.P. Reiser (Eds.): DAIS 2017, LNCS 10320, pp. 83–98, 2017.
DOI: 10.1007/978-3-319-59665-5_6

1   Introduction

Every time a user needs to create an account, he needs to provide a lot of private information, like name, birth date, gender, marital status, and so on. Even more, he needs to choose and answer to some security questions for account recovery in case he forgets the password or simply for user validation when performing sensitive actions. These security questions usually consist of private data as well.

This way, each user spreads his private data to a lot of organizations/companies/service providers. This raises two main issues: one is related to data protection and the other - to data duplication. In regards to data protection, each organization has its own ways of storing and protecting the data. Some are better than others. The user's data is as safe as the weakest organization to which the user provided his data. Thus an attacker can target the weakest link to learn private information. The data duplication issue consists mainly of the fact that changing a piece of private information (like changing the last name by getting married) requires updating it in all the places this particular piece of private information was saved, which is burdening and time consuming.

An existing way of solving these problems is by using single sign-on techniques. But this makes the user dependent on the single sign-on provider because losing access to the account used for single sign-on means losing access to all the accounts authenticating the user with this single sign-on account.

We propose a solution that enables users to keep full control over their private data. Private Data System (PDS) is a distributed scalable system composed of three types of nodes, transparently spread across the entire Internet: audit, index and storage nodes. Each node manages a local key-value database and each type of node has its own purpose in the system, as explained further.

Each piece of private information is split into undecipherable chunks. Each chunk is assigned a different partial key in a different key-value database managed by a different storage node. The association between these keys is stored under a master key in a key-value database managed by an index node. Since the data needs to be accessible by different processing nodes, the master key is referenced by different key references. The association between them is stored under a key reference in a key-value database managed by an audit node. The key references are the only points of access to the actual data. Hence it also contains information regarding who owns the referenced data, who was this particular key reference shared with, and metadata describing the referenced data.

The communication between nodes is achieved with the help of executable choreographies, which visit the needed nodes in the needed order, execute on each node the needed operations, and return to the user with the results.

An interesting use case of using PDS are social networks and other systems which, besides private data, manage also trust and reputation data [5].

We will start by reviewing the related work (Sect. 2) and introducing the system along with its elements (Sect. 3). Then, we'll explain how CRUD (create, read, update, delete) and sharing/revoking operations work (Sect. 4). In the end, we will analyze the proposed system from the privacy perspective (Sect. 5), conclude (Sect. 6), and present future directions in regards to the proposed system (Sect. 7).

2   Related Work

Smart systems integrate technology, organizations and people in order to accomplish complex processes that are controlled by computer systems. For a large number of integration points, integration is achieved through classical ESB (Enterprise Service Bus) - type systems [8], MOM (Message-Oriented Middleware) systems [9], systems based on EIP (Enterprise Integration Patterns) [11] or through the orchestration of services through custom code or languages used to model business processes [12].

All these methods tend to be sufficient to integrate the components belonging to one organization. On the other hand, the integration among multiple organizations should be addressed using choreographies as any centralized solution is risky in terms of security and private data protection. Composition of systems using orchestration tends to create centralized systems.

Although many authors perceive choreographies as a mechanism to describe in a more formal way the contracts among several organizations [1], the academic research proposed the concept of executable choreographies [4,6,7]. They suggest transforming the descriptions of the choreographies in code that is executed inside each organization participating in the choreography. As such, a choreography is not only a formal description of a contract among organizations but also a description of a workflow in an executable way. The same description (choreography) gets to run in several organizations in a decentralized manner (without the need for a centralized conductor) and therefore any need to translate the choreography into other programming languages disappears.

While PDS could be implemented outside the world of the executable choreographies, we believe that choreographies are suitable for the complex workflows operating across multiple organizations. The code of the executable choreographies is verifiable at a higher level and can provide confidence that the implementation provides the privacy properties of the theoretical model.

Another advantage of the executable choreographies is that it comes with a solution for the self sovereign identity. The Sovrin Foundation explains in [15] why the rise of the self sovereign identities was inevitable and details the path that had to be traversed for the community to come to this conclusion.

For PDS, the data owner must be identified and authorized. Supplementary benefits in the data leakage preventions could be achieved if the data owner is identified in all the other organizations contributing to a request without leaking its identity (using some anonymous aliases controlled by the data owner). The executable choreographies aim at offering these benefits without any supplementary implementation effort. However, detailing the way in which the self sovereign identities used by the data owners and processors are authenticated and authorized is not the purpose of this paper. It is a complex enough topic to require its own paper, so we will revisit this issue at a later date.

In regards to the advances related to data sovereignty, we would like to mention [10], which proposes storing encrypted data in cloud federations and [3], which proposes sovereign information sharing in order to integrate the information belonging to autonomous entities. Queries are executed on the databases and reveal only the results. The work is continued in [2] which enables sovereign information sharing using web services. This work applies to service providers which want to allow queries on their databases without sharing the content on which the queries are executed. Our work focuses on the average user which needs to own and store his data in a single place and provide/revoke access to it to various service providers as needed.

Note that [14] introduces the data sovereignty notion for establishing the nation-state where the cloud storage service providers are storing the data physically in order to ensure they are meeting their contractual geographic obligations. In this paper, we consider data sovereignty to be the ability of the user to have full control over his data and the entities to which it is shared or revoked.

States and international organizations start to gradually introduce principles and standards, the most notable being Privacy By Design [13]. Collecting information in parallel with the absence of technical constraints on how companies can use the data intentionally or unintentionally begins to be perceived as a risk. On the one hand, there are risks for companies because users could refuse to adopt privacy challenged technologies. On the other hand, we have risks regarding the whole society, the most obvious being represented by the potential that some companies can influence society in illegal and immoral manners.

Commercial exploitation of private data has come to create the impression that people are exploited commercially in ways that do not adequately compensate for the risks they take. A more transparent model that allows fair and equitable use of personal data is needed. Considering all these aspects, the article proposes a software architecture in which private data's storage places are under the strict control of the user or his delegates.

3   System Elements

In this section, we define the terminology used for the Private Data System throughout this paper. First, we define the following **roles:**

Data Owner (DO) represents the identity which owns the data.

Data Processor (DP) represents the identity which processes the data; the identity to which the data was shared.

Second, we define the following **types of data:**

Private Data (PD) represents the private data which is to be stored in the system; if a piece of private data PD is split into n undecipherable chunks, then PD_i, $i = 0$, n is an undecipherable chunk of data.

Metadata (MD) specifies the relationship between the Private Data and Data Processors by labeling the data according to the Data Owner and ontologies.

Third, since the system is based on key-value databases, we define the following **keys for data storage, associations, and references:**

Master Key (MK) represents and anonymizes a piece of private information.

Partial Key (PK) represents and anonymizes one undecipherable chunk from the set of undecipherable chunks in which a piece of private information was split. Thus, the MK is associated to the set of PKs which represent the set of undecipherable chunks needed to recombine the piece of private information.

Key Reference (KR) represents a reference to/an alias of a piece of private information (a reference to a Master Key).

Key Reference Hash (KRH) is obtained by applying a hash function on the Key Reference value and adding the address of the processing node which is to receive the results.

In the end, we define the following types of nodes:

Processing Node (PN) stores Key References and needs to retrieve and process the private data referenced by them. Processing nodes are forbidden by law to store the retrieved data on long term.

Audit Node (AN) manages a key-value database which stores the association between Key References and the Master Keys they reference along with the information describing the data referenced by the Master Key (Data Owner, Data Processor, and Metadata). In the database, the key is a Key Reference and the value is a tuple consisting of the Master Key, the Metadata, the Data Owner, and the Data Processor.

Index Node (IN) manages a key-value database which stores the association between Master Keys and its corresponding Partial Keys. In the database, the key is the Master Key and the value is the list of Partial Keys needed to reconstruct the piece of private information represented by the Master Key.

Storage Node (SN) manages a key-value database which stores the association between Partial Keys and Partial Messages. In the database, the key is the Partial Key and the value is the undecipherable chunk of data represented by this particular Partial Key.

4   System Operations

In this section we detail the way in which CRUD (Create, Read, Update, Delete) operations as well as copying, sharing, and revoking access to data are performed in the proposed system. For simplicity, we are going to use the following notations throughout this paper:

- $[E_1, E_2, ..., E_n]$ is a list containing the elements $E_1, E_2, ..., E_n$.
- $(E_1, E_2, ..., E_n)$ is a tuple containing the elements $E_1, E_2, ..., E_n$.
- $\{K_1 : V_1, K_2 : V_2, ..., K_n : V_n\}$ is a dictionary in which the value V_1 is stored under the key K_1, the value V_2 is stored under the key K_2, ..., and the value V_n is stored under the key K_n.

- $N_1 \rightarrow N_2 : M$ means the node N_1 sends to the node N_2 the message M, which corresponds to performing a step in the executable choreography.
- $DB[K] := V$ means the value V is stored under the key K in the key-value database DB by the node managing DB.
- $V := DB[K]$ means the value V associated to the key K is retrieved from the key-value database DB by the node managing DB.
- $N_1 : A$ means the node N_1 performs the action A.
- $M := gen()$ means the message M is generated (either randomly or according to an algorithm); this is an action.
- $PD_1, PD_2, ..., PD_n := split(PD)$ means the private data PD is split into n undecipherable chunks of data $PD_1, PD_2, ..., PD_n$; this is an action.
- $PD := recombine(PD_1, PD_2, ..., PD_n)$ means the n undecipherable chunks of data $PD_1, PD_2, ..., PD_n$ are recombined in order to obtain the initial piece of private data PD which was split to obtain them; this is an action.

4.1   Creating/Storing Private Data

The storage of private data is achieved in three phases, illustrated at a higher level in Fig. 1 and detailed in the following schema:

Phase 1

1. $PN \rightarrow AN : DO, MD$
2. $AN : MK := gen()$
3. $AN : KR := gen()$
4. $AN[KR] := (MK, MD, DO, DP)$
5. $AN \rightarrow PN : KR, MK$

Phase 2

1. $PN : PD_1, PD_2, ..., PD_n := split(PD)$
2. $PN :$ chooses randomly n SNs
3. $PN \rightarrow SN_i : PD_i, i = \overline{1, n}$
4. $SN_i : PK_i := gen(), i = \overline{1, n}$
5. $SN_i[PK_i] := PD_i, i = \overline{1, n}$
6. $SN_i \rightarrow PN : PK_i, i = \overline{1, n}$

Phase 3

1. $PN \rightarrow IN : MK, PK_1, PK_2, ..., PK_n$
2. $IN[MK] := [PK_1, PK_2, ..., PK_n]$
3. $PN[alias] := KR$

When a processing node needs to store private data, it starts the first phase by sending to an audit node the metadata describing the information it wants to store along with its identity (considered both data owner because it stores its information and data processor because it is the identity which is going to use the associated reference key for data retrieval). The audit node first generates a

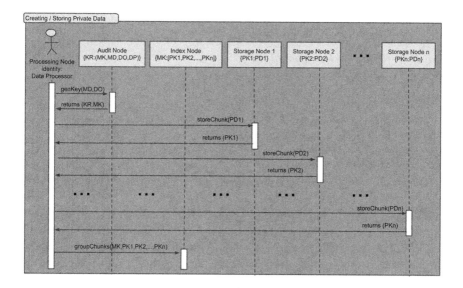

Fig. 1. Storing private data

master key and a key reference, then stores the generated master key, the received metadata, and the received data owner (as both data owner and data processor) under the generated key reference in its key-value database. The audit node completes this phase by sending the generated master key and the key reference to the processing node.

In the second phase, the processing node splits the private information into n undecipherable chunks $PD_1, PD_2, ..., PD_n$ and chooses randomly n storage nodes so that each storage node is responsible for storing a single undecipherable chunk of private data. Each storage node, upon receiving its undecipherable piece of private data, generates a partial key, stores its chunk of information under that key, and sends to the processing node the generated partial key.

In the third phase, the user sends to an index node the master key and its corresponding partial keys. The processing node stores the key reference under an alias because it is needed for subsequent private information retrieval.

4.2 Reading/Retrieving Private Data

If a processing node needs to access a private information, it must have a key reference. The way the processing node uses the key reference to retrieve the associated private information can be followed in Fig. 2 and is described in detail in the following schema:

Phase 1

1. $PN \rightarrow AN : DP, KR$

Phase 2

1. $MK := AN[KR]$
2. $HKR := (location(PN), hash(KR))$
3. $AN \rightarrow IN : DP, MK, HKR$

Phase 3

1. $PK_1, PK_2, \ldots, PK_n := IN[MK]$
2. $IN \rightarrow SN_i : DP, HKR, PK_i, i = \overline{1, n}$
3. $PD_i := SN_i[PK_i], i = \overline{1, n}$
4. $SN_i \rightarrow PN : HKR, PD_i, i = \overline{1, n}$
5. $PN : PD := recombine(PD_1, PD_2, ..., PD_n)$, where $PD_i, i = \overline{1, n}$ must have the same HKR as PD

The key reference might reference either a piece of private information of the processing node or a piece of private information shared to the processing node by another processing node. By sending his key reference to the audit node along with his (processing node's) identity, the processing node completes the first phase.

In phase two, the audit node retrieves the master key corresponding to the received key reference. Next, it computes HKR, which is a hash on the retrieved key reference prefixed with the location of the processing node. Then, the audit node sends the processing node's identity, the retrieved master key, and the computed HKR to the index node. This way, the index node doesn't learn the association between key references and master keys, but at the same time propagates HKR, which is information required by the processing node to identify the request being answered. Note that the processing node might issue multiple data retrieval operations at the same time and, without HKR, the processing node wouldn't know which undecipherable chunks correspond to which pieces of private data he requested at the same time.

In the third phase, the index node retrieves from its database the partial keys corresponding to the master key and sends each partial key along with the processing node's identity and HKR to the corresponding storage nodes. Each storage node retrieves the undecipherable value (PD_i) corresponding to the received partial key (PK_i) and sends to the processing node the retrieved undecipherable chunk and the HKR. The processing node, upon receiving the undecipherable chunks, groups them by HKR and recombines the grouped components in order to obtain the private piece of information. This information can be processed, but the law prevents the processing node to store it.

Thus HKR's purpose is to serve as an identifier so that a processing node which retrieves multiple private information pieces at the same time can associate the received undecipherable pieces of information to the requested key references.

4.3   Updating Private Data

The first two phases are identical for data retrieving and data updating, but starting with the third step of the third phase, things are performed differently as can be observed in the following schema:

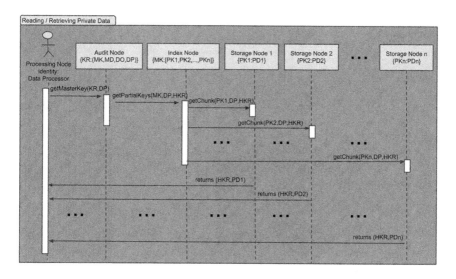

Fig. 2. Retrieving private data

Phase 1

1. $PN \rightarrow AN : DP, KR$

Phase 2

1. $MK := AN[KR]$
2. $HKR := (location(PN), hash(KR))$
3. $AN \rightarrow IN : DP, MK, HKR$

Phase 3

1. $PK_1, PK_2, ..., PK_n := IN[MK]$
2. $IN \rightarrow SN_i : DP, HKR, PK_i, i = \overline{1, n}$
3. $SN_i \rightarrow PN : HKR, i = \overline{1, n}$
4. $PN : PD_1, PD_2, ..., PD_n := split(PD)$
5. $PN \rightarrow SN_i : PD_i, i = \overline{1, n}$
6. $SN_i[PK_i] := PD_i, i = \overline{1, n}$

The storage nodes, upon receiving the partial keys from the index node, instead of retrieving the undecipherable chunks of private data corresponding to the partial keys and sending them along with HKR to the processing node for recombination as performed by the storing operation, for the updating operation they send the HKR alone to the processing node. Upon receiving the HKR from the storage nodes, the processing node splits the new information in undecipherable chunks and sends one chunk to each storage node which sent the HKR corresponding to this piece of private information. Then, the storage nodes update the values stored under the partial keys in their key-value database in accordance to the newly received undecipherable chunks.

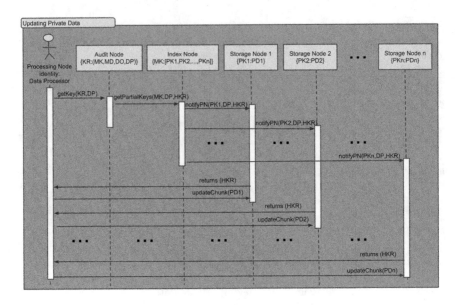

Fig. 3. Updating private data

The reason we decided to go with this approach rather than use an invalidation and a store operation is because we want all the existing key references to remain valid and, even more, to point to the updated private data.

The data flow between the nodes which are part of the system during an update operation can be observed in Fig. 3.

4.4   Deleting Private Data

Figure 4 illustrates the data flow and the following schema illustrates the actions performed during a delete operation:

1. $PN \rightarrow AN : KR, DO$
2. $MK := AN[KR]$
3. $AN \rightarrow IN : MK$
4. IN : invalidate $IN[MK]$

In order to perform a delete operation, a processing node sends to the audit node its identity (which must be the identity of the data owner) and its key reference of the data to be deleted. If the audit node would invalidate the received key reference, this would mean only revoking access to the private data for the data owner, while all the data processors which received access to this private data at some point in time would still be able to access the data. Thus, instead of doing this, the audit node sends the received key reference to the index node for it to invalidate the associated master key. In this way, neither the data owner, nor the data processors will be able to access this piece of private data anymore

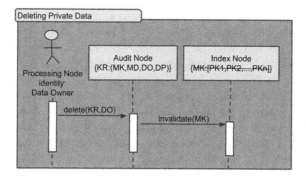

Fig. 4. Deleting private data

because all the key references they have for this piece of private data point to the same master key.

4.5 Sharing Access to Private Data

The sharing operation is described in Fig. 5 and follows the following steps:

1. $PN_1 \rightarrow AN : KR_1, DP_2$
2. $MK, MD, DO := AN[KR_1]$
3. $AN : KR_2 := gen()$
4. $AN[KR_2] := (MK, MD, DO, DP_2)$
5. $AN \rightarrow PN_2 : KR_2, MD$

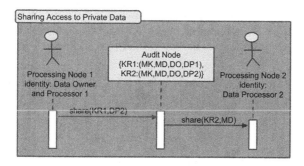

Fig. 5. Sharing access to private data

In order to share a piece of information, a processing node (PN_1) must send to an audit node its key reference (KR_1) of the private information it wants to share along with the identity of the processing node that is to receive access to the private information (DP_2). When this happens, the audit node retrieves the master key (MK) corresponding to the received key reference (KR_1), generates a new key reference (KR_2), and saves the retrieved master key (MK), the retrieved metadata (MD), the retrieved data owner (DO) and the received data processor (DP_2) under the newly generated key reference (KR_2). Of course, the initial association (between KR_1 and MK) remains in the database, as well.

Note that every association between a key reference and a master key also has information regarding the identity of the organization owning the data (Data Owner) and the identity of the organization with which data is shared (Data Processor). If data owner is the same with data processor, then this association is the initial key reference created when the private information was first stored.

Next, the audit node sends the newly generated key reference (KR_2) along with the received metadata (MD) to the processing node which is to receive access (PN_2) to the private data. In this way, neither data owner knows the data processor's key reference, nor the data processor knows the data owner's key reference.

4.6   Revoking Access to Private Data

The revocation operation is described in Fig. 6 and follows the following steps:

1. $PN \rightarrow AN : KR_1, DO, DP_2$
2. $MK := AN[KR_1]$
3. search KR_2 which contains MK, DO, DP_2 as values
4. invalidate $AN[KR_2]$

The data owner can revoke access to a private information by issuing a revocation request to the audit node. The revocation request contains the identity of the data owner and of the data processor to which access is being revoked as well as the data owner's key reference (KR_1). Note that we receive the data owner's key reference, while the revocation needs to be done on data processor's key reference (KR_2). This happens because each processing node knows its key reference, but it doesn't know the key references of the data processors which

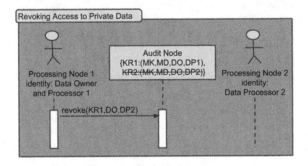

Fig. 6. Revoking access to private data

have access to its data. So, the audit node needs to retrieve the master key corresponding to the received key reference (KR_1) and search the key reference to be revoked (KR_2) knowing that it has associated the retrieved master key and the received data owner and data processor. After learning the value of the reference key to be revoked, the audit node simply invalidates it. Nothing is deleted.

4.7   Copying Private Data

By design, any copy operation on the private data should be done only through the sharing operation. Data derived from the private data should be stored in the PDS and assigned to the original data owner.

5   System Analysis from the Privacy Perspective

In this section we are going to analyze how powerful each type of node defined in the system is and how much information they can gather by themselves or by colluding with other types of nodes.

Each storage node has access to only one undecipherable chunk of each private piece of information it stores. Each chunk is saved under a partial key which has no meaning to the storage node. The storage node doesn't know which other storage nodes the other chunks of the same pieces of private information store, nor under which partial keys. Even more, the storage node doesn't know what type of information it stores. It may be a social security number, a password, a name, a birth date, and so on. A single storage node can't attack the system and neither can a collection of colluding storage nodes.

Index nodes store only the associations between master keys and partial keys. So, they know the partial keys whose corresponding undecipherable chunks can be recombined to form a private piece of information, but they don't know the values of the actual chunks, nor the type of information that will be obtained after recombining the chunks. A single index node can't attack the system and neither a collection of colluding index nodes.

Audit nodes have information regarding the meaning of the data, the owner of the data, and the identities with which the data was shared, but they don't have information regarding the way the data was split in chunks (the correspondence between master key and partial keys) and the locations where the data chunks are stored. So, a single audit node or a group of colluding audit nodes can't recombine the private data. However, audit nodes are able to create reference keys at their discretion and share them with legal or illegal organizations.

Processing nodes have access to the private data as they need it for normal operations. Privacy by Design principles are intended to regulate the usage of private data without reducing functionality. The main goal of the PDS is to make it obvious when a company is misusing the private data outside the purpose accepted by the user, but without reducing access to the private data. For example, if an organization collects private data by using PDS, it becomes visible if it is copying or using private data for other purposes than intended.

Only processing nodes and audit nodes know what the pieces of information referenced by key references mean. Encryption is not needed because the attackers see a huge pool of partial undecipherable messages. Traffic can't be used to obtain information because the traffic data is encrypted using TLS and can't be used to deduce information regarding which nodes communicate because of the huge amount of concurrent swarms flying from node to node.

If an index node colludes with all the storage nodes storing chunks of the same piece of private information, then together they can recombine the message, but without knowing its meaning, who owns it and with whom it was shared with, it is of no value to them. In order for the data to be of value, they need to collude also with the audit node, which stores the metadata, the data owner and the data processor of this particular piece of information.

6   Conclusions

In normal conditions only processing nodes should be able to read plaintext data. All the other node types involved in the PDS should not be capable of accessing private data. In special conditions, audit nodes should be able to read the data as well in order to enable legal access to the private data owned by other data owners for crime prevention or other legal usages. We imagine audit organizations offering public services that are controlled by the law and industry regulations. The level of access to the systems storing this metadata should be similar to the one for financial services. Special legal procedures should be followed when accessing private data outside of the normal flow.

Systems and approaches that are trying to obfuscate and encrypt too much are fighting an impossible fight with the common social interest and are blocking the normal evolution of the technologies in the privacy area. The interests of any citizen are to be protected from unfair usage of his data by the large Internet companies, to have control on who he shares his private data with, to be able to revoke access to his data to anyone at any time.

An Internet based on fully homomorphic encryption would not be what we need because it would create a world in which data can be too easily lost. It would provide a perfect method for criminals and terrorists to hide their data from the public interest. Fighting with dangerous, corrupted governments is important, but PDS is not supposed to have a role in this fight. PDS is a balanced solution which enforces Privacy by Design in code and maintains an equilibrium between public and private interests.

7   Future Work

As future work, we intend to pursue three different paths. First, we will develop a new self-sovereignty authentication technique which uses the advantages provided by the architecture of the system proposed in this paper. Secondly, as Privacy by Design and Privacy by Default (PbD) are being enforced by laws (e.g. in the General Data Protection Regulation), we intend to propose a Privacy Enhancing Technique (PET) that can ensure these principles directly in code. It is supposed to be a privacy estimation method for systems using the technique proposed in this paper for achieving self-sovereign storage of private data.

Thirdly, we will propose and describe a mechanism for the audit nodes to store the metadata so that it enables the implementation of personal assistants. The metadata will describe the schema of the stored objects (in the form of JSON schema or OWL) and the representation types that could enable type checking when data is shared. It will enable the use of specific Privacy Policies (which will control what entities are allowed to read the information and will contain revocation policies) and Security Policies (which will control what entities are allowed to modify the content of a Master Key). Both privacy and security policies will be enforced by the audit nodes, but the input (rules and policies) will be provided by the Data Owner himself. Giving up to the standard communication promoted by web technologies and moving towards a model of communication verifiable as the one proposed by executable choreographies, we have the opportunity to develop formal verifications methods on how the private data is used.

Acknowledgments. This work is partly funded by the **European Union's Horizon 2020 Research and Innovation Programme** under grant agreement No 692178.

It is also partially supported by the **Private Sky Project**, under the **POC-A1-A1.2.3-G-2015 Programme** (Grant Agreement no. P_40_371).

References

1. WSCDL specification. https://www.w3.org/TR/ws-cdl-10/
2. Agrawal, R., Asonov, D., Srikant, R.: Enabling sovereign information sharing using web services. In: Proceedings of the 2004 ACM SIGMOD International Conference on Management of Data, pp. 873–877. ACM (2004)
3. Agrawal, R., Evfimievski, A., Srikant, R.: Information sharing across private databases. In: Proceedings of the 2003 ACM SIGMOD International Conference on Management of Data, pp. 86–97. ACM (2003)
4. Akkawi, F., Fletcher, D.P., Cottenier, T., Duncavage, D.P., Alena, R.L., Elrad, T.: An executable choreography framework for dynamic service-oriented architectures. In: 2006 IEEE Aerospace Conference, p. 13. IEEE (2006)
5. Alboaie, L., Vaida, M.-F.: Trust and reputation model for various online communities. Stud. Inform. Control **20**(2), 143–156 (2011)
6. Alboaie, S., Alboaie, L., Panu, A.: Levels of privacy for ehealth systems in the cloud era (2015)
7. Besana, P., Barker, A.: An executable calculus for service choreography. In: Meersman, R., Dillon, T., Herrero, P. (eds.) OTM 2009. LNCS, vol. 5870, pp. 373–380. Springer, Heidelberg (2009). doi:10.1007/978-3-642-05148-7_26
8. Chappell, D.A.: Enterprise Service Bus - Theory in Practice. O'Reilly, Sebastopol (2004)
9. Curry, E.: Message-oriented middleware. In: Middleware for Communications, pp. 1–28 (2004)

10. Esposito, C., Castiglione, A., Choo, K.-K.R.: Encryption-based solution for data sovereignty in federated clouds. IEEE Cloud Comput. **3**(1), 12–17 (2016)
11. Hohpe, G., Woolf, B.: Enterprise Integration Patterns: Designing, Building, and Deploying Messaging Solutions. Addison-Wesley Professional, Reading (2004)
12. Ko, R.K.L.: A computer scientist's introductory guide to business process management (BPM). ACM Crossroads **15**(4) (2009). Article No. 4
13. McKean, R.: Eu data protection reform - privacy-by-design. http://www.olswang.com
14. Peterson, Z.N.J., Gondree, M., Beverly, R.: A position paper on data sovereignty: the importance of geolocating data in the cloud. In: HotCloud (2011)
15. Tobin, A., Reed, D.: The inevitable rise of self-sovereign identity (2016)

Roaming in Graph (Graph Processing)

Scalable Anti-KNN: Decentralized Computation of k-Furthest-Neighbor Graphs with HyFN

Simon Bouget[1]([✉]), Yérom-David Bromberg[1,2], François Taïani[1,2]([✉]), and Anthony Ventresque[3]([✉])

[1] Université de Rennes 1 - IRISA, Rennes, France
{simon.bouget,david.bromberg,francois.taiani}@irisa.fr
[2] ESIR, Rennes, France
[3] Lero@UCD, School of Computer Science,
University College Dublin, Dublin, Ireland
anthony.ventresque@ucd.ie

Abstract. The decentralized construction of k-Furthest-Neighbor graphs has been little studied, although such structures can play a very useful role, for instance in a number of distributed resource allocation problems. In this paper we define KFN graphs; we propose HyFN, a generic peer-to-peer KFN construction algorithm, and thoroughly evaluate its behavior on a number of logical networks of varying sizes.

1 Motivation

k-Nearest-Neighbor (KNN) graphs have found usage in a number of domains, including machine learning, recommenders, and search. Some applications do not however require the k closest nodes, but the k most dissimilar nodes, what we term the k-Furthest-Neighbor (KFN) graph.

Virtual Machines (VMs) placement —i.e. the (re-)assignment of workloads in virtualised IT environments— is a good example of where KFN can be applied. The problem consists in finding an assignment of VMs on physical machines (PMs) that minimises some cost function(s) [27]. The problem has been described as one of the most complex and important for the IT industry [3], with large potential savings [20]. An important challenge is that a solution does not only consist in packing VMs onto PMs — it also requires to limit the amount of interferences between VMs hosted on the same PM [31]. Whatever technique is used (e.g. clustering [21]), interference aware VM placement algorithms need to identify complementary workloads — i.e. workloads that are dissimilar enough that the interferences between them are minimised. This is why the application of KFN graphs would make a lot of sense: identifying quickly complementary workloads (using KFN) to help placement algorithms would decrease the risks of interferences.

The construction of KNN graphs in decentralized systems has been widely studied in the past [4,14,17,30]. However, existing approaches typically assume

© IFIP International Federation for Information Processing 2017
Published by Springer International Publishing AG 2017. All Rights Reserved
L.Y. Chen and H.P. Reiser (Eds.): DAIS 2017, LNCS 10320, pp. 101–114, 2017.
DOI: 10.1007/978-3-319-59665-5_7

Algorithm 1. Greedy decentralized KNN algorithm executing at node p

---

1 **each round do**
2     $q \leftarrow$ one random neighbor from $\Gamma(p)$
3   **send** $\langle \text{PUSH}, \Gamma(p) \cup \{p\} \rangle$ **to** q ; **request** $\Gamma(q)$ **from** q ▷ *push - pull*
4     $cand \leftarrow \Gamma(p) \cup \Gamma(q) \cup \{r \text{ random nodes}\} \setminus \{p\}$
5     $\Gamma(p) \leftarrow \text{argtop}_{g \in cand}^{k} \left(\text{sim}(p, g) \right)$

6 **on receiving** $\langle \text{PUSH}, \Gamma' \rangle$ **do**
7     $cand \leftarrow \Gamma(p) \cup \Gamma' \setminus \{p\}$
8     $\Gamma(p) \leftarrow \text{argtop}_{g \in cand}^{k} \left(\text{sim}(p, g) \right)$

---

a form of "likely transitivity" of similarity between nodes: if A is close to B, and B to C, then A is likely to be close to C. Unfortunately this property no longer holds when constructing KFN graphs. As a result, these approaches, as demonstrated in the remainder of the paper, are not working anymore when applied to this new problem.

To address this problem, this paper proposes HyFN (standing for *Hybrid KFN*, pronounced *hyphen*), an hybrid decentralized approach for the decentralized construction of k-furthest-neighbor graphs. We show that HyFN is able to construct a KFN graph with 3200 nodes in less than 17 rounds, when a traditional greedy approach is unable to converge. We also show that our proposal is highly scalable, with a convergence time evolving in $O(log(n))$ for larger graphs.

The remainder of this paper is organized as follows: we first discuss some background about k-nearest-neighbor (KNN) graphs and their decentralized construction in peer-to-peer networks, before presenting our intuition for the construction of a k-furthest-neighbor graph (KFN) in Sect. 2. In Sect. 3, we describe in more detail HyFN and its variants. We evaluate our approach in Sect. 4, discuss related work in Sect. 5 and conclude in Sect. 6.

2 Decentralized Construction of a KFN Graph

2.1 Background: Decentralized KNN Graph Construction

The problem of constructing a k-furthest-neighbor (KFN) graph can be seen as a variant of a k-nearest-neighbor (KNN) graph construction that uses an opposed similarity.

A large body of works have been proposed to construct KNN graphs in decentralized systems, with applications ranging from recommendation [4,14,19], to search [13], to news dissemination [6]. In such systems, nodes (e.g. representing a user) can connect to each other using point-to-point networking, but only maintain a small partial view of the rest of the system, typically a small-size neighborhood of other nodes. Each node also stores a profile (e.g. a user's browsing history), and uses a peer-to-peer epidemic protocol [1,4,17,30] to converge

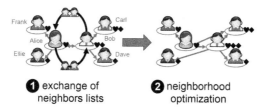

1 exchange of
neighbors lists

2 neighborhood
optimization

Fig. 1. A round of greedy decentralized KNN construction

towards an optimal neighborhood, i.e. a neighborhood containing the k most-similar other nodes in the system according to some similarity metric on profiles (e.g. cosine similarity, or Jaccard's coefficient).

The principle of a typical P2P protocol for KNN graph construction [9,30] is shown in Algorithm 1, in its push-pull variant[1]. Starting from a random neighborhood, individual nodes repeatedly select a random neighbor q (line 2), exchange their current neighborhood with that of q (noted $\Gamma(q)$, line 4), and use the gained information to select more similar neighbors (line 5)[2]. Similarly, when receiving a new neighborhood pushed to them, nodes update their local view with the new nodes they have just heard of (lines 6–8). The intuition behind this greedy procedure is that if A is similar to B, and B to C, C is likely to be similar to A as well. To avoid local minima, this greedy procedure is often complemented with a few random peers (returned by a *peer sampling service* [18], tuned with parameter r at line 4).

This mechanism is illustrated in Fig. 1. In this example, node *Alice* is interested in hearts (*Alice*'s profile), and is currently connected to *Frank*, and to *Ellie*. During this round, Alice selects *Bob* as her exchange partner. After exchanging her neighbors list with *Bob*, *Alice* finds out about *Carl*, who appears to be a better neighbor than *Ellie*. As such, *Alice* replaces *Ellie* with *Carl* in her neighborhood. Similarly *Bob* detects that *Ellie* is a better neighbor than *Alice*, and drops *Alice* in favor of *Ellie*.

2.2 Moving to Decentralized k-Furthest-Neighbor Graph Construction

Algorithm 1 can be easily adapted to compute a decentralized k-furthest-neighbor (KFN) graph by using a negative similarity at line 5:

$$\Gamma(p) \leftarrow \underset{g \in cand}{\operatorname{argtop}^{k}} \big(-\operatorname{sim}(p,g) \big) \tag{1}$$

---

[1] The presented model is close to the *Vicinity* algorithm [30], but variations exist, most notably the T-Man algorithm [17], which buffers and selects nodes differently.

[2] argtop^k returns a k-tuple of nodes that maximizes the similarity function $\operatorname{sim}(p, -)$. Said differently, argtop^k generalizes the concept of argument of the maximum (argmax for short) to the k top values of a function over a finite discrete set.

Unfortunately, with this modification, one of the key premises of Algorithm 1 disappears: the far neighbors of a far neighbor are not so likely to be interesting candidates to construct a KFN graph. Said differently, if A is far from B, and B far from C, this does not imply that A is far from C (or further from C than any other node taken randomly in the dataset).

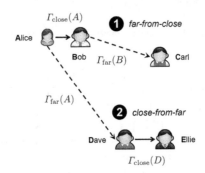

Fig. 2. The two heuristics we propose to construct a KFN graph

Starting from this observation, we propose instead to use a *dual strategy* that constructs an *intermediate KNN graph* in order to construct *a final KFN graph*. In our approach, each node p maintains two views containing k nodes each: $\Gamma_{\text{close}}(p)$ and $\Gamma_{\text{far}}(p)$.

$\Gamma_{\text{close}}(p)$ uses the algorithm shown in Algorithm 1 to converge towards the k most similar other nodes in the system. $\Gamma_{\text{far}}(p)$ employs two greedy optimization heuristics that exploits $\Gamma_{\text{close}}(p)$ to progressively discover the k furthest neighbors from p. The intuition behind these two heuristics (shown in Fig. 2 in the case of the node *Alice*) is as follows:

- The first heuristic (termed *far-from-close* and labeled **1** in the figure) requests the "far neighborhood" $\Gamma_{\text{far}}(B)$ of a node *Bob* found in *Alice*'s "close neighborhood" $\Gamma_{\text{close}}(A)$. The idea is that if *Bob* is close to *Alice*, then nodes that are far from *Bob* (such as *Carl* in Fig. 2) will also be far from *Alice*.
- The second heuristic (termed *close-to-far* and labeled **2** in the figure) requests the "close neighborhood" $\Gamma_{\text{close}}(D)$ of a node *Dave* found in *Alice*'s "far neighborhood" $\Gamma_{\text{far}}(A)$. The idea is that if *Dave* is far from *Alice*, then nodes that are close to *Dave* (such as *Ellie* in Fig. 2) will also be far from *Alice*.

In the following we present HyFN, a general algorithm that combines the two heuristics described above in various measures.

3   Algorithms

3.1   General Framework

Algorithm 2 provides an overview of the approach we propose, termed HyFN, as executed by Node p. For a fair comparison with a traditional greedy approach,

---

Algorithm 2. HyFN: A generic algorithm to implement a KFN computation, executing at node p

---

1 **Init:** For each p, $\Gamma_{\text{close}}(p)$ and $\Gamma_{\text{far}}(p)$ are heaps of size k, initialized as empty.

2 **each round do**
3   **with probability α do**
4 | UPDATECLOSEVIEW()
5   **otherwise**
6   UPDATEFARVIEW()

7 **procedure** UPDATECLOSEVIEW() **is**
8     $q \leftarrow$ one random neighbor from $\Gamma_{\text{close}}(p)$
9   **send** $\langle \text{CLOSE}, \Gamma_{\text{close}}(p) \cup \{p\}\rangle$ **to** q ; **request** $\Gamma_{\text{close}}(q)$ **from** q ▷ push-pull
10     $cand_{\text{close}} \leftarrow \Gamma_{\text{close}}(p) \cup \Gamma_{\text{close}}(q) \cup \{r \text{ random nodes}\} \setminus \{p\}$
11     $\Gamma_{\text{close}}(p) \leftarrow \text{argtop}^k_{g \in cand_{\text{close}}}(\text{sim}(p, g))$

12 **on receiving** $\langle \text{CLOSE}, \Gamma'_{close}\rangle$ **do**
13     $cand_{close} \leftarrow \Gamma_{close}(p) \cup \Gamma'_{close} \setminus \{p\}$
14     $\Gamma_{close}(p) \leftarrow \text{argtop}^k_{g \in cand_{close}}(\text{sim}(p, g))$

15 **procedure** UPDATEFARVIEW() **is**
16     $cand_{\text{far}} \leftarrow \Gamma_{\text{far}}(p) \cup \text{FARCANDIDATESXX}(p) \cup \{r \text{ random nodes}\}$
17     $\Gamma_{\text{far}}(p) \leftarrow \text{argtop}^k_{g \in cand_{\text{far}}}(-\text{sim}(p, g))$

---

we limit ourselves to *one* push-pull exchange per round and per node (as in Algorithm 1). This limitation is key to properly assess the interest of our approach: an algorithm that exchanges more information is naturally advantaged against its more frugal competitors. It would for instance be unfair to compare an algorithm using multiple push-pull exchanges to maintain multiple views against Algorithm 1, as such an algorithm would be more costly in terms of network traffic.

To ensure only one push-pull exchange is performed per round we use the construct **with probability α do .. otherwise** at line 3. This construct executes with a given probability (here α) the first statement, and with a probability $(1 - \alpha)$ the second. In this particular case, Algorithm 2 randomly alternates between invoking UPDATECLOSEVIEW() at line 4, and invoking UPDATEFARVIEW() at line 6. Both procedures (discussed below), only generate one network exchange per node and per round, thus enforcing our communication limit. UPDATECLOSEVIEW() maintains $\Gamma_{\text{close}}(p)$, p's close neighborhood, while UPDATEFARVIEW() uses $\Gamma_{\text{close}}(p)$ to construct $\Gamma_{\text{far}}(p)$. The parameter α (contained in $[0, 1]$) measures out how much effort each node will spend on $\Gamma_{\text{close}}(p)$ rather than $\Gamma_{\text{far}}(p)$.

UPDATECLOSEVIEW(), shown at lines 7–11, uses Algorithm 1 (discussed in Sect. 2.1) to construct $\Gamma_{\text{close}}(p)$. UPDATEFARVIEW() depends on a pluggable pro-

---

Algorithm 3. A far-from-close strategy to select far candidates (at p)

1 **procedure** FARCANDIDATESFARFROMCLOSE(node p) **is**
2     $q_{close} \leftarrow$ one random neighbor from $\Gamma_{close}(p)$
3   **send** $\langle \text{FAR}, \Gamma_{far}(p) \rangle$ **to** q_{close} ; **request** $\Gamma_{far}(q_{close})$ **from** q_{close} $\triangleright$ *pull*
4   **return** $\Gamma_{far}(q_{close})$

Algorithm 4. A close-to-far strategy to select far candidates (at p)

1 **procedure** FARCANDIDATESCLOSETOFAR(node p) **is**
2     $q_{far} \leftarrow$ one random neighbor from $\Gamma_{far}(p)$
3   **send** $\langle \text{FAR}, \Gamma_{close}(p) \cup \{p\} \rangle$ **to** q_{far} ; **request** $\Gamma_{close}(q_{far})$ **from** q_{far} $\triangleright$ *pull*
4   **return** $\Gamma_{close}(q_{far})$

Algorithm 5. Reception of a FAR push message (at p)

1 **on receiving** $\langle \text{FAR}, \Gamma'_{far} \rangle$ **do**
2     $cand_{far} \leftarrow \Gamma_{far}(p) \cup \Gamma'_{far}$
3     $\Gamma_{far}(p) \leftarrow \operatorname{argtop}^k_{g \in cand_{far}} \left(-\operatorname{sim}(p,g) \right)$

---

cedure FARCANDIDATESXX(p), which exchanges potential new candidate nodes using a push-pull approach to update p's far neighborhood, $\Gamma_{far}(p)$ at line 16. The current far neighborhood of p, the nodes received by FARCANDIDATESXX(p), and r random nodes are stored in the intermediate $cand_{far}$ variable (line 16). The k furthest nodes from $cand_{far}$ then become p's new far neighborhood (line 17; note the minus sign before $\operatorname{sim}(p,g)$, in contrast to line 11). (We discuss the push part of the exchange just below.)

3.2 Instantiating the Selection of Far Candidates

The pluggable method FARCANDIDATESXX(p) can be instantiated in three different manners, with the procedures FARCANDIDATESFARFROMCLOSE(p), FARCANDIDATESCLOSETOFAR(p) and FARCANDIDATESMIXED(p), shown in Algorithms 3, 4, and 6.

- FARCANDIDATESFARFROMCLOSE(p) (Algorithm 3) implements the *far-from-close* strategy discussed in Sect. 2.2: the local node p first selects one of its close neighbors q_{close} (line 2), and returns the far neighbors of q_{close}, $\Gamma_{far}(q_{close})$, as new candidates to update $\Gamma_{far}(p)$. In addition, the procedure pushes towards q_{close} the far neighbors of p, as nodes far from p are likely to lay far from q_{close} as well. The receipt of the corresponding FAR message is handled by the code shown in Algorithm 5.
- FARCANDIDATESCLOSETOFAR(p) (Algorithm 4) implements the *close-to-far* strategy presented above: this time, p picks one of its current far neighbors

---

Algorithm 6. A mixed strategy to select far candidates (at node p)

---

1 **procedure** FARCANDIDATESMIXED(node p) **is**
2   **with probability** β **do**
3 | **return** FARCANDIDATESCLOSETOFAR(p)
4   **otherwise**
5 | **return** FARCANDIDATESFARFROMCLOSE(p)

---

q_{far}, and returns the close neighbors of q_{far}, $\Gamma_{\text{close}}(q_{\text{far}})$ in order to improve $\Gamma_{\text{far}}(p)$. The procedure also pushes towards q_{far} the close neighborhood of node p, $\Gamma_{\text{close}}(p)$, as those are likely to lay far from q_{far}. The push message, of type FAR, is handled as above.

- FARCANDIDATESMIXED(p) (Algorithm 6) combines the two above strategies in one single heuristics. As in Algorithm 2, we use the **with probability** construct to switch between the *far-from-close* and *close-to-far* strategies with probability β, thus insuring that only one push-pull exchange occurs every time FARCANDIDATESMIXED(p) is invoked. The parameter β further controls how much each strategy is used, and allows FARCANDIDATESMIXED(p) to generalize the previous two procedures: the extreme case $\beta = 0$ corresponds to the *far-from-close* strategy, while $\beta = 1$ implements a *close-to-far* approach.

Considered all-together, Algorithms 2 to 6 capture a family of decentralized k-furthest-neighbor (KFN) graph construction protocols, controlled by two stochastic parameters, α and β. Parameter α controls the distribution of efforts between the intermediate KNN view and the final KFN view, while β arbitrates between the *far-from-close* and *close-to-far* strategies.

Note that some gossip protocols, such as the original T-Man, tailor the candidates they send to the specific node that requested them, while we do not. For instance, in FARCANDIDATESFARFROMCLOSE, q sends back the same set $\Gamma_{\text{far}}(q)$ as potential new neighbors for p, whatever node p sent the request. This set is not tailored to a specific node p. This is because those other protocols work with an unbounded view that keeps all data received but fixed-size messages, and so they want to send back the best information they have available. As our approach works with fixed-size view, we simply send the full set of node.

4 Evaluation

We evaluate our framework using the simulator PeerSim [23], and compare its behavior against a basic greedy epidemic protocol (Algorithm 1) that uses a negative similarity metric (Eq. 1). We term this baseline solution *Far From Far* and we note that this is strictly better than taking purely random nodes: it selects the best neighbors from candidates specifically including random nodes from the peer-sampling service, but also some additional nodes known from one-hop neighbors.

We are essentially interested in two aspects of our solution: (i) *its convergence*, i.e. how fast our framework is able to converge to a good KFN graph, and (ii) *its scalability*, i.e. how does this convergence speed evolve with growing network sizes. The code used for our experiments can be found on-line at https://gitlab.inria.fr/ASAP/HyFN.

4.1 Experimental Set-Up and Metrics

Unless stated otherwise our default set-up involves 3200 nodes regularly positioned on a $[0, 1)$ ring. By default, we use views of $k = 14$ nodes, and fetch $r = 3$ random nodes in each round. We set the parameters of HyFN to $\alpha = \beta = 0.5$. These values mean that on average nodes spend the same number of rounds constructing their KNN and KFN views (α at line 3 of Algorithm 2), and that the construction of the KFN view uses the heuristics *far-from-close* and *close-from-far* in equal measure (β at line 2 of Algorithm 6). We assume a random peer sampling service (RPS) [18] is available, which we use to initialize all views with random nodes before the protocol starts, and to provide r random nodes in each round.

To measure the convergence of the approximate KFN graph constructed by HyFN we use the following four metrics:

- **Number of missing links:** We count for each node how many of its k furthest neighbors are missing from its KFN view. The count of all these *missing links* over the network yields our first metric.
- **Number of converged nodes:** As a second measure of convergence, we consider that a node is converged when at least 80% of its k furthest neighbors (taking into account ties) are contained in its KFN view. As a measure of the network's convergence, we count in each round how many nodes are converged.
- **Average KFN distance:** For each node, we compute the average distance between this node and the nodes in its KFN view. This metric should tend toward 0.5 in a ring of perimeter 1 (our default topology). Note that even a perfectly converged network won't actually reach 0.5 though, with the exact value depending on the density of the network.
- **Convergence time:** Finally, we consider that the whole network is converged when at least 80% of all nodes are converged, according to the above criterion. We count the number of rounds until this convergence condition is fulfilled.

We do not report the communication overhead of either HyFN or our baseline: the protocols are all designed to initiate one single push-pull exchange in each round, and therefore present the same communication costs.

In the following we first evaluate HyFN on our default scenario (3200 nodes on a regular ring, $k = 14$, $r = 3$, $\alpha = \beta = 0.5$, the values for k and r being the smallest values still providing functional results) and compare it against

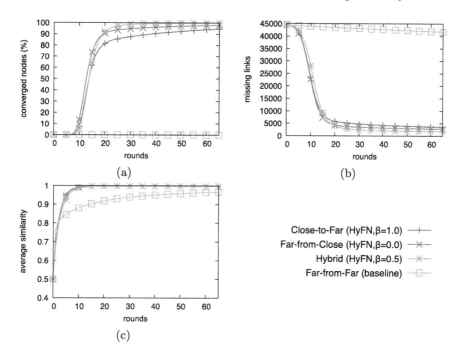

Fig. 3. Converged nodes, missing links, and average similarity of the baseline (*Far-from-Far*) and of three versions of HyFN (corresponding to $\beta = 1$ for *Close-to-Far*, $\beta = 0$ for *Far-from-Close* and $\beta = 0.5$ for *Hybrid*) on a 3200-node regular ring.

our baseline. We then analyze the impact of the mixing parameters α and β. Finally, we study the scalability of HyFN up to networks of 12800 nodes, both on a ring and grid topology. All reported values are averages computed over 25 experimental runs.

4.2   Results

Figure 3 shows the convergence of HyFN in our default scenario (3200 nodes on a regular ring), according to three convergence metrics: the percentage of converged nodes (Fig. 3a), the number of missing links (Fig. 3b), and the average KFN similarity (normalized to 1, Fig. 3c). The behavior of three variants of HyFN are shown, which correspond to the three heuristics presented in Algorithms 3 (*Far-from-Close*), 4 (*Close-to-Far*), and 6 (*Hybrid*), discussed in Sect. 3.2.

Comparison to the Far-from-Far Baseline. From the three convergence metrics, it appears that the three versions of HyFN clearly outperform the baseline. More precisely, all HyFN variants have reached 80% of converged nodes after at most 20 rounds whereas the baseline is unable to converge even after 65 rounds (Fig. 3a). Interestingly, the hybrid variant has the best performances in terms of overall convergence. From the average similarity metric (Fig. 3c), the baseline has the worst performances, even if it gets decent results in a reasonable time. In fact, it doesn't get the farthest neighbors, but still it gets far neighbors. Moreover, the metric of missing links (Fig. 3b) shows clearly that the baseline does not work: it just converges linearly only due to the couple of random neighbors that are fetched at each turn. Finally, among all HyFN variants, the *Hybrid* approach seems to converge most closely to the theoretically ideal network at the price of being a slightly slower than *Close-to-Far*.

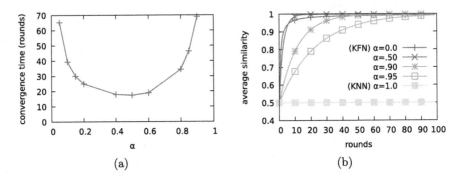

Fig. 4. Impact of the α stochastic parameter on a 3200-node regular ring.

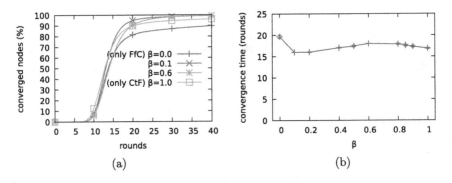

Fig. 5. Impact of the β stochastic parameter on a 3200-node regular ring.

Influence of the parameters α and β. Our key aim is to evaluate the effective impact of the stochastic parameters α and β on the KFN graph and to set them accordingly. Figure 4 outlines the impact of the α parameter, and shows that $\alpha = 0.5$ is close to the optimal. This value provides: (i) the best convergence time (Fig. 4a), and (ii) the best tradeoff between the convergence speed and the quality of the neighborhood (Fig. 4b). Concerning the impact of fine tuning β (Fig. 5), having β close to 0.2 gives the best network convergence, and convergence speed.

Note that, we are not able to reach 100% of converged nodes when we choose a β value of either 0 or 1. As a result having a non hybrid heuristic is not the most suitable choice, although the results of these kind of heuristics is still better than the baseline. Furthermore, as soon as we use the hybrid strategy, the value of $0 < \beta < 1$ has a little impact on the convergence time.

Consequently, it appears that fine tuning α is predominant compared to β. In other terms, once we have set α to its best value (i.e. 0.5), the value of β has a little impact as long as $0 < \beta < 1$, so as long as we are actually using an hybrid approach.

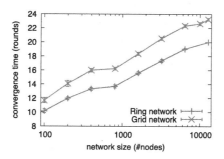

Fig. 6. Behavior of HyFN with the hybrid heuristic for networks from s = 100 nodes to s = 12800 nodes, for a variety of network topologies (Ring and Grid in the above figure).

Scalability. We have investigated the applicability of the hybrid heuristic on both a ring and grid logical networks of varying sizes from 100 to 12800 nodes (Fig. 6). The values for k and r in the default 3200-node configuration where the smallest possible while still providing good performances, and it is a known property that this parameters evolve logarithmically with respect to the size of the network s. So for every configuration, we set up $k = 1.2 * \log_2(s)$ and $r = 0.3 * \log_2(s)$, both rounded to the closest integer — in order to give back $k = 14$ and $r = 3$ for $s = 3200$. As a result, it appears that HyFN converges as expected in logarithmic time relative to the network total size, demonstrating thus that our approach scales well.

5   Related Work

To the best of our knowledge, HyFN is the first decentralized protocol specifically designed to compute a distributed k-furthest-neighbor (KFN) graph.

In terms of related mechanisms, a distributed KFN graph is a form of peer-to-peer network overlay. Peer-to-peer overlays have been widely applied in the past to implement distributed services, ranging from distributed storage [25, 26, 28], and streaming [12, 22], through to pub/sub [2, 24] and environmental sensing [15]. Among peer-to-peer overlays, k-nearest neighbor (KNN) overlays

[4,17,30] come closest to HyFN, although they converge poorly when applied to the KFN graph construction problem, as our evaluation shows. KNN overlays have been extensively studied in the past, as they provide decentralized self-organization properties which have been exploited to implement a large number of resilient and scalable services, from recommendation systems [4,14,30], to collaborative caching [11] and generic topology construction [5,17].

Epidemic topology construction protocols such as the ones presented in this work are typically highly scalable and efficient due to their inherent concurrency (each node executes the protocol in parallel) and locality (nodes only perform a few interactions per round). These two properties (concurrency and locality) render these algorithms also attractive for high-end parallel machines, and have given rise to several highly effective parallel KNN graph construction algorithms [7,8,10].

VM placement (the main technique for data centre optimisation) aims at assigning VMs to PMs in data centres — so that some cost function(s) is minimised [3,27], such as, electricity cost, resource (e.g. CPU or memory) wastage, maintenance cost. The problem is often described as an instance of the general bin packing problem, and most techniques in the literature pack as many VMs as possible on PMs. However, in practice, piling up VMs may not be such a good idea as all resources cannot be perfectly isolated. This lack of isolation generates contentions between VMs hosted in the same PM; for instance, pressure on cache or I/O by one VM will have an impact on the other VMs sharing this PM. Most studies in the literature use time series analysis to compare two VMs' workloads. For instance, Halder et al. [16] propose an interference aware first fit decreasing using a large correlation matrix – keeping track of the VMs' time series and the composition of those time series in each PM. Verma et al. [29] simplify the time series using a concept of *envelop*, recording only the peaks of utilisation and not the full time series. They then cluster similar workloads and make sure they do not end up in the same PMs. Li et al. [21] propose a two phase clustering that addresses the scalability issues that previous approaches suffer from. They also propose a placement algorithm that minimises the number of required PMs and the number of interferences. Their solution[3] would certainly benefit from the concept of KNN and the algorithms proposed in the current paper – we are working on an adaptation to an industry setting, with large and hosting departments running complex workloads.

6   Conclusion

In this paper, we propose HyFN, a novel and generic decentralized protocol to compute k-furthest-neighbor (KFN) graphs. HyFN exploits an intermediate k-nearest-neighbor (KNN) graph, which is constructed in parallel, to progressively converge towards an optimal solution. We have in particular proposed

---

[3] Note that one of the co-authors of the present paper was senior author of [21].

three heuristics to exploit this KNN graph. Our evaluation shows that our proposal clearly outperforms a naive greedy implementation based on existing KNN epidemic protocols.

Beyond its application to decentralized and pair-to-pair systems, we believe our KFN construction framework holds a strong potential for the computation of KFN graphs on highly parallel machines. Its inherent properties of locality and high concurrency are likely to make it a worthwhile approach in cases in which a KFN graph is required, including resource allocation problems such as those encountered in VM allocation services.

Acknowledgement. This work was supported, in part, by Science Foundation Ireland grant 13/RC/2094 to Lero - the Irish Software Research Centre (www.lero.ie), and by the ANR (Agence Nationale de la Recherche) Project PAMELA n. ANR-16-CE23-0016.

References

1. Bai, X., Bertier, M., Guerraoui, R., Kermarrec, A.-M., Leroy, V.: Gossiping personalized queries. In: EDBT 2010 (2010)
2. Baldoni, R., Beraldi, R., Quéma, V., Querzoni, L., Piergiovanni, S.T.: TERA: topic-based event routing for peer-to-peer architectures. In: DEBS 2007, pp. 2–13. ACM (2007)
3. Beloglazov, A., Abawajy, J., Buyya, R.: Energy-aware resource allocation heuristics for efficient management of data centers for cloud computing. In: FGCS, pp. 755–768 (2012)
4. Bertier, M., Frey, D., Guerraoui, R., Kermarrec, A.-M., Leroy, V.: The gossple anonymous social network. In: Gupta, I., Mascolo, C. (eds.) Middleware 2010. LNCS, vol. 6452, pp. 191–211. Springer, Heidelberg (2010). doi:10.1007/978-3-642-16955-7_10
5. Bouget, S., Kervadec, H., Kermarrec, A.-M., Taïani, F.: Polystyrene: the decentralized data shape that never dies. In: ICDCS'14, pp. 288–297, June 2014
6. Boutet, A., Frey, D., Guerraoui, R., Jégou, A., Kermarrec, A.-M.: WhatsUp decentralized instant news recommender. In: IPDPS (2013)
7. Boutet, A., Frey, D., Guerraoui, R., Kermarrec, A.-M., Patra, R.: HyRec: leveraging browsers for scalable recommenders. In: Middleware, pp. 85–96 (2014)
8. Boutet, A., Kermarrec, A.-M., Mittal, N., Taïani, F.: Being prepared in a sparse world: the case of KNN graph construction. In: ICDE 2016, pp. 172–181 (2016)
9. Demers, A., Greene, D., Hauser, C., Irish, W., Larson, J., Shenker, S., Sturgis, H., Swinehart, D., Terry, D.: Epidemic algorithms for replicated database maintenance. In: PODC 1987 (1987)
10. Dong, W., Moses, C., Li, K.: Efficient k-nearest neighbor graph construction for generic similarity measures. In: WWW, pp. 577–586 (2011)
11. Frey, D., Goessens, M., Kermarrec, A.-M.: Behave: behavioral cache for web content. In: Magoutis, K., Pietzuch, P. (eds.) DAIS 2014. LNCS, vol. 8460, pp. 89–103. Springer, Heidelberg (2014). doi:10.1007/978-3-662-43352-2_8
12. Frey, D., Guerraoui, R., Kermarrec, A.-M., Koldehofe, B., Mogensen, M., Monod, M., Quéma, V.: Heterogeneous gossip. In: Bacon, J.M., Cooper, B.F. (eds.) Middleware 2009. LNCS, vol. 5896, pp. 42–61. Springer, Heidelberg (2009). doi:10.1007/978-3-642-10445-9_3

13. Frey, D., Jégou, A., Kermarrec, A.-M.: Social market: combining explicit and implicit social networks. In: Défago, X., Petit, F., Villain, V. (eds.) SSS 2011. LNCS, vol. 6976, pp. 193–207. Springer, Heidelberg (2011). doi:10.1007/978-3-642-24550-3_16

14. Frey, D., Kermarrec, A.-M., Maddock, C., Mauthe, A., Roman, P.-L., Taïani, F.: Similitude: decentralised adaptation in large-scale P2P recommenders. In: Bessani, A., Bouchenak, S. (eds.) DAIS 2015. LNCS, vol. 9038, pp. 51–65. Springer, Cham (2015). doi:10.1007/978-3-319-19129-4_5

15. Grace, P., Hughes, D., Porter, B., Blair, G.S., Coulson, G., Taïani, F.: Experiences with open overlays: a middleware approach to network heterogeneity. In: Eurosys 2008, Glasgow, Scotland UK, 31 March-4 April 2008, pp. 123–136. ACM (2008)

16. Halder, K., Bellur, U., Kulkarni, P.: Risk aware provisioning and resource aggregation based consolidation of virtual machines. In: CLOUD, pp. 598–605 (2012)

17. Jelasity, M., Montresor, A., Babaoglu, O.: T-man: gossip-based fast overlay topology construction. Comput. Netw. **53**(13), 2321–2339 (2009)

18. Jelasity, M., Voulgaris, S., Guerraoui, R., Kermarrec, A.-M., Van Steen, M.: Gossip-based peer sampling. ACM ToCS **25**(3), 8 (2007)

19. Kermarrec, A.-M., Taïani, F.: Diverging towards the common good: heterogeneous self-organisation in decentralised recommenders. In: SNS 2012 (2012)

20. Koomey, J., Taylor, J.: New data supports finding that nearly a third of capital in enterprise data centers is wasted (2015)

21. Li, X., Ventresque, A., Iglesias, J.O., Murphy, J.: Scalable correlation-aware virtual machine consolidation using two-phase clustering. In: HPCS, pp. 237–245 (2015)

22. Liu, J., Zhou, M.: Tree-assisted gossiping for overlay video distribution. J. Multimedia Tools Appl. **29**(3), 211–232 (2006)

23. Montresor, A., Jelasity, M.: Peersim: a scalable p2p simulator. In: P2P 2009 (2009)

24. Patel, J.A., Riviere, E., Gupta, I., Kermarrec, A.: Rappel: exploiting interest and network locality to improve fairness in publish-subscribe systems. Comput. Netw. **53**(13), 2304–2320 (2009)

25. Ratnasamy, S., Francis, P., Handley, M., Karp, R., Shenker, S.: A scalable content-addressable network. In: SIGCOMM 2001, pp. 161–172. ACM, New York (2001)

26. Rowstron, A., Druschel, P.: Pastry: scalable, decentralized object location, and routing for large-scale peer-to-peer systems. In: Guerraoui, R. (ed.) Middleware 2001. LNCS, vol. 2218, pp. 329–350. Springer, Heidelberg (2001). doi:10.1007/3-540-45518-3_18

27. Saber, T., Ventresque, A., Brandic, I., Thorburn, J., Murphy, L.: Towards a multi-objective VM reassignment for large decentralised data centres. In: UCC (2015)

28. Stoica, I., Morris, R., Karger, D., Kaashoek, M.F., Balakrishnan, H.: Chord: a scalable peer-to-peer lookup service for internet applications. ACM SIGCOMM Comput. Commun. Rev. **31**(4), 149–160 (2001)

29. Verma, A., Dasgupta, G., Nayak, T.K., De, P., Kothari, R.: Server workload analysis for power minimization using consolidation. In: USENIX ATC, p. 28 (2009)

30. Voulgaris, S., van Steen, M.: Epidemic-style management of semantic overlays for content-based searching. In: Euro-Par 2005 (2005)

31. Xu, F., Liu, F., Jin, H., Vasilakos, A.V.: Managing performance overhead of virtual machines in cloud computing: a survey, state of the art, and future directions. Proc. IEEE **102**(1), 11–31 (2014)

Lifting Low-Level Workflow Changes Through User-Defined Graph-Rule-Based Patterns

Alexander Jahl$^{(\boxtimes)}$, Harun Baraki, Huu Tam Tran,
Ramaprasad Kuppili, and Kurt Geihs

Distributed Systems Group, University of Kassel, Kassel, Germany
{jahl,baraki,tran,rkuppili,geihs}@vs.uni-kassel.de

Abstract. In dynamic service-oriented architectures, services and service compositions underlie constant evolution that may not only affect the own workflow but dependent services too. Subsequently, required adaptations necessitate an effective detection of the changes and their effects. Merely capturing a sequence of low-level changes and analyzing each of them demands much coordination and may lead to an incomplete picture. An abstraction that summarizes a combination of low-level changes will facilitate the detection and reduce the number of changes that shall be considered for adaptation. In this paper, we propose an abstraction that is formulated through graph-based patterns, since service compositions are workflows that can be mapped to directed labeled graphs. The characteristics and granularity of a graph pattern can be adjusted by domain experts to the respective workflow language and application case. In particular, graph-based patterns are crucial when workflows are represented in two different formats. This could be the case if there exists one representation for the execution and one for the verification. We present implementation details and a detailed example that shows the feasibility and simplicity of our solution.

Keywords: Graph transformation · Graph matching · Pattern matching · Change Impact Analysis · Dependency graph · Web services · Service evolution · Answer set programming

1 Introduction

It is common wisdom that actively used software must be evolved continuously in order to maintain its utility and quality [12]. Adding new features, removing obsolete features, fixing bugs, closing security holes, improving performance all require updating a software product from time to time. Certainly, this is also true for services provided via a computer network. However, services seldom work in isolation in a stand-alone fashion. They may be part of business processes where services depend on other services and may be composed of other services.

These manifold interdependencies make on-the-fly service evolution a particularly difficult and challenging problem because the evolution of one service may

© IFIP International Federation for Information Processing 2017
Published by Springer International Publishing AG 2017. All Rights Reserved
L.Y. Chen and H.P. Reiser (Eds.): DAIS 2017, LNCS 10320, pp. 115–128, 2017.
DOI: 10.1007/978-3-319-59665-5_8

incur changes in other dependent services and clients. In analogy to biology, we call this service co-evolution. Our goal is to provide a general solution for coordinated decentralized service co-evolution. Such a solution is lacking. For heavily used services in business-critical application scenarios upgrade-related downtime is not acceptable in most cases, but often the reality. Hence, on-the-fly, zero downtime service co-evolution is a major objective for our research.

This demands, first and foremost, an examination of the effects and consequences of each alteration in a formalized way. Current formal specification methods for Change Impact Analysis (CIA) apply logic programs, state machines, and semantic annotations. In [4] compositions are formulated in Prolog. This enables developers to perform consistency checks through atomic Prolog queries. Ryu et al. [15] map protocols of service compositions to finite state machines. After a change occurs, the protocol compatibility of the participating services will be tested to decide about a migration to the updated protocol version. Likewise, other works in this area also focus on updates which encompass a single removal or addition of a service or parameter, check the consistency after the update or inform affected parties [1]. However, the consideration of single update steps impedes detecting and processing complex changes like replacements, swaps, or the addition of new branches and subgraphs to the workflow. These changes are still treated as a sequence of low-level updates. Lifting a sequence of low-level changes to a complex change captures additional information that would be lost otherwise. By lifting we refer to the conversion of low-level changes to a more abstract, conceptional description of model modifications. A sequence of removals and additions of services at the same position would not be interpreted as a replacement. The detection of a complex change would allow triggering tailored actions for handling and checking them. In case of a replacement, the pre- and post-conditions of the replaced and the replacing service could be checked for compliance.

This work provides a practical solution for developers to define complex change patterns by means of a simply applicable graphical approach. The change patterns are formulated in terms of hierarchically organized graph rules. This enables identifying and categorizing changes with different granularities. Hence, nested rules are feasible that trigger actions for each level of the hierarchy, e.g. log removal and insertion and verify replacement. Just considering detected higher level changes, e.g. the replacement, would lead to a comprehensive view that compacts dealing with changes. Further applications, which will not be discussed in this work, include the storage and the communication and dissemination of changes in a flexible and dense format.

In this paper, we present our change pattern definition and detection approach. Both are implemented by means of our DiCORE: CIA (Distributed Cooperative Evolution: Change Impact Analysis) module. Additionally, we extend this module by an Answer-Set-Programming-based logic programming reasoner to verify the updated model and to draw conclusions about dependent components. Throughout the paper, a comprehensive example is used consistently to illustrate the course of action and demonstrate the practicability of our solution.

The remainder of this paper is organized as follows. Section 2 introduces our graph-rule-based change patterns and justifies the need for them. Thereafter, Sect. 3 presents the architecture and functionality of our first DiCORE:CIA prototype. Related work is discussed in Sect. 4. Finally, the main findings of this paper and future work are summarized in Sect. 5.

2 Graph-Rule-Based Patterns

We will start with the illustration of a service workflow that is changed and extended by the responsible service provider. With the aid of this running example, the subsequent sections demonstrate the definition and viability of our graph-rule-based patterns (GPs).

2.1 Scenario

The workflow depicted in Fig. 1 is an orchestration that can be executed on a client or service provider machine. Workflows usually encompass different types of nodes which are commonly termed *activities*. An activity may be the invocation of a local or remote service and may also encompass user interaction. Workflow WF1 includes one remote service invocation. The *getMap* function of service *S1* is requested. The other operations are executed locally. *choosePOI* and *getGPScoord* enable a user to select a Point of Interest and acquire its GPS coordinates. These are processed remotely by service *S1* that returns a detailed map of the corresponding area. The following activities create a suitable route plan (pedestrian, car, public transport, bicycle) and display it accordingly. Now let us assume that a workflow update provides a more precise localization and an additional map type is offered. This new workflow WF2 is shown in the lower part of Fig. 1. Additionally, service *S1* is replaced by service *S2*. The pollution map in workflow WF2 allows users to choose routes with low emission levels.

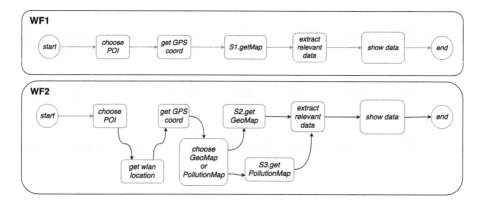

Fig. 1. Scenario: original workflow WF1 and revision WF2

Note that the workflows WF1 and WF2 in Fig. 1 are represented by a directed graph. This restricts the search area for the following graph matching approach significantly, increases its accuracy and reduces its faults. Nevertheless, it should be pointed out here that our GPs are applicable for undirected graphs, too.

2.2   Graph Comparison and Reduction

Before explaining GPs and their application in detail, our graph comparison and reduction approach is presented. The graph comparison matches nodes of two subsequent versions of a workflow to detect atomic changes, more precisely, it generates a list of added and removed nodes. The graph reduction is required to consider the addition or removal of subgraphs as the addition or removal of one node. This enables, for instance, that the replacement of a node by a subgraph is detected correctly.

Graph Comparison. Subgraph matching is the challenge to find all matches of a query graph. This task is known to be an NP-complete problem. A comparison between two graphs G_1 and G_2, where:

- $G = (N, E)$,
- N is a set of nodes,
- E is a set of edges,

consists in the determination of a mapping M that associates nodes of G_1 with nodes of G_2 in compliance with some predefined constraints. The mapping M is represented by a set of pairs $(m \in G_1, n \in G_2)$, each pair representing the mapping of a node m from G_1 with a node n from G_2. A mapping $M \subset N_1 \times N_2$ is an isomorphism if M is a bijective function that preserves the branch structure of the two graphs. For comparing the two versions of a graph, we compute the minimal graph edit distance [6] between them by using an A* algorithm and calculating the string edit distance (syntactical analysis) [13] for a structural matching of each corresponding graph node pair. Additionally, a semantic analysis [9] calculates a degree of similarity based on the equivalence between the words they consist of.

In our graph comparison algorithm depicted in Algorithm 1, this functionality is implemented by the *searchEquivalent* function listed in line 2. The algorithm starts with a start node N of the source graph and returns by use of *searchEquivalent* the best match as *equivalentN*. The match precision is obtained through an invocation of *getPercentFor*. The matching and its similarity assessment are stored into M as a triple. The *compare* function is invoked recursively for neighbour nodes found through direct edges (line 7). Finally, M contains the best matches between node $n \in N_1$ of a source graph G_1 and node $m \in N_2$ of the target graph G_2. Matches whose similarities fall below a threshold, will be discarded in a subsequent step. Applying the graph comparison method to our scenario in Fig. 1 results in a pairwise mapping of corresponding nodes of the source and the target graph. The outcome of the comparison depicted in Fig. 3

Algorithm 1. Subgraph comparison

```
 1 function compare (N, G);
   Input  : N, start node from source graph; G, target graph
   Output: M, mapping result
 2 equivalentN = searchEquivalent(N, G);
 3 percent = getPercentFor(N, G);
 4 if  equivalentN then
 5 │    M.put (N, equivalentN, percent);
 6 │    foreach edge in N.edges do
 7 │    │    nodes = edge.nodes;
 8 │    │    foreach node in nodes do
 9 │    │    │    if  node != N then
10 │    │    │    │    M.putall(compare (node, G));
11 │    │    │    end
12 │    │    end
13 │    end
14 end
15 return M;
```

reveals that not all nodes have compliant counterparts. These nodes are marked Green when added and Red when removed (Fig. 3). The graph matching and the marked nodes form the starting points for the application of our change patterns.

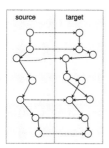

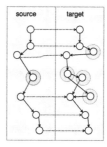

Fig. 2. Matching of Source graph G_1 nodes and the corresponding target graph G_2 nodes

Fig. 3. Graph matching with marked added and deleted nodes (Color figure online)

Graph Reduction. Preparatory steps that summarize the addition or removal of directly connected nodes will improve the scalability of our graph matching by reducing the search space. Besides that, the definition and application of GPs will be simplified. For instance, a developer may create a replacement GP by means of a removed and inserted node at the same position. A single node that is replaced by a subgraph would be identified by this GP because the insertion of the subgraph is reduced by our approach to an insertion of one single node. The two middle columns in Fig. 4 illustrate this amalgamation. Contracted nodes and their connections will be saved as subgraphs that are analyzed in subsequent steps.

A subgraph H is defined as a subset of vertices and edges of a graph $G = (N, E)$, with $H = (N_H, E_H, \mu, \nu, L_\mu, L_\nu)$ where:

- $N_H \subseteq N$,
- $E_H = E \cap (N_H \times N_H)$,
- μ function matching label $l \in L_\mu$ to node $n \in N_H$,
- ν function matching label $l \in L_\nu$ to edge $e \in E_H$,
- $L_\mu = L_\nu = \{x | x = green\} \oplus \{x | x = red\}$.

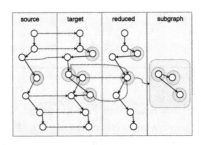

Fig. 4. Identify subgraph of new added nodes and contract to one node

2.3   Graph-Rule-Based Patterns

Our GPs are formulated by the usage of graph rules that are organized hierarchically and which enable identifying changes with different granularities. The GP notation is based on the graph rule syntax of [5, 10].

Graph Rules. (GRs) are undirected labeled graphs defined as a 6-tuple $R = (N, E, \mu, \nu, L_\mu, L_\nu)$ where:

- N is a set of nodes,
- E is a set of edges,
- μ function matching label $l \in L_\mu$ to node $n \in N$,
- ν function matching label $l \in L_\nu$ to edge $e \in E$,
- L_μ is a set of symbolic labels to mark nodes.
- L_ν is a set of symbolic labels to mark edges.

In general, graph rules can be used to transform a graph from one domain to another. Therefore, they connect corresponding nodes and edges and mark new and deleted components. In our case, the source and target domain of our GRs may be equal. A GR combines and includes information about added and deleted nodes and edges, e.g. in parallel or as a new branch, and their context.

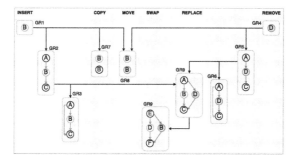

Fig. 5. Example set of graph rules to detect low- and high-level changes

GRs are formulated through a graphical representation. Figure 5 presents an example set of GRs and their interdependencies. GR1 stands for the insertion of a single node. Further information is gained, if, for instance, subsequently GR2 and GR3 can be matched. This represents the replacement of a direct connection between a node A and C by a node B and its connections to A and C.

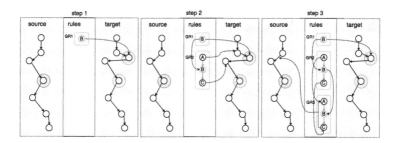

Fig. 6. Example of the application of successive and interrelated graph rules to detect the kind of change as precisely as possible

The application of this GR set to our example scenario is illustrated in Fig. 6. After the execution of the aforementioned graph matching (Figs. 2, 3 and 4), GR1 is detected in the first step. This can be interpreted programmatically as an added node. In the second step, further GRs reachable from GR1 are tried to be matched. Here, GR2 is fired which indicates an insertion between two existing nodes. Finally, GR3 identifies that these two existing nodes were directly connected before and, hence, the direct connection was replaced. Figures 7 and 8 demonstrate the described procedure or the other two identified nodes.

The colors in these GRs are part of the syntax. In our case, L_μ and L_ν have the same set of labels. We define L_μ and L_ν as follows:

- $L_\mu = L_\nu = \{black, green, red\}$.

They indicate which elements are added, removed or remained unchanged. Elements marked **Black** are used to find corresponding elements in both graphs.

Hence, they serve as context. Green elements were added in the target graph and do not exist in the source graph at the same position. Red elements exist in the source graph but do not exist at that position in the target graph. In the depicted examples, node names refer to the corresponding functionality, that is, same names stand for the same functionality type.

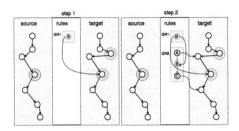

Fig. 7. Detection added node (step 1), identification neighbour nodes (step 2)

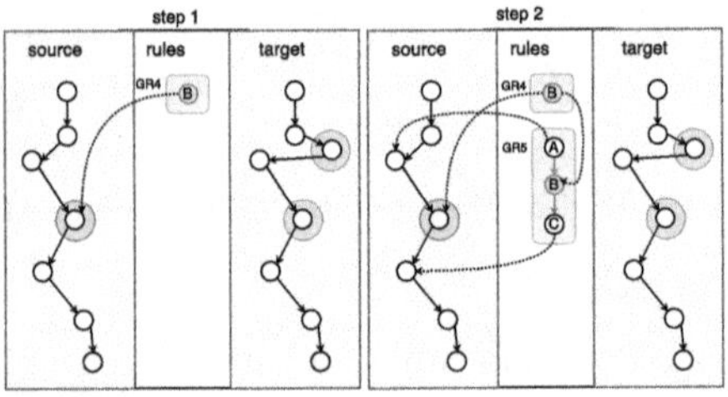

Fig. 8. Detection removed node (step 1), identification neighbour nodes (step 2)

GR-Based Change Patterns. GPs can be considered as a combination of GRs. A GP may stand for a specific statement. For instance, GR1 to GR3 are subsumed as an *Insert GP*. Formally, a GP is a directed graph that contains GRs as nodes:

- $P = (N_R, E)$
- N_R is a set of R,
- E is a set of edges, formulated as $E \subseteq N_R \times N_R$.

GPs can build on one another so that more details and information are captured. Linking GPs means to share related GRs. Figure 9 demonstrates this by connecting the *Insert GP* and *Remove GP* with the *Replace GP*. Coming back to our scenario, let us assume that a developer or user replaced an existing node D by a new node B. In Fig. 9, node B represents a subgraph. Initially, GR1 and GR4 match the added and removed nodes. These are included in the *Insert GP* and *Remove GP*. Subsequently, GR2 and GR5 identify the context nodes. GR3 will not be activated in this case since there was no direct connection between node A and C beforehand. The *Replace GP* is confirmed only if both GR2 and GR5 fire with the same context nodes A and C. The bidirectional arrows in the *Replace GP* indicate that it cannot be valid if merely one GR matches. Starting with simple rules, developers can extend them by adding GRs and GPs in a hierarchical manner to detect more complex changes. This allows, inter alia, the recognition of patterns like swaps, parallelizations and other domain specific structures.

The hierarchical GRs shown in Fig. 9 specify the search path for each change pattern. Starting at node GR1 or GR4, the algorithm presented in Algorithm 2 checks after a successful matching if one of the following rules can be applied.

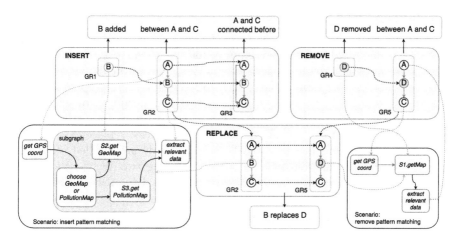

Fig. 9. GR-based change patterns *Insert, Remove* and *Replace*

In our example, that would be GR2 or GR5. If a GR matches, all relevant information like context nodes or added or removed edges are set at that point. Following GRs will use the same context information. Our match checking applies

---

Algorithm 2. GP graph matching

---

1 function findMatching (*G, R*);
    Input   : *G*, graph with included change marker; *R*, current rule from GP
    Output: *A*, map of all matched rules and connected G nodes
2 *match* = checkMatch(*G, R*);
3 **if** *match* **then**
4   A.put(*R, match*);
5   **foreach** *childR in R.children* **do**
6   A.put(findMatching(*G, childR*));
7   **end**
8 **end**
9 **return** *A*;

---

exact subgraph isomorphism to resolve this kind of pattern matching. Any successful executed graph rule provides new and additional informations.

Answer Set Programming follows the Declarative Programming paradigm and has its roots in logic programming, non-monotonic reasoning, and databases. It is used for planning and diagnosis of NP-hard search problems. ASP provides the possibility of simple ASP code generation in a readable format and reasoning about temporal and structural dependencies in a workflow. A detailed explanation can be found in [8].

Our framework translates process graphs to ASP in order to verify locally the workflow after changes are performed. If a consistency violation is detected, the change is discarded and the developer is notified. If changes affect the in- or output of a workflow, they may affect clients using this workflow. Since in- and outputs of workflows are formulated in ASP too, they serve as change description for these affected clients. Our DiCORE framework is also running on client side. This allows us to receive and process ASP fragments and check for consistency on the client side. Consistency violations will cause a service replacement so that pre- and post-conditions of each activity on client side are fulfilled. Figure 10 shows the transition diagram of a workflow including two Web service invocations. Transition diagrams can be directly translated to ASP [8]. The ASP translation of the transition diagram is given in Listing 1.1.

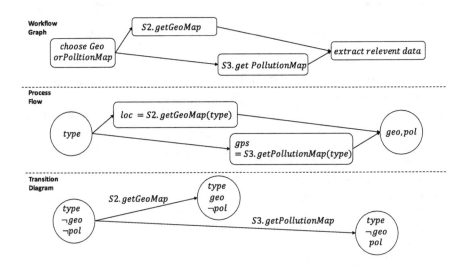

Fig. 10. Process graph to ASP

The translation to ASP is only executed for the original workflow. Whenever changes occur in the workflow graph, they will be detected, condensed and mapped to GPs. Each GP holds a corresponding translation in ASP which is generated automatically during the GP creation phase. This ensures that ASP descriptions can be updated instead of being generated anew.

Assuming that *S2* and *S3* are inserted into an existing workflow, our Graph Reduction would summarize this event as an insertion of a subgraph. This simplification step is also reflected automatically in ASP (Listing 1.2). It results in a shortened ASP description which reduces the search space for valid models. Eventually, the subgraph can be resolved into its original composition.

Listing 1.1. ASP translation

```
1 fluent(inertial,type)
2 fluent(inertial,geo)
3 fluent(inertial,pol)
4
5 action(getGeoMap)
6 action(getPollutionMap)
7
8 holds(geo, t+1) :- holds(
    type, t), holds(-geo, t
    ),holds(-pol, t),
    occurs(getGeoMap, t)
9 holds(pol, t+1) :- holds(
    type, t), holds(-geo, t
    ),holds(-pol, t),
    occurs(getPollutionMap,
    t)
10
11 holds(type, 0)
12 holds(-geo,0)
13 holds(-pol,0)
14 occurs(getGeoMap,0)
15 occurs(getPollutionMap,0)
```

Listing 1.2. ASP after reduction

```
1 fluent(intertial,type)
2 fluent(intertial,m)
3
4 action(Subgraph#getMap)
5
6 holds(m, t+1) :- holds(type,
    t), holds(-m, t),
    occurs(Subgraph#getMap,
    t)
7
8 holds(type, 0)
9 holds(-m,0)
10 occurs(Subgraph#getMap,0)
```

3 DiCORE:CIA

The DiCORE framework determines the kind of changes and the affected components in a business process and communicates them with dependent clients. DiCORE:CIA detects functional changes by analyzing the structure of the workflow. This module is implemented as a Java library and is part of our DiCORE framework. In combination with our ASP component (based on clingo [7]), it supports the developer conveniently through assistance for recognizing changes and their consequences. Furthermore, a graphical editor for visualizing, customizing and extending the GPs to particular requirements is provided. The following sections present an overview of the DiCORE:CIA module architecture and explain the main features.

3.1 Architecture Overview

DiCORE:CIA includes the following four packages: (1) Process Graph Converter, (2) Graph Matching, (3) Graph UI, (4) ASP Analyzer.

The Process Graph Converter uses a data model, imported from one of the well-known workflow languages, e.g. UML, BPMN, BPEL, YAWL, or EPC, to generate a process graph, based on the process graph syntax in [3].

The Graph Matching package consists of three main components: (1) Graph Comparator, (2) Graph Reduction, (3) Pattern Matching. The Graph Comparator matches two versions of a process graph and extracts the differences. The Graph Reduction component contracts the outputs of the Graph Comparator. Finally, the Pattern Matching component applies the GR graph to match GPs.

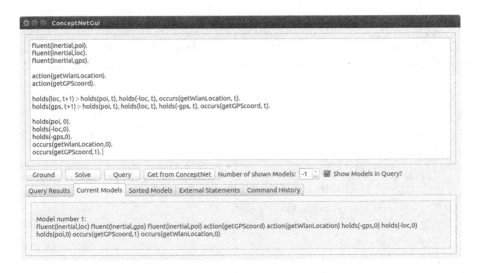

Fig. 11. ASP viewer [14]

The Graph UI package encompasses three components: (1) DiCORE GR Editor, (2) DiCORE Visualization, (3) ASP Viewer. The DiCORE GR Editor is the UI interface for designing the graph-based change patterns. The implementation is based on JavaFX[1]. The graphical interface provides functions for creating and editing hierarchically structured GRs as well as tools to import them from and export them to JSON and XML. DiCORE Visualization shows live information about process graphs and their changes. The ASP Viewer depicted in Fig. 11 shows the corresponding ASP models and allows further analytical steps not discussed in this work.

The ASP Analyzer contains three components: (1) ASP Converter, (2) ASP Query Generator, (3) ASP Updater. The process graph serves as input for the ASP Converter which generates the ASP description needed for further analytical steps. The ASP Query Generator executes consistency checks through automatically created queries and identifies after performed changes affected nodes inside the process graph.

4 Related Work

Workflows are always prone to different kinds of changes, such as new regulatory laws, changes in policies or strategies, or emerging technologies. Therefore, detecting, logging and notifying about functional changes in processes is a critical step in change analysis. This section will present a brief review of research work dealing with the detection and handling of functional changes.

---

[1] Standard GUI library for Java.

For detecting functional changes, various works applied comparisons between processes to extract different kind of information. These, however, do not provide tools to developers to define their own patterns or change types, but consider a fixed set of possible atomic changes.

Aamas et al. [2] propose the Bp-diff tool for a comparison of business models. The Bp-Diff tool may identify discrepancies involving pairs of tasks and provides both textual and visual feedback to help users understand each discrepancy. The textual feedback explains how a given pair of tasks is related in the given model versions. The visual feedback allows users to pinpoint the exact state where the discrepancy occurs. Similarly, Sergey et al. [11] present their tool BPMNDiffViz which compares process models represented in BPMN. The authors provide a web-based tool that finds business process discrepancies and visualizes them. However, this tool is applied only for BPMN formats and only considers atomic changes.

Further alternative approaches are based on predefined sets of change patterns. The authors in [16] suggest a set of change patterns like the addition and removal of process fragments or moving or replacing fragments. Our approach encompasses these patterns and is additionally editable and extendable through our GPs.

5   Conclusions

This paper presents a new contribution for formulating and detecting user-defined change patterns in complex service graphs. The patterns can be structured hierarchically and allow a categorization of changes. The hierarchic structure enables to capture additional information with each GP that could be matched to a change. Furthermore, our solution allows an intuitive and graphical formulation of patterns while other existing tools completely ignore user-defined change patterns. Our DiCORE framework presents a first implementation of the GPs. It communicates workflow changes with affected parties and triggers adaptations in case of inconsistencies. Therefore, we employ logic programming by automatically generated ASP descriptions that are processed by an ASP solver. GPs are not restricted to this application scenario but can be applied in general for detection, compression, logging and communication of simple and complex changes in a graph-based description expressed as interconnected graph rules.

In a future work, a special multi-agent system shall communicate the changes and coordinate possible adaptations with affected parties. Therefore we extend our DiCORE framework and continue to promote this research area.

Acknowledgment. This work is supported by the German Research Foundation (DFG) under the project PROSECCO, grant number 5534111. The authors would like to thank the DFG for supporting their participation in worldwide research networks.

References

1. Alam, K.A., Ahmad, R., Akhunzada, A., Nasir, M.H.N.M., Khan, S.U.: Impact analysis and change propagation in service-oriented enterprises: a systematic review. Inform. Syst. **54**, 43–73 (2015)
2. Armas-Cervantes, A., Baldan, P., Dumas, M., Garcıa-Banuelos, L.: Bp-diff: a tool for behavioral comparison of business process models. In: Proceedings of the BPM Demo Sessions, pp. 1–6 (2014)
3. Bouchaala, O., Yangui, M., Tata, S., Jmaiel, M.: Dat: Dependency analysis tool for service based business processes. In: 2014 IEEE 28th International Conference on Advanced Information Networking and Applications, pp. 621–628. IEEE (2014)
4. Dai, W., Covvey, D., Alencar, P., Cowan, D.: Lightweight query-based analysis of workflow process dependencies. J. Syst. Softw. **82**(6), 915–931 (2009)
5. Ehrig, H., Heckel, R., Rozenberg, G., Taentzer, G.: Graph Transformations. Springer, Heidelberg (2008)
6. Fischer, A., Suen, C.Y., Frinken, V., Riesen, K., Bunke, H.: Approximation of graph edit distance based on Hausdorff matching. Pattern Recogn. **48**(2), 331–343 (2015)
7. Gebser, M., Kaminski, R., Kaufmann, B., Ostrowski, M., Schaub, T., Wanko, P.: Theory solving made easy with Clingo 5. In: OASIcs-OpenAccess Series in Informatics, vol. 52. Schloss Dagstuhl-Leibniz-Zentrum fuer Informatik (2016)
8. Gelfond, M., Kahl, Y.: Knowledge Representation, Reasoning, and the Design of Intelligent Agents: The Answer-Set Programming Approach. Cambridge University Press, Cambridge (2014)
9. Gomaa, W.H., Fahmy, A.A.: A survey of text similarity approaches. Int. J. Comput. Appl. **68**(13), 13–18 (2013)
10. Grunske, L., Geiger, L., Zündorf, A., Van Eetvelde, N., Van Gorp, P., Varro, D.: Using graph transformation for practical model-driven software engineering. In: Beydeda, S., Book, M., Gruhn, V. (eds.) Model-driven Software Development, pp. 91–117. Springer, Heidelberg (2005)
11. Ivanov, S., Kalenkova, A., van der Aalst, W.M.: BPMNDiffViz: a tool for BPMN models comparison. In: BPM (Demos), pp. 35–39 (2015)
12. Lehman, M.M.: Programs, life cycles, and laws of software evolution. Proc. IEEE **68**(9), 1060–1076 (1980)
13. Lu, W., Du, X., Hadjieleftheriou, M., Ooi, B.C.: Efficiently supporting edit distance based string similarity search using B+ -Trees. IEEE Trans. Knowl. Data Eng. **26**(12), 2983–2996 (2014)
14. Opfer, S., Jakob, S., Geihs, K.: Reasoning for autonomous agents in dynamic domains. In: 9th International Conference on Agents and Artificial Intelligence, ICAART 2017 (2017)
15. Ryu, S.H., Casati, F., Skogsrud, H., Benatallah, B., Saint-Paul, R.: Supporting the dynamic evolution of web service protocols in service-oriented architectures. ACM Trans. Web (TWEB) **2**(2), 13 (2008)
16. Weber, B., Reichert, M., Rinderle-Ma, S.: Change patterns and change support features-enhancing flexibility in process-aware information systems. Data Knowl. Eng. **66**(3), 438–466 (2008)

Building Collaborative Services
(Services)

Packaging Microservices
(Work in Progress)

Fabrizio Montesi$^{(\boxtimes)}$ and Dan Sebastian Thrane

University of Southern Denmark, Odense, Denmark
`fmontesi@imada.sdu.dk`

Abstract. We describe a first proposal for a new packaging system for microservices based on the Jolie programming language, called the Jolie Package Manager (JPM). Its main features revolve around service interfaces, which make the functionalities that a service provides and depends on explicit. For the first time, JPM supports binding a service to an externally-provided package, and a notion of interface parametricity that can be used to develop generic service libraries that can modify the behaviour of arbitrary services. We illustrate the latter with a generic circuit breaker package.

1 Introduction

Microservices is an emerging paradigm where that components (even the internal ones) are autonomous and reusable services [4]. Applications are built by composing services as black boxes, using message passing.

The nature of microservices fosters granularity, and a MicroService Architecture (MSA) typically consists of many individual services. Since services are independent and their coordination happens only through message exchanges, code reuse (the focus of this work) takes a different form than that found in standard approaches based on software packages. Typically, in other paradigms, packages are software libraries, i.e., pieces of source or compiled code that become a part of the execution of the main application (e.g., through source inclusion, or static/dynamic linking). While this approach can be used for developing an "atomic" microservice (a service that does not contain other services), it falls short of capturing the essence of the paradigm and how it is used.

There are two key aspects that we need to keep in mind when dealing with code reuse in microservices. First, a common pattern in service development is to resolve the dependency of a service simply by *binding* it to an externally-provided service (available somewhere else in the network), instead of importing code to be run locally. Second, if we do decide to import some code to be run locally, that code should still be run as a separate and independent "local" service. This way, if we need to change strategy later on (say, when we go from development to production) and switch from running a dependency locally to binding our service to an external provider, we can do it without changing our implementation.

© IFIP International Federation for Information Processing 2017
Published by Springer International Publishing AG 2017. All Rights Reserved
L.Y. Chen and H.P. Reiser (Eds.): DAIS 2017, LNCS 10320, pp. 131–137, 2017.
DOI: 10.1007/978-3-319-59665-5_9

Package managers for mainstream technologies were not built with MSAs in mind, so these two patterns are not natively supported. Microservice developers must instead typically resort to ad-hoc conventions to deal with these problems.

In this paper, we report on the development of a package management system for the Jolie programming language [5][1]: the Jolie Package Manager (JPM). Jolie supports microservices natively, so it is a prime case study for the development of a package system for microservices that deals with the aforementioned aspects. We illustrate how JPM supports the configuration and use of service packages. Furthermore, JPM supports a notion of interface parametricity (polymorphism), which can be used to develop services whose behaviour is determined by the interfaces of the other services that they are bound to at deployment time. Parametricity is necessary because these interfaces are known only when packages are "linked" to each other (to solve dependencies).

2   A Simple Example

We briefly introduce Jolie with a small e-shop example.

Listing 1.1. shop.ol: A small microservice for a shop.

```
1   include"paymentprocessor.iol"
2
3   inputPort Shop { ... }
4   outputPort Warehouse { ... }
5   outputPort PaymentProcessor {
6       Location: "socket://paymentprocessor.com:443"
7       Protocol: https
8       Interfaces: IPaymentProcessor }
9
10  main {
11      checkout(order)(response) {
12          charge@PaymentProcessor( /* ... */ )()
13      }
14  }
```

Listing 1.1 shows a simple Shop service. It has a single checkout operation, defined in Lines 11–13. The Shop has two dependencies: the PaymentProcessor and the Warehouse, given as output ports. An output port dictactes how we can invoke another service. The output port PaymentProcessor is defined in Lines 5–8. This includes a Location attribute, which defines where the service can be contacted, a Protocol attribute, which defines the transport protocol to be used, and a list of statically defined Interfaces, which types the API of the service.

The current practice to make Jolie services configurable is based on ad-hoc conventions. For example, we may include a file named config.iol that contains some constant definitions (representing configuration parameters). Listing 1.2 shows the configuration file for the PaymentProcessor.

---

[1] http://www.jolie-lang.org/.

Listing 1.2. config.iol: Configuration for the PaymentProcessor.

```
1  constants {
2      PAYMENT_PROCESSOR_TEST_MODE = false,
3      PAYMENT_PROCESSOR_ACCOUNT_ID = "xxxxx-xxxxx-xxxxx",
4      PAYMENT_PROCESSOR_LOC = "socket://localhost:443",
5      PAYMENT_PROCESSOR_PROTOCOL = "https"
6  }
```

Here we provide a few fields for the behaviour of the service (TEST_MODE and ACCOUNT_MODE) and configuration for the input port of the service (LOC and PROTOCOL). The main problem of this approach is that this file needs to be included as source code by the service that we are configuring. This hides what the parameters mean (Are they bindings or not? What is the resulting architecture?). It also opens to security risks: since we are importing source code, an attacker may insert arbitrary malicious code in the configuration file and it would be executed.

3   Packages and the Package Manager

We introduce a *package* abstraction to the Jolie language and provide a tool that combines packages with configurations to achieve our aims from the Introduction, the Jolie Package Manager (JPM). A package is a folder containing Jolie source code. The code of a package is read-only when used as a dependency, to enable potential updates and integrity checks when packages are installed.

JPM distributes packages following a relatively standard approach. A package in a repository is equipped with a package manifest. A manifest contains information about the package, used for indexing (e.g., name, description, purpose, etc.) and package management (e.g., dependencies and version). We omit the details of manifests and how they are used to install packages from repositories, since these are similar to those in mainstream package managers. In the remainder, we focus on features that are peculiar to JPM.

3.1   Configuration

Jolie packages are configured by *configuration profiles*, which we introduce here. Crucially, profiles do not need to be included as source code by packages. They are instead given in separate *deployment files* (written by the user of the package) that are processed by the Jolie toolchain in a controlled way, when we need to run the services given inside of the package. The syntax of profiles recalls that of the Jolie constructs that can be configured. In Listing 1.3, we show an example of a configuration profile for the PaymentProcessor, which replaces the ad-hoc source-included configuration file given in Listing 1.2.

Listing 1.3. pp.col: Configuration for the PaymentProcessor in JPM.

```
1  profile "pp-production" configures "PaymentProcessor" {
2      inputPort PaymentProcessor {
3          Location: "socket://localhost:443"
4          Protocol: https }
5      PAYMENT_PROCESSOR_TEST_MODE = false
6      PAYMENT_PROCESSOR_ACCOUNT_ID = "xxxxx-xxxxx-xxxxx"
7  }
```

This snippet shows a single profile named "pp-production". A profile provides binding information (location, protocol) for communication ports and configuration values to a particular package. A user can provide different configuration profiles, e.g., one for development and one for production, and select among them at deployment time.

We require that the configurable elements of a Jolie program are marked with a new keyword, #ext. This allows the developer to omit binding information in communication ports; the omitted field need then to be provided externally by a configuration profile. We do not allow setting the Interfaces part of a port externally, since this would prevent type checking of programs until they know their deployment setup (typing how they use ports inside of their behaviours). Thus in the PaymentProcessor its input port is defined as:

#ext inputPort PaymentProcessor { Interfaces:IPaymentProcessor }.

3.2   Embedded Dependencies

In Jolie, all components are services that run independently. Sometimes, for performance or convenience, it is useful to *embed* a service in the same local VM (Jolie is implemented in Java). Services in the same VM still exchange messages, but they can use efficient in-memory channels, as opposed to the network.

Our new package system allows us to embed pre-configured Jolie packages in two ways. These two ways give a system administrator the freedom to choose and apply the best deployment strategy without any changes required to the services. We start by looking at the externally configurable approach.

Figure 1 shows a development configuration for the Shop. In this configuration, we embed the PaymentProcessor and its dependencies inside the Shop. Listing 1.4 depicts the desired deployment. When we state that a service should be embedded, we simply pass the name of the configuration profile to be used.

Listing 1.4. Embedding services from a configuration.

```
1  profile "shop-development" configures "Shop" {
2      outputPort PaymentProcessor embeds "pp-development"
3  }
4  profile "pp-development" configures "PaymentProcessor" {
5      inputPort PaymentProcessor { Location: "local" }
6      outputPort FakeCCProcessor embeds "fake-processor"
7  }
8  profile "fake-processor" configures "FakeCCProcessor" { ... }
```

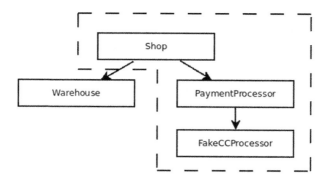

Fig. 1. Desired deployment configuration for our development build. The dashed region represents services inside of the same VM.

4   Parametric Interfaces

Proxy services delegate the computation of replies for their requests to other services. A notable example is circuit breaker [8]. We summarise this pattern in the following (see [7] for a thorough discussion in Jolie).

Circuit breakers attempt to protect against some of the problems that occur when using remote calls, such as connection problems, timeouts, and critical faults. During normal operation, a `CircuitBreaker` functions like a normal proxy between a `Client` and a `TargetService`. Monitoring code inside of the `CircuitBreaker` attempts to detect problems. If enough problems are detected, the `CircuitBreaker` will start failing immediately without attempting to proxy the call. After a period of time it will start allowing some calls through, and eventually transition back to the normal state and allow all calls through.

Packaging proxy services like circuit breakers raises a particular problem. Intuitively, the proxy should only accept calls for operations that are declared in the interface of the target service. However, this interface is known only at deployment time, since we may want to reuse the same circuit breaker package to protect different services. Proxy services are thus inherently *parametric* on the interfaces of the target services that we choose at deployment time. To address this problem, we introduce the notion of configurable interface to Jolie.

Listing 1.5. `cb.ol`: An externally defined interface.

```
1  #ext interface ITarget
```

In Listing 1.5 we define an externally configurable interface. A concrete interface is bound to it at deployment time by reading the configuration, giving the service, in this case `CircuitBreaker`, the information needed to correctly proxy operations. Observe that since we want Jolie services to be type-checkable without knowing their configuration (since configuration may change in different deployment setups), this means that the behaviour of the service is necessarily defined as polymorphic, i.e., it cannot assume any specific operation in the configurable interfaces (this is obtained through aggregation in Jolie, see [5]).

To create a circuit breaker running in a client, we would embed the circuit breaker locally and have it bound to our external payment processor, this is shown in Listing 1.6.

Listing 1.6. cb.col: Shop configuration with client-side circuit breaker for PaymentProcessor.

```
1    profile "shop-production" configures "Shop" {
2        outputPort PaymentProcessor embeds "cb-pp"
3    }
4    profile "cb-pp" configures "CircuitBreaker" {
5        interface ITarget = PaymentProcessIface from "PaymentProcessor"
6        outputPort TargetSrv { ... }
7    }
```

We can just as easily create a circuit breaker that operates server-side (intercepting incoming calls), or as a proxy in the network, by adopting different deployment files for "cb-pp".

5   Related Work

A common approach to simulate bindings to external services in mainstream languages is to communicate with services via stub libraries. A stub library provides an interface that resembles that of the target service, and internally delegates all work to the latter. In web architectures, these libraries can be synthesised from specifications, for example using OpenAPI [1] specifications in tools like Swagger [9]. Our approach applies directly to web development through Jolie [6].

Seneca [2] is a microservice toolkit for Node.js, where business logic is enclosed in a plugin typically distributed as a Node.js module. By including these plugins as dependencies, a server can essentially embed the logic of these plugins, similarly to JPM. Seneca uses pattern matching to determine which service should handle a particular message. This makes the bindings of a Seneca service implicit, in contrast to JPM, where bindings are explicit. A similar mechanism may nevertheless be implemented in Jolie and JPM by adopting proxy services, cf. [3].

Acknowledgments. This work was partially supported by CRC (Choreographies for Reliable and efficient Communication software), grant no. DFF–4005-00304 from the Danish Council for Independent Research, and by the Open Data Framework project at the University of Southern Denmark.

References

1. Open api website. https://www.openapis.org/. Accessed 22 Feb 2017
2. Seneca Authors. Seneca official website. http://senecajs.org. Accessed 22 Feb 2017

3. Dalla Preda, M., Gabbrielli, M., Guidi, C., Mauro, J., Montesi, F.: Interface-based service composition with aggregation. In: Paoli, F., Pimentel, E., Zavattaro, G. (eds.) ESOCC 2012. LNCS, vol. 7592, pp. 48–63. Springer, Heidelberg (2012). doi:10.1007/978-3-642-33427-6_4

4. Dragoni, N., Giallorenzo, S., Lluch-Lafuente, A., Mazzara, M., Montesi, F., Mustafin, R., Safina, L.: Microservices: yesterday, today, and tomorrow. In: Present and Ulterior Software Engineering (PAUSE). Springer(2017, to Appear). https://arxiv.org/abs/1606.04036

5. Montesi, F., Guidi, C., Zavattaro, G.: Service-oriented programming with Jolie. In: Bouguettaya, A., Sheng, Q.Z., Daniel, F. (eds.) Web Services Foundations, pp. 81–107. Springer, New York (2014)

6. Montesi, F.: Process-aware web programming with Jolie. Sci. Comput. Program. **130**, 69–96 (2016). Also: SAC, pp. 761–763 (2013)

7. Montesi, F., Weber, J.: Circuit breakers, discovery, and API gateways in microservices. CoRR, abs/1609.05830 (2016)

8. Nygard, M.T.: Release It!: Design and Deploy Production-Ready Software (Pragmatic Programmers). Pragmatic Bookshelf, Raleigh (2007)

9. SmartBear Software. Swagger website. http://swagger.io/. Accessed 22 Feb 2017

formic: Building Collaborative Applications with Operational Transformation
(Work in Progress)

Tim Jungnickel$^{(\boxtimes)}$ and Ronny Bräunlich

TU Berlin, Berlin, Germany
tim.jungnickel@tu-berlin.de, r.braeunlich@campus.tu-berlin.de

Abstract. As part of the ongoing revolution of the way people work in distributed teams, the need of applications for real-time collaboration is increasing. Commercial products like Google Docs set the landmark for modern web-based collaboration. In this work we provide a library that utilizes the underlying technology, namely Operational Transformation, to simplify the development of collaborative web applications. Our library *formic* features a novel transformation function that enables simultaneous editing of JSON objects.

Keywords: Consistency control · Operational Transformation · Collaboration · Web development

1 Introduction

The Internet has changed the way we work together and collaboration is no longer restricted to face-to-face meetings. Hence, working in geographically distributed teams will be the predominant part of our future work life [18]. Moreover, due to the increasing number of internet devices everyone uses, we will easily become collaborators with ourselves.

The only way to technically realize usable collaborative applications in high latency networks, like the Internet, is to use a local replica of the application state on every collaborating device. Hence, users can directly access and update the local replica on the device without any noticeable latency. All changes are propagated in the background. Unfortunately, having multiple replicas of the application state raises fundamental questions in distributed systems research. Most important is the need of a consistency control mechanism to ensure convergence among replicas [3].

Successful collaborative applications like Google Docs or Etherpad use Operational Transformation (OT) [7] to allow simultaneous editing of shared documents. We illustrate the mechanics of OT with the following simple text editing scenario. Two users u_1 and u_2 maintain their own replica of the character sequence abc. Both users simultaneously invoke edit operations on their local

© IFIP International Federation for Information Processing 2017
Published by Springer International Publishing AG 2017. All Rights Reserved
L.Y. Chen and H.P. Reiser (Eds.): DAIS 2017, LNCS 10320, pp. 138–145, 2017.
DOI: 10.1007/978-3-319-59665-5_10

replica. The user u_1 inserts an X at position 0, resulting in Xabc. The user u_2 deletes the character b at position 1, resulting in ac. A naïve interchange of the invoked edit operations would result in diverging replicas: u_1 results in Xbc, whereas u_2 results in Xac. In OT, remote operations are *transformed* based on previously executed local operations. Hence, u_1 needs to transform the position of the remote delete operation to respect the effect of the local insert operation, i.e. u_2's delete operation on position 1 needs to be transformed to a delete operation on position 2 to ensure convergence.

In modern web development, single-page applications based on JavaScript become more and more popular. In frameworks like AngularJS or React essential business logic is executed in the browser at client site, allowing fully responsive user interfaces, even if the network connection is unstable. The major challenge for building collaborative web applications is to combine the chosen web framework with a fitting consistency control mechanism like OT.

Contributions: In this work we contribute to close the gap between the conceptual and formal descriptions of OT systems and real world web development by providing the missing details of an OT extension that supports simultaneous editing of JSON objects. Since JSON is the de facto standard data interchange format of the web, we expect that a combination of JSON with OT encourages the design of more complex collaborative web applications. Ultimately we present and evaluate a programming library that utilizes provably correct transformations and simplifies the development of collaboration systems.

Related Work: OT has been introduced by Ellis and Gibbs in 1989 [7], followed by multiple decades of research around the mechanism and very valuable contributions from various groups. Prominent example applications are Google's document editing suite Google Docs and the free competitor Etherpad. In recent work, Dang and Ignat showed, that the performance of both systems with a larger number of collaborators is limited [6]. Hence, our library must be able to compete with such systems, which we evaluate in Sect. 4.

We have seen notable work outside the academic community that aims to use OT for the development of new collaborative applications. The JavaScript library ShareDB [9] offers the OT mechanism with support for various datatypes such as lists or JSON objects. However, especially the JSON datatype misses a verification of the necessary transformation property (namely TP1).

Apart from OT, other consistency control systems are interesting for collaborative applications, for example Conflict-Free Replicated Data Types [20]. Several benchmarks have been conducted to show the suitability of CRDTs for document editing [1,4]. In recent work, Nédelec et al. introduced a web-based collaborative editor CRATE that enables collaboration without the need of a central server [17]. Kleppmann and Beresford presented a very promising JSON CRDT [15] which has, to the best of our knowledge, not been demonstrated in a collaborative application. In this work, however, we focus on OT systems and compare the performance of Google Docs and ShareDB against our library.

An alternative but noteworthy mechanism is Differential Synchronization by Fraser [8], which is a state based synchronization mechanism based on diffing and patching. An implementation of Jan Monschke demonstrates the applicability to JSON documents [16]. So far we have not seen much academic attention to it.

In earlier research, we presented the conceptual extension of OT to support operations on JSON objects [14]. In this paper, we deliver the missing implementation and evaluation.

2 Preliminaries

In general, OT is an operation based consistency control system, i.e. edit operations on the local replicas of the collaborators are propagated through the network and applied at remote sites. An OT system is composed of a *control algorithm* and a *transformation function* [21]. The control algorithm determines the operations to be transformed and the transformation order. The transformation function determines how the operations are transformed to include the effects of previous operations.

We demonstrate an extract of a transformation function for operations on lists in Listing 1.1, which was initially introduced by Ellis and Gibbs in [2] and improved by Ressel et al. in [8]. We recall the example from the introduction where u_1 inserts a character at position 0 and u_2 simultaneously deletes a character at position 1. According to line number 2 of Listing 1.1, the position of the delete operation must be increased by one. In this example, the *transformation* of the delete operation ensures convergence among replicas.

Listing 1.1. Pseudo code of the transformation function

```
1  function XFORM(insert(i, k1), delete(k2)):
2    if k1 < k2: return(insert(i, k1), delete(k2 + 1))
3    if k1 > k2: return(insert(i, k1 - 1), delete(k2))
4    if k1 == k2: return(insert(i, k1), delete(k2 + 1))
```

One essential and necessary property of a transformation function is the *Transformation Property 1* (TP1) [19]. In essence, TP1 describes that the transformation function needs to repair the inconsistencies that occur if two operation instances are applied in different orders, loosely formalized as:

$$\forall O_1, O_2. \, \text{XFORM}(O_1, O_2) = (O_1', O_2') \Rightarrow (O_2' \circ O_1 = O_1' \circ O_2)$$

OT Systems are not restricted to operations on linear data structures such as lists. However, more complex data structures result in more complex transformation functions, which makes it difficult to prove that TP1 is satisfied. For the rest of this paper, we focus on operations on JSON objects, because we identified them to be most relevant for modern web applications.

JSON (JavaScript Object Notation) is a hierarchically structured data interchange format [10]. A JSON object is an unordered set of key/value pairs. Values can be of primitive type (such as string, number, or boolean) or complex structures, such as arrays or other objects. An array is an ordered list of values.

3 *formic*'s JSON Transformation

Our goal is to provide the necessary mechanics to build collaborative web applications easier and based on solid formal guarantees. Therefore, we implemented *formic* [5], a free software library that features collaboration on list structures, ordered *n*-ary trees, and JSON. In this section we report on *formic*'s architecture and provide the missing details of the transformation of operations on JSON objects.

Architecture: Our library *formic* utilizes the Wave OT control algorithm, which has been introduced by Google [2]. The algorithm provably ensures convergence among replicas as long as the used transformation function satisfies TP1. Our library implements the client and the server part of the Wave algorithm. Updates among server and client are sent via WebSockets, i.e. a communication protocol for bidirectional communication over a single TCP connection. In case of disconnection, a client can continue to operate *offline* based on the state of the local replica. If the client reconnects, all operations are exchanged and the replicas converge. In contrast to ShareDB and Etherpad, *formic* is, to the best of our knowledge, the first free software OT library that supports an offline mode.

In *formic*, we implemented transformation functions for operations on lists and *n*-ary trees that are proven[1] to satisfy TP1. Moreover, we developed a transformation function for operations on arbitrary JSON objects.

JSON Transformation: In *formic*, we introduce a novel transformation function, which features insert, delete, and replace operations on arbitrary JSON objects. Since JSON is a hierarchical format, we derive essential parts from the transformation function on *n*-ary trees, which is already proven to be TP1-valid. The major difference is, that the position parameter, which indicates where an item should be edited, is no longer an *access path*, i.e. a vector with numeric parameters. Since a position inside a JSON is identified with a vector of keys and positions inside an array, the operations must be translated to operations on trees accordingly. For example, the position parameter of an operation on the JSON object in Fig. 1, that aims to insert an item at position 0 of the array with the key `"key5"`, would be translated in the following way:

$$["key3", "key5", 0] \rightarrow [2, 0, 1, 0, 0]$$

The complete translation mechanism from a JSON object to an *n*-ary tree is documented in the *formic* repository [5]. The transformation function for replace operations can be found in the updated version of the technical report in [13].

---

[1] For list operations, we implemented a proof in the theorem prover Isabelle [11]. For operations on *n*-ary trees, we refer to our technical report [13].

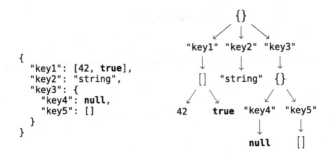

Fig. 1. Tree representation of a JSON object [14]

4   Evaluation

We evaluated the performance of our library by reusing the experiment of Dang and Ignat [6], which was initially used to explore the performance of Google Docs at large scale. In their experiment, real users have been simulated with Selenium, a widely accepted web-based testing tool. The simulated users are divided into one Writer, one Reader, and up to 50 DummyWriters. The DummyWriters write random strings to a shared document. The Writer writes a specific string to the document and the Reader waits until the specific string is present and reports the delay. Dang and Ignat measured the delay with different numbers of DummyWriters and various type speed (1–8 keystrokes per second). We used a similar setup to evaluate *formic* by installing the server and the Selenium users on several virtualized machines on our local cluster (16 servers with 2 x Intel Xeon X5355 (2 × 4 cores), 32 GB Memory).

Note that the original experiment design of Dang and Ignat is based on *simple* insertions of characters and strings to an empty document. Hence, no functionality of a rich text editor is utilized in this experiment. Therefore we decided to compare the performance measurement of Google Docs in [6] to the performance of the transformation of list operations in *formic*. We present the results in Fig. 2.

In contrast to Google Docs, *formic* offers the OT mechanism in a way that web developers can enable simultaneous and collaborative editing of arbitrary objects, as long as the objects can be serialized into JSON. In order to evaluate the transformation of operations on JSON objects properly, we decided to compare the performance of *formic* to ShareDB in an collaborative JSON editing scenario. For this run, we modified the mentioned experiment design so that the DummyWriters are now invoking operations to a shared JSON object over a test website. To ensure comparability, we implemented an identical test website with *formic* and ShareDB and installed both systems on the same local cluster. We present the results in Fig. 3.

Results: In Fig. 2, we show a comparison between the results of Dang and Ignat and the performance of *formic* in an identical setup. We see that *formic* is able to compete with the performance of Google Docs and even shows a better

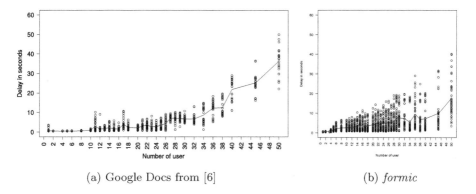

(a) Google Docs from [6]   (b) *formic*

Fig. 2. The performance of collaborative editing with one keystroke per second.

performance at large scale. In Fig. 3 we show the comparison between *formic* and ShareDB in a JSON editing scenario. We see that ShareDB performs slightly better. In contrast to the first experiment, the delay of both systems remains relatively low and does not exceed 10 s.

Discussion: With respect to text editing scenarios, we can confirm the finding of Dang and Ignat, that the performance of OT in collaborative web applications is limited at large scale. However, the performance of *formic* is comparable with Google Docs. We note that the used local cluster for the evaluation of *formic* is relatively old. Hence, we would expect even better results with modern hardware. Unfortunately, Google provides no insight into the used infrastructure and the underlying OT implementation and it is therefore difficult to reason about the performance results of Google Docs.

In the JSON editing scenario, our library performs slightly worse than the competitor ShareDB. We explain the difference in the performance by the used optimizations in ShareDB which are not implemented in *formic* yet. For example, multiple operations on the local replica can be combined before they are sent to the server. This reduces the amount of necessary communication and leads to faster response times. One major bottleneck in *formic* is the mapping of a JSON object to an ordered n-ary tree. The mapping enforces a total order in every layer of the tree, which is technically not necessary for every JSON component. For example, key/value pairs inside a JSON object do not require ordering, whereas elements inside an array must be ordered. This issue can be solved by introducing a more complex data model, which leads, as mentioned in Sect. 2, to more complex proofs. The most interesting solution would use a combination of different consistency control systems to best suit the JSON definition, e.g. a combination of the Observed-Remove Set CRDT [20] and OT.

Ultimately, *formic* is a considerable tool to develop collaborative web applications that are able to compete with established collaborative solutions. The very next step is to improve the accessibility of *formic* by providing examples and developer friendly integrations for commonly used web frameworks.

As a first step, we implemented a collaborative Battleship game based on a shared JSON object and published the source code along with the library [5]. Moreover, we plan to integrate the JSON transformation into a collaborative patient documentation system [12].

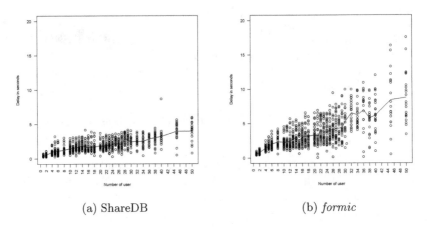

<table>
<tr><td>(a) ShareDB</td><td>(b) formic</td></tr>
</table>

Fig. 3. JSON editing with one modification per second.

5   Conclusion

With *formic*, we presented an open-source library that simplifies the development of web-based collaborative applications by providing a fully working OT system with implemented transformation functions for operations on lists, trees and JSON objects. Moreover, *formic* is composed of tested and verified components. Especially the used transformation functions are proven to be TP1-valid, which makes *formic* an attractive tool to solve the consistency-related challenges in collaborative applications.

The conducted experiment has demonstrated that our library is able to compete against Google Docs, the most successful collaborative application that utilizes OT. However, the underlying client-server architecture limits the performance at large scale.

Ultimately, the development of collaborative web applications will become more important in the future. The use of a single service for web-based collaboration, such as Google Docs, is highly questionable in terms of privacy and confidentiality, especially for sensitive data. Therefore, we expect to see more organizations, which use in-house applications for the collaborative work in distributed teams. The presented library simplifies the development and enables the design of collaborative applications that are not restricted to collaborative text editing, but rather fully flexible due to the JSON transformation. Future work includes the improvement of the accessibility and the development of more features, such as undo/redo or move operations.

References

1. Ahmed-Nacer, M., Ignat, C.-L., Oster, G., Roh, H.-G., Urso, P.: Evaluating crdts for real-time document editing. In: ACM Symposium on Document Engineering (2011)
2. Apache. Wave Protocol (2014). https://incubator.apache.org/wave
3. Brewer, E.: Towards robust distributed systems. In: Principles of Distributed Computing, PODC 2000 (2000). (Invited Talk)
4. Briot, L., Urso, P., Shapiro, M.: High responsiveness for group editing crdts. In: International Conference on Supporting Group Work, pp. 51–60 (2016)
5. Bräunlich, R.: formic (2017). https://github.com/rbraeunlich/formic
6. Dang, Q.V., Ignat, C.L.: Performance of real-time collaborative editors at large scale: user perspective. In: IFIP Networking Conference and Workshops, pp. 548–553 (2016)
7. Ellis, C.A., Gibbs, S.J.: Concurrency control in groupware systems. SIGMOD Rec. **18**(2), 399–407 (1989)
8. Fraser, N.: Differential synchronization. In: ACM Symposium on Document Engineering, pp. 13–20 (2009)
9. Gentle, J., Smith, N.: ShareDB (2016). https://github.com/share/sharedb
10. JSON. JavaScript Object Notation (1999). http://json.org
11. Jungnickel, T.: A proof of tp1 for transformations of list operations (2015). https://gitlab.tubit.tu-berlin.de/jungnickel/isabelle
12. Jungnickel, T., Cabello, J., Raile, K.: Hotpi: open-source collaborative patient documentation. In: Companion of ACM Conference on Computer Supported Cooperative Work and Social Computing, pp. 219–222 (2017)
13. Jungnickel, T., Herb, T.: Tp1-valid transformation functions for operations on ordered n-ary trees (2015). http://arxiv.org/abs/1512.05949
14. Jungnickel, T., Herb, T.: Simultaneous editing of JSON objects via operational transformation. In: ACM Symposium on Applied Computing, pp. 812–815 (2016)
15. Kleppmann, M., Beresford, A.R.: A conflict-free replicated JSON datatype (2016). http://arxiv.org/abs/1608.03960
16. Monschke, J.: DiffSync (2015). https://github.com/janmonschke/diffsync
17. Nédelec, B., Molli, P., Mostefaoui, A.: Crate: writing stories together with our browsers. In: International Conference Companion on World Wide Web, pp. 231–234 (2016)
18. Powell, A., Piccoli, G., Ives, B.: Virtual teams: a review of current literature and directions for future research. SIGMIS Database **35**(1), 6–36 (2004)
19. Ressel, M., Nitsche-Ruhland, D., Gunzenhäuser, R.: An integrating, transformation-oriented approach to concurrency control and undo in group editors. In: ACM Conference on Computer Supported Cooperative Work, pp. 288–297 (1996)
20. Shapiro, M., Preguiça, N., Baquero, C., Zawirski, M.: Conflict-free replicated data types. In: Défago, X., Petit, F., Villain, V. (eds.) SSS 2011. LNCS, vol. 6976, pp. 386–400. Springer, Heidelberg (2011). doi:10.1007/978-3-642-24550-3_29
21. Sun, C., Jia, X., Zhang, Y., Yang, Y., Chen, D.: Achieving convergence, causality preservation, and intention preservation in real-time cooperative editing systems. ACM Trans. Comput. Hum. Interact. **5**(1), 63–108 (1998)

Filament: A Cohort Construction Service for Decentralized Collaborative Editing Platforms

Ariyattu C. Resmi[1(✉)] and François Taiani[1,2(✉)]

[1] Université de Rennes 1 - IRISA, Rennes, France
{rariyatt,francois.taiani}@irisa.fr
[2] ESIR, Rennes, France

Abstract. Distributed collaborative editors allow several remote users to contribute concurrently to the same document. Only a limited number of concurrent users can be supported by the currently deployed editors. A number of peer-to-peer solutions have therefore been proposed to remove this limitation and allow a large number of users to work collaboratively. These approaches however tend to assume that all users edit the same set of documents, which is unlikely to be the case if such systems should become widely used and ubiquitous. In this paper we discuss a novel cohort-construction approach that allow users editing the same documents to rapidly find each other. Our proposal utilises the semantic relations between peers to construct a set of self-organizing overlays to route search requests. The resulting protocol is efficient, scalable, and provides beneficial load-balancing properties over the involved peers. We evaluate our approach and compare it against a standard Chord based DHT approach. Our approach performs as well as a DHT based approach but provides better load balancing.

1 Introduction

A new generation of low-cost computers known as *plug computers* has recently appeared, offering users the possibility to create cheap nano-clusters of domestic servers, host data and services and federate these resources with other users. These nano-clusters of autonomous users brings closer the vision of *self-hosted on-line social services*, as promoted by initiatives such as ownCloud [4] or diaspora [1]. But the initiatives so far primarily focused on the sharing and diffusion of *immutable* data (pictures, posts, chat messages) and offer much less in terms of real-time collaborative tools such as collaborative editors. In order to fill this gap, several researchers have proposed promising approaches [9, 22, 30] to realize decentralized peer-to-peer collaborative editors.

Most of these works, generally assume that all nodes in the system edit the same document or the same set of documents, and typically propagate updates using a uniform broadcast primitive. This is unlikely to be the case in very large

© IFIP International Federation for Information Processing 2017
Published by Springer International Publishing AG 2017. All Rights Reserved
L.Y. Chen and H.P. Reiser (Eds.): DAIS 2017, LNCS 10320, pp. 146–160, 2017.
DOI: 10.1007/978-3-319-59665-5_11

systems. Propagating changes about every document to the entire system is highly counter-productive and unnecessary. Instead we argue that users editing the same document should be able to first locate each other in order to exchange updates between themselves. This finding procedure, which we term *cohort construction*, should be efficient, reactive to changes and robust to failures.

A straightforward choice to realize such a cohort-construction mechanism consists in using a DHT (*Distributed Hash Table*) [25,27,31] to act as an intermediate rendezvous point between nodes editing the same document. This choice is however sub-optimal: it adds an extra level of indirection in the document peering procedure, and creates potential hot-spots for nodes handling highly popular documents. It also uses a DHT in a context for which DHTs are typically not designed for: a decentralized collaborative editor will typically host fewer documents than nodes, leading to fewer keys than nodes being stored in the DHT, in contrast to a typical DHT, which is designed to handle the reverse situation, with more keys than nodes.

In this paper we propose *Filament*, a *decentralized cohort-construction protocol* adapted to the needs of large-scale collaborative editors. Filament eliminates the need for any intermediate DHT, and allows nodes editing the same document to find each other in a rapid, efficient, and robust manner by generating an adaptive *routing field* around themselves. Filament's architecture hinges around a set of collaborating self-organizing overlays exploiting a novel document-based similarity metric. Beyond its intrinsic merits, Filament's design further demonstrates how the horizontal composition of several self-organizing overlays can lead to richer and more efficient services. Simulation results show that in a network of 2^{12} nodes, Filament is able to reduce the document latency by around 20% compared to a Chord-based DHT approach.

The paper is organized as follows. We first present the problem we address and our intuition (Sect. 2); we then present our algorithm (Sect. 3), and its evaluation (Sect. 4). We finally discuss related work (Sect. 5), and conclude (Sect. 6).

2 Background, Problem, and Intuition

2.1 Collaborative Editing and Cohort Construction

Distributed collaborative editors allow several remote users to contribute concurrently to the same document. Most of the currently deployed distributed collaborative editors are centralized, hosted in tightly integrated environments and show poor scalability [2,3] and poor fault tolerance. For instance, typical collaborative editors such as Google Doc [3] or Etherpad [2] are limited in the number of users they can support concurrently.

To overcome this limitation, several promising works have been proposed to host collaborative editing platforms in decentralized peer-to-peer architectures [9,22,30]. However, most of these approaches assume that all users in a system edit the same document. In a large community, this assumption is unrealistic, and users editing the same document need a mechanism to find each

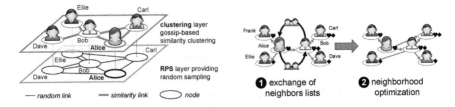

Fig. 1. Overlay architecture

Fig. 2. P2P neighborhood optimization

other. This is a particular case of peer-to-peer search, which has been extensively researched in the past both in unstructured [11,12,19,23] and structured systems, in particular in DHT [25–27,31]. Unstructured approaches have probabilistic guarantees: a resource might be present in the system, but it may not get found unless a flooding or exhaustive multicast strategy is used, which might be very costly in massive systems.

Structured approaches such as DHTs typically have deterministic guaranties in the sense that they are correct and complete, but they assume that the number of items to be stored is much higher than the number of storage nodes available. This is in stark contrast to distributed collaborative platforms, in which the number of documents being edited is smaller than the number of users. Furthermore, these systems use consistent hashing techniques in which a node's role in the system is independent of this node's particular interests (in our case here documents), thus adding an additional layer of redirection. In case of a highly requested resource, DHTs use load-balancing techniques [16,24] that typically use virtual nodes or modified hash function [10] to spread the load more evenly. These functions are however reactive, and well suited for content that is mostly read, but less suitable when interest in a document might vary rapidly.

To address these challenges, we propose a novel decentralized service that connects together users interested in the same document without relying on the additional indirection implied by DHTs, while delivering deterministic guarantees, contrary to the unstructured networks. Our solution exploits self-organizing overlays with a novel document based similarity metric and is proactively load balancing, in that nodes working on the same documents naturally add their resources to help route their requests to the corresponding document editing community (which we call a *document cohort*) and more generally illustrate how an advanced behaviour can be obtained by combining several sub self-organizing overlays to create a routing structure that matches both the expected load and document interests of individual nodes.

2.2 Self-organizing Overlays

Our proposal, called Filament, composes together several self-organizing overlay networks to deliver its service. Overlay networks connect computers (aka *nodes* or *peers*) on top of a standard point-to-point network (e.g. TCP/IP) in order to add additional properties and services to this underlying network [9,25–27,30].

A self-organizing overlay [14, 28] seeks to organize its nodes so that each nodes is eventually connected to its k closest other nodes, according to some similarity function. A self-organizing overlay typically uses a two-layer structure to organize peers (Fig. 1). Each layer provides a peer-to-peer overlay, in which users (or peers) maintain a fixed list of neighbors (or *views*). For instance, in Fig. 1, Alice is connected to Bob, Carl, and Dave in the bottom RPS (Random Peer Sampling) layer, and to Carl and Bob in the upper layer (clustering).

RPS layer allows each peer to periodically obtain a random sample of the rest of the network and thus guaranties the convergence of the second layer (clustering), while making the overall system highly resilient against churn and partitions. Peers exchange and shuffle their neighbors list in *periodic gossip rounds* to maximise the randomness of the RPS graph over time [15]. For efficiency, each peer does not however communicate with all its neighbors in each round, but instead randomly selects one of its neighbors in its RPS view to interact with.

The clustering layer implements a local greedy optimisation procedure that leverages both neighbors returned by the RPS, and current neighbors from the clustering views [14, 28]. A peer will periodically update its list of similar neighbors with new neighbors found to be more similar to them in the RPS layer. This guarantees convergence under stable conditions, but can be slow in large systems. This mechanism is therefore complemented by a swap mechanism in the clustering layer (Fig. 2), whereby two neighboring peers (here Alice and Bob) exchange their neighbors lists (Step 1), and seek to construct a better neighborhood based on the other peer's information (Step 2 in Fig. 2).

In Fig. 2(1) the interests of each user is shown as a symbol associated with them. Thus Frank, Alice, Bob and Carl share the same interests. So instead of a communication link to Ellie as shown in the random network, it is beneficial for Alice to have a communication link to Carl who shares the same interest as shown in Fig. 2(2). Bob applies a similar procedure, and decides to drops Alice for Ellie.

3   System

In a large CE system, users editing the same document need to find each other in order to propagate modifications between themselves. Our approach *Filament* relies on a novel set of similarity metric, and exploits self-organizing overlays to allows the rapid, efficient, and robust discovery of document communities in large scale decentralized collaborative editing platforms. Each node in the system further maintains a specific view for each document it is currently editing, in order to rapidly propagate the edits: the aim of Filament is to fill this view as rapidly as possible. In addition to this we also need mechanisms that help the system react to changes, and reconnect nodes as required i.e. in cases where a new node joins the system or in cases where a new document is added to a node in the system.

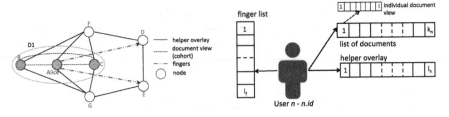

Fig. 3. Overlay view   **Fig. 4.** Illustration of the system model

3.1   System Model

We consider a network consisting of a large number of nodes representing users $\mathcal{N}$ = $\{n_1, n_2, .., n_N\}$. The network is dynamic: nodes may join or leave at anytime. Nodes are assigned unique identifiers and communicate using messages over an existing network, such as the Internet, allowing every node to potentially communicate with any other node as soon as it knows the other node's identifier. Nodes are organized in a set of interdependent overlay networks (termed *suboverlays* in the following). For each suboverlay, individual node know the identifiers of a set of other nodes, which forms its *neighbourhood* (or *view*) in this suboverlay. This neighbourhood can change over time to fulfil the overlay network's objectives. Each node/user n is editing a set of zero or more documents (noted $n.\mathcal{D}$) at a time according to their interests. For the sake of uniformity, both the node ids and document ids are taken from the same id space.

3.2   Filament

As mentioned previously, our approach makes use of a hierarchy of self-organizing overlays inorder to allow the rapid, efficient, and robust discovery of document communities. All the nodes in the system are part of several suboverlays as shown in Fig. 3. A *helper overlay* ($\mathcal{H}$) is associated with each node. This helper overlay provides short distance routing links within the system, and relies on a document-based similarity function, i.e. a similarity function that uses the set of documents edited by individual nodes in order to compute whether two nodes are close or far. The helper overlay view is initially filled using random peers taken from Random Peer Sampling layer (RPS). As the system executes, $n.\mathcal{H}$ is progressively filled with nodes that are similar to but not identical to node n in terms of the documents they edit.

Each node in the system further maintains a specific view for each document it is currently editing, in order to rapidly propagate new edits on these documents (These edits can then be used to maintain a converged document state at each interested node using existing algorithms [9, 22, 30]). In Fig. 3, nodes Alice, B and C will form a document overlay as all of them are editing document D1. Likewise, the system should insure that a node takes part in all the document overlays pertaining to the documents it is currently editing.

Table 1. Notations and Entities

$n.id$	Node identifier of node n
k_n	Number of documents being edited by node n
$n.\mathcal{D}$	List of documents edited by node n depicted as $\{d_1^n, d_2^n, ..., d_{k_n}^n\}$
$n.\mathcal{H}$	Helper overlay associated with node n
$n.\mathcal{F}$	Fingers of node n
$n.view(d)$	Set of collaborators for document d contained in node n
$F_n[i]$	Node which is the ith finger of node n
l	Maximum size of the collaborators list associated with each document
lh	Size of helper overlay
lf	Size of finger list

In addition to the above helper and document overlays, each node maintains a set of *fingers* ($\mathcal{F}$), which acts as long distance links within the system, in order to create a small world topology, and provide fast routing. Similar to a traditional ring-based DHT, these links also help to rapidly locate collaborating nodes, and to avoid disjoint partitions. A simplified view of the system model is shown in Fig. 4. It shows the overlays that are associated with a node in the system. Table 1 summarizes the notations that are being used in this paper.

The basic algorithm behind our approach is shown with the help of Figs. 5 and 6. Figure 5 shows how the system is initialized while Fig. 6 shows what the system does in each round.

The proposed algorithms hinge on a novel similarity metric based on document ids. This similarity metric is described in procedure $\Delta(n, u)$ in Fig. 6. Each node n has a list of documents $n.\mathcal{D}$ associated with it. This list contains the documents that are being currently edited by that node.

Given two nodes and the list of documents being edited by those nodes, the similarity metric in our approach is the smallest distance between the non-identical documents contained by it. For example, suppose node A is editing documents 5, 3 and 8, while node B is editing documents 3, 11 and 9, then the similarity between them is taken as 1 which is the difference between 8 and 9. The identical documents being edited by them are not taken into consideration here. The key to the faster convergence of our system is the novel similarity metric which helps in finding nodes which are similar but not identical in their interests.

The initialization stage is pretty straightforward. The helper overlay associated with each node is filled randomly using Random Peer Sampling. The number of nodes in the helper overlay is truncated to lh. The documents that each node is editing is also selected randomly. In the initial stage, as we don't know the collaborators, the helper overlay is used to fill all the document views associated with each node. The node which is the farthest in the helper overlay forms the first entry of the finger list. Based on how far this node is, the other entries are also filled.

Figure 6 shows how our system progresses after initialization. All the sub overlays contained in the system follow the same generic procedure. In each cycle all the suboverlays get updated so as to reach an optimal stage. Procedure $Update\_Overlay(O, dist, c, s, so, base)$ is used for updating the overlay networks. Six arguments are being passed to this function. Here O represents the overlay being updated. $dist$ represents the function used for calculating the similarity between the nodes. s is the size of the resulting overlay. so is the sort order. This sorts the resulting array in ascending or descending order on the basis of similarity metric. $base$ is used to get the nodes which are similar but non-identical. An important argument that is being passed to this function is c, which represents the candidate list that is used to update the overlay. This contains a list of nodes that can be used to update a given overlay. For generality, we are truncating the candidate list to the desired size(s) of the resulting overlay. A good set of candidates can significantly affect the convergence speed of our system.

In each round, node n randomly selects a node p from its helper overlay and gets the neighbourhood information of p. $p.\mathcal{H}$ along with one randomly selected node in the system is used as the candidate list for the updation of helper overlay associated with node n. A random entry is added with the hope that the system converges faster. Measures are taken to remove n from the candidate list associated with updation of overlays associated with node n. The randomly filled helper overlay is modified as the simulation progresses so as to fill it with nodes similar to themselves but non-identical. Likewise the finger list is also updated with another set of carefully selected candidate list. Fingers help in providing links to non-similar nodes; in other words they provide long distance routing links to nodes further away. They also help in preventing disjoint clusters. The finger lists are used in cases where a node needs to find collaborators for a newly added document. A node can look in its finger list in order to find someone editing the newly added document or to find some one who might be editing a document similar to the newly added document. Individual document views are also updated in each round. If the current document view already has a node with that document then that node's document view is used to update the document overlay or else a randomly selected node is made use of.

1: **System initialization**
2:     $n.\mathcal{H} \leftarrow$ random R.P.S of size lh
3:     **for all** $d \in n.\mathcal{D} : n.view(d) \leftarrow n.\mathcal{H}$
4:     $Update\_Overlay(F[0], \Delta, n.\mathcal{H}, 1, -1, 1)$
5:     **for** i from 1 to log $F[0]$
6:         $Update\_Overlay(F[i], \Delta, n.\mathcal{H}, 1, 1, \Delta(F[0], n)/2^i)$

Fig. 5. Initialization

```
 1: In round(r) do
 2:     p ← random node from n.H
 3:     ch ← p.H∪ {one random R.P.S} \ {n}
 4:     Update_Overlay(n.H, Δ, ch, lh, −1, 1)
 5:     for i from 1 to lf
 6:         cf ← F[i].F ∪ F[i].H∪ {one random R.P.S} \ {n}
 7:         Update_Overlay(F[i], Δ, cf, 1, 1, 1)
 8:     for all d from n.D
 9:         if ∃p ∈ n.view(d) so that d ∈ p.D
10:             select p ; c ← p.view(d)
11:         else select a random node p from n.view(d)
12:             c ← p.H ∪ p.F∪ {one random R.P.S} \ {n}
13:         Update_Overlay(n.view(d), Δ, c, l, −1, 0)

14: Procedure Δ(n, u)
15:     S₁ ← n.D \ u.D
16:     if S₁=∅ then S₁ ← n.id
17:     S₂ ← u.D \ n.D
18:     if S₂=∅ then S₂ ← u.id
19:     S₃ ← S₁ × S₂
20:     m ← min(|x − y|)∀(x, y) ∈ S₃
21:     return m

22: Procedure δ(d, n, u)
23:     if d ∈ n.D ∩ q.D
24:         return 0
25:     else
26:         return Δ(n, u)

27: Procedure Update_Overlay(O, dist, c, s, so, base)
28:     O ← argmaxˢₚ∈c(dist(n, p) − base) * so
```

$$14:\ \textbf{Procedure } \Delta(n, u)$$
$$15:\quad S_1 \leftarrow n.\mathcal{D} \setminus u.\mathcal{D}$$
$$16:\quad \textbf{if } S_1=\emptyset \textbf{ then } S_1 \leftarrow n.id$$
$$17:\quad S_2 \leftarrow u.\mathcal{D} \setminus n.\mathcal{D}$$
$$18:\quad \textbf{if } S_2=\emptyset \textbf{ then } S_2 \leftarrow u.id$$
$$19:\quad S_3 \leftarrow S_1 \times S_2$$
$$20:\quad m \leftarrow min(|x - y|)\forall(x, y) \in S_3$$
$$21:\quad \textbf{return } m$$

Fig. 6. Filament

After a certain number of rounds the system kind of stabilizes i.e., all the document views get filled. Procedure $\delta(d, n, u)$ helps when a new document gets added to a node or when a new node is added to the system. When a new document d gets added to a node n, what we aim to do is to find its collaborators in a fast manner. Procedure $\delta(d, n, u)$ checks whether the document d which is newly added to node n is present in node u. If it is present then n uses the document view of u to find collaborators for d. We can use $Update\_Overlay(n.view(d), \delta(d, -, -), n.\mathcal{F} \cup n.\mathcal{H}, l, 1, 0)$ for this purpose. If none of the nodes in the candidate list contains document d, then node n makes use of the similarity metric Δ to find collaborators.

4   Evaluation

4.1   Experimental Setting and Metrics

Unless otherwise indicated, the default network size is taken as 2^{12}. We assume that the system has converged when all the document sub-overlays are filled i.e. all the nodes have successfully found collaborators for the documents they are currently editing. For generality, the value of l (document view) and lh (size of the help overlay) is taken as 10 in all the experiments. For all the network sizes, we assume that a total of 10 documents are there in the system. It is also assumed that each document is being edited by 10% of the network size number of nodes. The results obtained during the evaluation are shown in this section.

We assess the performance of our approach using two metrics:

- **Document latency** - captures the number of rounds it takes for the system to find l collaborators for a newly added document.
- **Load** associated with each node - measures the load associated with each node based on the communication cost associated with them. This is directly related to the number of times a node is accessed during simulation.

4.2   Baselines

The performance of our approach is compared against a chord-based DHT [20] approach. The main reason for this is that a DHT is commonly used in similar applications and they perform really well providing deterministic guaranties. The document id is hashed and based on the hash value obtained, a node gets selected. The collaborators list for that document gets stored in the selected node. So in order to find the collaborators for a document all we have to do is hash the document id and send a message to the corresponding node for the collaborators list. The main delay here is to find a node given its node id. Chord based topology helps in this by providing faster routing. Node ids are ordered in an ID space modulo 2^t. We say that id a follows id b in the ring, if $(a - b + 2^t) \bmod 2^t < 2^{t-1}$; otherwise a precedes b. Given an id a, its successor is defined as the nearest node whose id is equal to a or follows a in the ring. The notion of predecessor is defined in a symmetric way. Each node maintains two sets of neighbors, called leaves and fingers. Leaves of node n are its lh nearest successors. For each node n, its jth finger is defined as successor$(n + 2^j)$, with $j \in [0, t-1]$. Routing in Chord works by forwarding messages in the ring following the successor direction; when receiving a message targeted at node k, node n forwards it to its furthest leaf or finger that precedes successor(k). Fingers help in reducing the number of nodes traversed to reach the destination node.

4.3   Results

All the results (Figs. 7, 8, 9, 10, 11, 12 and Tables 2, 3) are computed with Peersim [21] and are averaged over 10 experiments. The source code is made

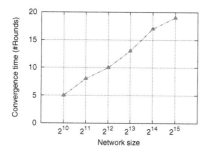

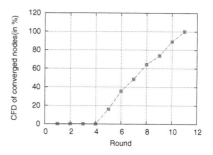

Fig. 7. Convergence time of Filament for varying network sizes

Fig. 8. Cumulative frequency distribution of converged nodes for Filament in the base case

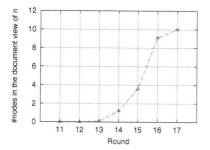

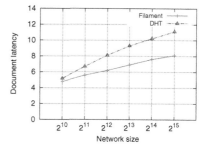

Fig. 9. No: of nodes in the document view of n for Filament in the base case

Fig. 10. Filament vs DHT based on document latency

available in http://armi.in/resmi/ce1.zip. The comparison to the baseline is done with the help of a base case setting. When shown, intervals of confidence are computed at a 95% confidence level using a student t-distribution.

Figure 7 shows the convergence time of Filament with varying network sizes. As the network size increases the time taken for the system to converge also increases. We assume that the system is converged when all the document overlays are completely filled. From the graph it is clear that Filament works well for very large network sizes. Figure 8 shows the cumulative frequency distribution of converged nodes for Filament in the base case. A small number of converged nodes causes a chain effect causing a larger number of nodes to converge in the following rounds. Thus once the nodes start converging, the system progresses towards convergence in a faster manner. Figure 9 shows the number of nodes in the document view of n when a new document is added to n and it tries to find l collaborators.

Figure 10 and Table 2 show how our approach fares compared to a chord based DHT approach. Our approach has lower document latency compared to a DHT. The document latency varies from 4.8 to 8.1 as the network size grows from 2^{10} to 2^{15} for Filament while it varies from 5.2 to 11.1 for DHT. DHT provides

Table 2. Filament vs DHT based on document latency (#rounds)

Network Size	Filament	DHT
2^{10}	4.8($\pm$1.3)	5.2($\pm$1.4)
2^{11}	5.6($\pm$1.2)	6.7($\pm$1.3)
2^{12}	6.2($\pm$1.1)	8.1($\pm$1.2)
2^{13}	6.9($\pm$1.1)	9.3($\pm$1.1)
2^{14}	7.6($\pm$1.1)	10.2($\pm$1.1)
2^{15}	8.1($\pm$0.9)	11.1($\pm$0.9)

Table 3. Load associated with nodes for Filament and DHT (in bytes)

Load	Filament	DHT
Minimum	8	8
Mean	64	96
Maximum	176	880

an additional level of indirection. The document id is used for hashing and the collaborator list associated with a document might be stored in a node which is not editing that document at all. Moreover DHT is not exactly an optimal solution in this scenario as the number of documents being edited is significantly smaller compared to the number of nodes in the system. The latency in the case of DHT is mainly associated with routing to the node with the collaborators list. Compared to DHT, Filament shows a better performance with the help of document sub-overlays and finger list.

The Table 3 shows the maximum, minimum and mean load associated with a node for both Filament and DHT when a new document is added to the system. When a new document is added to a node, the node tries to find l collaborators for that document. Inorder to do that, it has to exchange messages with other nodes. Here we assume that a single message has a size of 8 bytes which is the size of node id. The results show the case when a document d is added to a node that doesn't contain it and 10 experiments are conducted with the same document id. The cumulative result is shown in the table. In the case of DHT the same node is getting accessed multiple times for the collaborators list of d while in the case of Filament the load is divided as all the nodes editing the document will have collaborators list in them. The average load associated with a node is slightly lesser for Filament. But the maximum load of DHT is very high which can lead to bottle necks in the network.

Effects of Variants. Figure 11 shows the effect of varying the number of documents in the system. As we can see increasing the number of documents in the system helps it to converge in a faster manner. This is to be expected as the number of sub-overlays associated with each node increases with the increased number of documents. Making use of these additional sub-overlays, a node can optimize its neighbourhood and finger list. But there is also a disadvantage associated with this; the amount of overlays to be managed in each round increases leading to an increased load for the nodes.

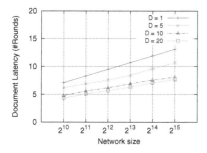

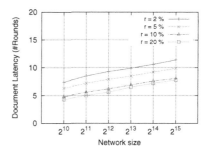

Fig. 11. Effect of varying the number of documents for Filament

Fig. 12. Effect of varying the number of nodes editing a document

Figure 12 shows the effect of varying the number of nodes editing a document or in other words the size of collaborators in the system. From the graph it is clear that as the number of nodes editing a given document increases it helps the system to converge faster. This is mainly because we can easily get the information about the collaborators if more and more nodes are editing the same document.

5   Related Work

Researchers have been looking into peer-to-peer collaborative editing platforms [9,13,17,18,22,30] for some time. Most of these approaches in decentralized peer-to-peer collaborative editing assume that all users in a system participate in the same edition which may not be the case in most systems. Search techniques to find collaborators in peer-to-peer system has been extensively researched in the past in both unstructured [11,12,19,23] and structured overlays, in particular in the context of *Distributed Hash Tables* (DHT) [25–27,31]. Most of the works assume a static network which is a rather strong assumption considering the rather dynamic nature of CE systems. DHTs typically provide deterministic guaranties, but usually assume that the number of items to be stored is much higher than the number of storage nodes available. Furthermore, these systems use consistent hashing techniques in which a node's role in the system is independent of this node's interests. Unstructured approaches have probabilistic recall rate. Flooding or exhaustive multicast strategy are used in these systems but they are very costly. Works by Pascal et al. [9,22,30] study structured collaborative editing platforms and routing techniques.

Our problem is very similar to peer clustering. Publish/subscribe systems are mainly used for distributed and selective content delivery. Content based pub/sub systems and routing are also actively studied [5–8,29]. In pub/sub systems subscribers express their interest by registering subscriptions and they will be notified of any events(issued by publishers) which match their subscription. The work by Voulgaris et al. [29], proposes Sub-2-Sub, a solution to implement a content based pub/sub system. Subscribers sharing the same interests are clustered to form a ring-shaped overlay network which is updated continuously by analyzing the interests of users. The work mainly focuses on interest clustering and the content dissemination. The TERA system [5] was designed with a general overlay (similar to Filament's helper overlay) that is used to keep track of given topic ids used to maintain topic-overlays and perform topic based routing. The problem of building overlays for users with possibly intersecting interests was formalized in works like [8] and then used to define the Spidercast system [7]. In this case, a single overlay is built but the connectivity between users interested in the same topic is guaranteed. Starting from this initial trend, several other papers [6] have appeared in this line of research. Many of these search and routing techniques can be adapted for CE systems but is not optimal because of the structural difference between CE and pub/sub systems.

6   Conclusion and Future Work

In this paper, we presented Filament, a novel cohort-construction approach that allows users editing the same documents to rapidly find each other. Filament utilises the semantic relations between peers to construct a set of self-organizing overlays which can be used to route search requests. The resulting protocol is efficient, scalable, and provides beneficial load-balancing properties over the involved peers. Simulation results show that in a network of 2^{12} nodes, Filament is able to reduce the document latency by around 20% compared to a Chord-based DHT approach.

One aspect we would like to explore in future is to deploy Filament in a real system and see how it fares. A thorough analytical study of the behaviour of our approach is also intended.

Acknowledgments. This work was partially funded by the DeSceNt project granted by the Labex CominLabs excellence laboratory of the French Agence Nationale de la Recherche (ANR- 10-LABX-07-01).

References

1. Diaspora. https://en.wikipedia.org/wiki/Diaspora_(software)
2. Etherpad. https://en.wikipedia.org/wiki/Etherpad
3. Google docs. https://en.wikipedia.org/wiki/Google_Docs,_Sheets,_and_Slides
4. ownCloud. https://owncloud.org/
5. Baldoni, R., Beraldi, R., Quema, V., Querzoni, L., Tucci-Piergiovanni, S.: Tera: Topic-based event routing for peer-to-peer architectures. In: Proceedings of the 2007 Inaugural International Conference on Distributed Event-based Systems, DEBS 2007, pp. 2–13 (2007)
6. Chen, C., Tock, Y.: Design of routing protocols and overlay topologies for topic-based publish/subscribe on small-world networks. In: Proceedings of the Industrial Track of the 16th International Middleware Conference. Middleware Industry 2015 (2015)

7. Chockler, G., Melamed, R., Tock, Y., Vitenberg, R.: Spidercast: a scalable interest-aware overlay for topic-based pub/sub communication. In: Proceedings of the 2007 Inaugural International Conference on Distributed Event-based Systems, DEBS 2007, pp. 14–25 (2007)
8. Chockler, G.V., Melamed, R., Tock, Y., Vitenberg, R.: Constructing scalable overlays for pub-sub with many topics. In: Proceedings of the Twenty-Sixth Annual ACM Symposium on Principles of Distributed Computing, PODC 2007, Portland, Oregon, USA, 12–15 August 2007, pp. 109–118 (2007)
9. Davoust, A., Skaf-Molli, H., Molli, P., Esfandiari, B., Aslan, K.: Distributed wikis: a survey. Concurrency Comput. Pract. Experience 27(11), 2751–2777 (2015)
10. DeCandia, G., Hastorun, D., Jampani, M., Kakulapati, G., Lakshman, A., Pilchin, A., Sivasubramanian, S., Vosshall, P., Vogels, W.: Dynamo: amazon's highly available key-value store. In: SOSP 2007 (2007)
11. Dorrigiv, R., Lopez-Ortiz, A., Prałat, P.: Search algorithms for unstructured peer-to-peer networks. In: 32nd IEEE Conference on Local Computer Networks, LCN 2007, pp. 343–352. IEEE (2007)
12. Gkantsidis, C., Mihail, M., Saberi, A.: Random walks in peer-to-peer networks: algorithms and evaluation. Perform. Eval. 63(3), 241–263 (2006)
13. Gupta, A., Sahin, O.D., Agrawal, D., El Abbadi, A.: Meghdoot: content-based publish/subscribe over P2P networks. In: Jacobsen, H.-A. (ed.) Middleware 2004. LNCS, vol. 3231, pp. 254–273. Springer, Heidelberg (2004). doi:10.1007/978-3-540-30229-2_14
14. Jelasity, M., Montresor, A., Babaoglu, O.: T-man: gossip-based fast overlay topology construction. Comput. Netw. 53(13), 2321–2339 (2009)
15. Jelasity, M., Voulgaris, S., Guerraoui, R., Kermarrec, A.M., van Steen, M.: Gossip-based peer sampling. ACM Trans. Comput. Syst. 25, 8 (2007). http://doi.acm.org/10.1145/1275517.1275520
16. Karger, D.R., Ruhl, M.: Simple efficient load balancing algorithms for peer-to-peer systems. In: Proceedings of the Sixteenth Annual ACM Symposium on Parallelism in Algorithms and Architectures, pp. 36–43. ACM (2004)
17. Kermarrec, A.-M., Triantafillou, P.: Xl peer-to-peer pub/sub systems. ACM Comput. Surv. (CSUR) 46(2), 16:1–16:45 (2013). Article no 16
18. Lakshman, A., Malik, P.: Cassandra: a decentralized structured storage system. SIGOPS Oper. Syst. Rev. 44(2), 35–40 (2010). ACM
19. Lv, Q., Cao, P., Cohen, E., Li, K., Shenker, S.: Search and replication in unstructured peer-to-peer networks. In: Proceedings of the 16th International Conference on Supercomputing, pp. 84–95. ACM (2002)
20. Montresor, A., Jelasity, M., Babaoglu, O.: Chord on demand. In: P2P 2005 (2005)
21. Montresor, A., Jelasity, M.: PeerSim: a scalable P2P simulator. In: P2P 2009 (2009)
22. Oster, G., Mondéjar, R., Molli, P., Dumitriu, S.: Building a collaborative peer-to-peer wiki system on a structured overlay. Comput. Netw. 54(12), 1939–1952 (2010)
23. Otto, F., Ouyang, S.: Improving search in unstructured P2P systems: intelligent walks (I-Walks). In: Corchado, E., Yin, H., Botti, V., Fyfe, C. (eds.) IDEAL 2006. LNCS, vol. 4224, pp. 1312–1319. Springer, Heidelberg (2006). doi:10.1007/11875581_156
24. Rao, A., Lakshminarayanan, K., Surana, S., Karp, R., Stoica, I.: Load balancing in structured P2P systems. In: Kaashoek, M.F., Stoica, I. (eds.) IPTPS 2003. LNCS, vol. 2735, pp. 68–79. Springer, Heidelberg (2003). doi:10.1007/978-3-540-45172-3_6
25. Ratnasamy, S., Francis, P., Handley, M., Karp, R., Shenker, S.: A scalable content-addressable network. SIGCOMM Comput. Commun. Rev. 31(4), 161–172 (2001)

26. Rowstron, A., Druschel, P.: Pastry: scalable, decentralized object location, and routing for large-scale peer-to-peer systems. In: Guerraoui, R. (ed.) Middleware 2001. LNCS, vol. 2218, pp. 329–350. Springer, Heidelberg (2001). doi:10.1007/3-540-45518-3_18

27. Stoica, I., Morris, R., Karger, D., Kaashoek, M.F., Balakrishnan, H.: Chord: a scalable peer-to-peer lookup service for internet applications. In: SIGCOMM 2001 (2001)

28. Voulgaris, S., van Steen, M.: Epidemic-style management of semantic overlays for content-based searching. In: Euro-Par 2005 (2005)

29. Voulgaris, S., Rivière, E., Kermarrec, A.M., Steen, M.V.: Sub-2-sub: self-organizing content-based publish subscribe for dynamic large scale collaborative networks. In: IPTPS 2006: the Fifth International Workshop on Peer-to-Peer Systems (2006)

30. Weiss, S., Urso, P., Molli, P.: Logoot-undo: distributed collaborative editing system on P2P networks. IEEE Trans. Parallel Distrib. Syst. **21**(8), 1162–1174 (2010)

31. Zhao, B., Kubiatowicz, J., Joseph, A.: Tapestry: an infrastructure for fault-tolerant wide-area location and routing. Computer **74** (2001)

Making Things Safe (Security)

Benchmarking Cryptographic Schemes for Securing Public Cloud Storages
(Practical Experience Report)

Stefan Contiu[1,2]($^\boxtimes$), Emmanuel Leblond[1], and Laurent Réveillère[2]

[1] Scille, 94250 Gentilly, France
{stefan.contiu,emmanuel.leblond}@scille.fr
[2] LaBRI, Université de Bordeaux, 33400 Talence, France
laurent.reveillere@u-bordeaux.fr

Abstract. Much research has focused during the last years on the security and privacy concerns of public cloud storages. Cryptographic primitives are commonly used to ensure user data confidentiality, authenticity and integrity. Confidentiality has been addressed by the use of symmetric-key encryption algorithms, while integrity and authenticity have been achieved by using message authentication codes, secure hashes or digital signatures. The choice of a specific configuration for securing an untrusted cloud storage highly depends on the expected security level, the size and type of data to store and the access pattern to these data. In this work, we are interested in overcoming the lack of comprehensive comparison of the costs and effectiveness of cryptographic primitives for securing public cloud storage, and ease an informed choice between them based on target usage conditions. We describe the results of an independent experimental study of six cryptographic schemes, representative of the principal design alternatives. Our practical experience report reveals that the best scheme for a given situation, such as a write-heavy workload of mostly small files, is not necessarily the most appropriate for a different situation such as a read-only workload of large files. We identify the scheme characteristics that are correlated with these differences and discuss the pros and cons of each design. Our experimental framework and results are available in the open for use by the community.

Keywords: Cloud storage · Security · Block cipher modes · Digital signatures

1 Introduction

Public clouds storage services such as Dropbox or Google Drive provide a convenient way for users to store and share personal data. As a result, we have witnessed a rapid adoption of these services in recent years [19]. Indeed, the cloud storage market is forecasted to grow from about $24 billion in 2016 to

© IFIP International Federation for Information Processing 2017
Published by Springer International Publishing AG 2017. All Rights Reserved
L.Y. Chen and H.P. Reiser (Eds.): DAIS 2017, LNCS 10320, pp. 163–176, 2017.
DOI: 10.1007/978-3-319-59665-5_12

about \$75 billion in 2021 [1]. However, despite its success, public cloud storage space is commonly assumed to be entirely untrusted, providing no guarantees over unauthorized exposure of user sensitive data. Therefore, it is not surprising that security and privacy issues in that context has gained increasing momentum within research community [24].

A traditional approach to ensure user data confidentiality, authenticity and integrity is the use cryptographic primitives. Confidentiality is addressed by the use of symmetric-key encryption algorithms, while authenticity and integrity are achieved by using message authentication codes, secure hashes or digital signatures. Cryptographic schemes are then constructed by selecting among these primitives depending on the expected level of security and privacy.

Among existing solutions, different configurations have been explored. For example, CloudProof [18] relies on AES in CTR mode for symmetric-key encryption, SHA-1 for hashing and RSA with 1024 bits key for signing. DepSky [3] uses similar cryptographic schemes except that it relies on AES in CBC mode instead of CTR. BlueSky [21] relies on AES for encryption and uses a message authentication code based on SHA-256 to provide both authenticity and integrity. In SafeSky [23] the encryption and authentication are combined by using AES in CCM mode.

Although widely used for general purpose usage, there exists very few studies comparing the costs and effectiveness of cryptographic primitives for securing public cloud storage. In this practical experience report, we are interested in overcoming this lack of a comprehensive comparison between them. We argue that the choice of a specific cryptographic construction has a direct impact on the performance and scalability of the secured cloud storage system, thus requiring a sound knowledge of its intrinsic properties. We consider different usage conditions such as various data size models and cloud workload scenarios and describe the results of an independent experimental study of six cryptographic schemes, representative of the principal design alternatives. We consider three different block cipher modes for AES encryption: chaining mode (CBC), counter mode (CTR), and an authenticated encryption mode that also covers integrity (GCM). For the public-key signature primitives, we evaluate the usage of cryptosystems based on RSA and Elliptic Curve Cryptography (ECC).

In our experiments, we perform both a set of micro-benchmarks and macro-benchmarks. Micro-benchmarks measure the intrinsic performance of a cryptographic primitive when varying the size of the cryptographic key. Macro-benchmarks assess how cryptographic primitives perform when a user interacts with a secured public cloud. We perform read and write operations on three large data sets modeled by considering different block sizes: uniform sizes, mostly small sizes, and mostly large sizes. The interaction between the user and the cloud is modeled based on four cloud workloads inspired from Yahoo! Cloud Serving Benchmark (YCSB) [7]. The workloads mimic mostly-write, write-heavy, read-heavy, and read-only operations.

The contributions of our performance comparison study aim at helping practitioners to decide which is the most appropriate cryptographic scheme for a target security level under certain usage conditions. Firstly, our results show that there is no one-size-fits-all to security in public cloud storage. Secondly, we identify which are the schemes that better match the studied usage scenarios. Although AES in CBC in conjunction with RSA is the preferred cryptographic scheme in the literature [3,5,21], we show that other algorithms can out-perform it by a factor of 10 under specific conditions. These findings can further be used to design a cryptographic approach that changes its behavior at runtime based on contextual information.

The rest of this paper is organized as follows. Section 2 presents the cryptographic primitives we evaluate in our experiments. We describe our experimental setup in Sect. 3. Section 4 presents our evaluation results and discusses the pros and cons of each cryptographic scheme with respect to target usage conditions. Section 5 reviews related work. Finally, Sect. 6 concludes.

2 Cryptographic Building Blocks

Various cryptographic primitives are used together for ensuring confidentiality, authenticity, and integrity of user data stored in public clouds. As illustrated in Fig. 1, securing data for public cloud storage is commonly a three step process. First, the data bock is encrypted using symmetric-key algorithm (step ❶). Second, a fixed size message digest is produced by using a one-way collision resistant function (step ❷) on the input data block. Third, a digital signature algorithm is used to prove the authenticity of the message digest with respect to the user private key (step ❸). In the remainder of this section, we describe in more details each step and related cryptographic algorithms.

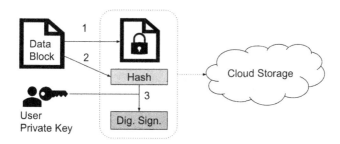

Fig. 1. Securing data for public cloud storage

2.1 Symmetric-Key Algorithms

A symmetric-key algorithm provides data confidentiality by the use of the same secret key for both encrypting and decrypting the data. Among existing algorithms, the one specified by the AES specification has become the de facto standard and is used worldwide [6]. It is a block cipher algorithm, operating on fixed-length group of 128 bits called a block with a key size of 128, 192 or 256 bits. To securely transform amounts of data larger than a block, the cipher's single-block operation needs to be repeatedly applied accordingly to a block cipher mode. Many modes of operation have been defined [9], each one offering a different level of performance and robustness. We now describe the three major modes that we cover in our study.

CBC. Cipher Block Chaining (CBC) works by *chaining* each block to its predecessor. At each step, the current block of plaintext is xor-ed with the ciphertext of the previous block, and then encrypted with the secret key. Since the first block has no predecessor, a random initialization vector is used instead. The initialization vector can then be publicly stored together with the ciphertext. Due to the chaining nature of this mode, the encryption is sequential and can not be parallelized. However, because each block is xor-ed with the ciphertext of the previous block, not the plaintext, decryption can be parallelized. Note that the reuse of the same initialization vector can leak information only about the first block.

CTR. Counter (CTR) mode generates keystream blocks, which are then xor-ed with the plaintext blocks to get the ciphertext. It generates the next keystream block by encrypting successive values of a *counter*. The counter can be any function which produces a sequence which is guaranteed not to repeat for a long time, although an actual increment-by-one counter is the simplest and most popular. A nonce is combined together with the counter to produce the actual unique counter block for encryption. Since counter values at different block offsets are known, this mode can be fully parallelized. However, reusing the same nonce can leak information about all blocks, making the implementation of CTR more sensitive than CBC. Nevertheless, this mode is proven to respect tight security requirements and is formally approved by NIST [8].

GCM. Galois Counter Mode (GCM) is a block cipher mode that performs both encryption and authentication by combining counter mode and operations in a finite (Galois) field. GCM is defined for block ciphers with a block size of 128 bits. Implementing GCM can make efficient use of Carry-less Multiplication (CLMUL), an extension to the ×86 instruction set used by microprocessors from Intel and AMD [11]. Similarly to CTR mode, GCM takes as input a nonce and thus reusing the same nonce with the same key leaks information about the whole message.

2.2 Message Digests

Message digests or simply hash functions are one-way collision resistant functions, mapping an input data block to a short fixed size output. The role of hash functions is to provide integrity guarantees over the data. Also, they are utilized as a preceding operation in digital signature schemes, reducing an arbitrarily large amount of data to a small output on which the signature is applied.

Hash functions work by splitting the data into fixed size blocks, and iteratively applying a compression function with an intermediate state [9]. Secure Hash Algorithms (SHA) are a class of secure hashes standardized by NIST in three family sets (SHA-1, SHA-2, and SHA-3). The first set has been proved insecure due to collision attacks [22]. The second set is a popular choice, coming with 32 and 64 bits processing variants, and producing outputs of 256, 384, and 512 bits. Lastly, the third family SHA-3 was recently standardized by NIST, not as a replacement to the previous SHA-2, but as an alternative [17].

2.3   Digital Signatures

Digital signature algorithms are employed for proving the authenticity of a data block with respect to the user private key. Moreover, they provide the properties of non-repudiation and integrity, meaning that the signing user can not deny herself as the signer and that the data block content is not altered. The verification of the message and signature pair can be openly performed by anybody knowing the user public key.

RSA is a public key cryptosystem, based on the difficult mathematical problem of factoring the product of two arbitrarily large prime numbers. The key sizes employed by RSA require a much larger length as compared to symmetric encryption, because solving the mathematical problem is faster than a brute force attack iterating over all possible keys.

Elliptic Curve Cryptography. (ECC) is a relatively novel direction in public key cryptosystems [15], that besides a considerable interest from academia, has also been integrated within technical solutions like Bitcoin, SSH, and TLS [4]. The advantage of ECC over the traditional RSA is the small nature of key sizes, implying an increase of computational speed. ECC is based on the difficult mathematical problem of discrete logarithm when the computations are performed over the points of an elliptic curve. The security of the ECC cryptosystem is highly correlated to the choice of the curve equation. Various curves have been proposed and formally reviewed, such as the ones standardized by NIST [14].

2.4   Cryptographic Strength of Key Sizes

The size of the cryptographic key is the principal factor affecting the performance and the security level of cryptographic primitives. Sufficiently large key sizes protect the cryptographic algorithms from brute force attacks on the key values. Therefore, the security strength of a cryptographic algorithm is upper-bounded by the size of the key used.

Table 1 lists three strength levels (Low, Medium, High) as specified by NIST [2]. The security strength level represents the upper bound protection

Table 1. Computational equivalence of key sizes (in bits).

Security strength	AES	RSA	ECC	SHA-2
Low	128	128	3,072	256–383	256
Medium	192	192	7,680	384–511	384
High	256	256	15,360	≥512	512

in bits for a brute force attack employed on the key values. The key sizes displayed within the same row are computationally equivalent with respect to the same security strength level. The strength for symmetric encryption is by design identical to the key size. RSA requires much larger key sizes up to 15,360 bits for a security strength of 256 bits, because solving the factorization problem is faster than a brute force attack on the key. Elliptic curve cryptography and secured hash methods require roughly the double in length.

3   Experimental Cloud-Based Data Store

In order to easily and efficiently evaluate the wide spectrum of cryptographic schemes described previously, we designed and implemented an experimental testbed, consisting of a single client accessing data on a public cloud storage. We assume that only the client can be trusted and thus data must be encrypted prior transmission to the storage node. The client component performs the actual processing and transformation (e.g., encryption, hashing) of data blocks before they are stored, as well as the reverse decoding operation (e.g., decryption, digital signature). We describe in the remainder of this section the cryptographic schemes we used in our evaluation, the model of data and the cloud workloads.

3.1   Cryptographic Schemes

We constructed six cryptographic schemes (CBC-RSA, CTR-RSA, GCM-RSA, CBC-ECC, CTR-ECC, GCM-ECC) using the main primitives described in Sect. 2. The schemes are constructed by varying the block cipher mode (CBC, CTR, and GCM) for AES symmetric encryption, and the digital signature algorithm (RSA and ECC). Message digests are generated using the SHA-2 secure hash algorithm. For each scheme, we use three different cryptographic key sizes covering the security strength levels defined in Table 1. Each key is pre-generated before the experiments using a pseudo random generator.

3.2   Data Sets

Users use cloud storage services for data files of various types among them most popular ones are photos, documents, and music [19]. Such files commonly have sizes from few hundreds of kilo bytes to several mega bytes. Smaller block sizes, of the magnitude of tens of kilo bytes, are specific for systems that perform de-duplication [16] or for modeling the entire set of files on a user machine [20]. On the other hand, larger block sizes such as 64 MB are utilized by distributed file systems operating on fixed size chunks [10]. To cover this variety of file sizes, we defined three different data sets, as depicted in Table 2, by varying the probability distribution of sizes.

Table 2. Data sets.

Data set	Probability distribution	Mean	Files	Size (GB)
Mostly-small	Log normal	256 KB	2,000	0.5
Mixed-sizes	Uniform	32 MB	100	3.1
Mostly-large	Reversed log normal	64 MB	20	1.2

The mostly-small data set follows a log normal distribution with a mean at 256 KB and contains a total of 0.5 GB of data. The mostly-large data set follows a reversed log normal distribution of files sizes for a total amount of 1.2 GB of data. The mixed-sizes data set follows a uniform distribution holding 3.1 GB of data. For all the three data sets the file sizes range from 1 KB to 64 MB.

3.3   Cloud Workloads

The ratio of read and write operations that a client performs over a cloud storage is specific to a given usage scenario. For example, when using the cloud storage to backup local files, the workload is governed by write operations. On the other hand, when sharing files such as photos with a large number of users, the workload is dominated by read operations.

To model the diversity of cloud workloads, we leverage on YCSB [7], a reference framework for benchmarking cloud storages. In addition to the three workloads defined by YCSB (write-heavy, read-heavy, read-only), we introduced a fourth one (mostly-write) composed of 5% or reads and 95% of write operations to mimic the behavior of backup scenarios. Table 3 lists the four workloads of our study and the corresponding ratios of read and write operations. The mostly-write workload performs a small number of reads (5%). The write-heavy workload consists of an even number of writes and reads. The two intensive read workloads, read-heavy and read-only, consider a small amount of writes (5%) and no writes respectively.

3.4   Implementation

Our implementation of the cryptographic schemes under evaluation relies on the open-source `openssl`[1] (v1.1.1) library. This library is implemented in a mix of

---

[1] https://www.openssl.org/.

Table 3. Cloud workloads

	Reads	Writes
Mostly-write	5%	95%
Write-heavy	50%	50%
Read-heavy	95%	5%
Read-only	100%	0%

C and hand-written Assembly and can take advantage of hardware acceleration provided by AES-NI and CLMUL extension instruction sets.

To test in isolation the raw performance of each cryptographic primitive, we have implemented a set of microbenchmarks in C. Our implementation uses rtdsc processor instruction to collect the number of cycles from the time stamp counter (TSC) register.

To evaluate the primitives in realistic settings, we have implemented a testbed in Python to facilitate the integration with the cryptography.io[2] (v1.8) the reference Python binding for openssl.

The cloud storage implementation contains both a Dropbox interface and a locally simulated cloud provider as an in-memory key-value store. To prevent variations of real cloud access latencies interfering with the observed outcomes and to better isolate the performance of cryptographic primitives, we report the results when utilizing the simulated cloud storage. To mimic the behavior of a public cloud storage, we added a delay of 50ms to each request to simulate a realistic round-trip latency.

4   Results

This section presents our extensive evaluation of the previously described cryptographic schemes. We perform our experiments on a 4-Core Intel i7-6600U processor at 3.4 GHz with 16 GB of RAM, and operating on Ubuntu v16.04 LTS. We first test in isolation the cryptographic primitives via a set of microbenchmarks, and we finally evaluate the primitives in realistic settings.

4.1   Micro-Benchmark

Our first set of experiments evaluate the intrinsic performance of cryptographic primitives for increasing security strength levels. In this scenario, the primitives are tested in isolation via a specialized client that sequentially perform an operation (e.g., encryption, signature) on block sizes from 512 KB to 64 MB. We repeatably execute 50 times each operation on randomly generated data and averaging the consumed CPU cycles. Our preliminary results confirm that the number of CPU cycles is always linear with respect to the size of the input data. In the remainder, we thus only show the average number of cycles per byte.

---

[2] https://cryptography.io/.

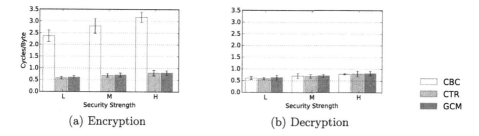

Fig. 2. Performance of AES (cycles per byte)

Figure 2 presents our results for AES encryption and decryption. We notice that parallelizable operations have a considerable performance improvement compared to the non-parallelizable encryption in CBC mode. This large performance improvement by a factor of 4.5 for encryption is due to the pipelining technique supported by the **AES-NI** instruction set at the processor level. We also notice that the performance overhead increases almost linearly with the targeted security strength level.

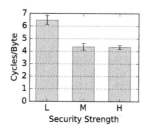

Fig. 3. Performance of SHA-2 (cycles per byte)

The cost of the SHA-2 hashing function is shown in Fig. 3. The SHA-256 method, for a low security strength level, requires on average 6.4 cycles per byte. Hashing for stronger security strength levels always perform better with an improvement of about 33%. The reason is that the calculation is done on a larger length of data at a time. Performances of SHA-384 is comparable to SHA-512, confirming that it uses the same algorithm, but truncating the hash to a smaller output. As SHA-512 offers both the higher security strength and the best performance, we use it in our macrobenchmark.

The performance results of digital signatures based on RSA and ECC are depicted in Fig. 4. Both signing and verification operations work over the secured hash produced using a hashing function such as SHA-2. Therefore, the time does not depend on the size of the input data. We thus consider only the total number of cycles required to perform the operation. The cost of the signing operation using RSA drastically increases with the size of the key. For example, the performance cost increases up to 614 millions of cycles for the strongest security

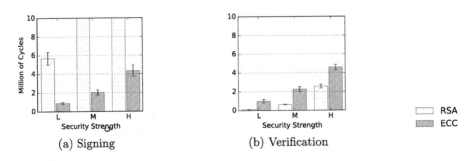

Fig. 4. Performance of digital signature

strength level (values are truncated to 10 millions in Fig. 4a), more than 100 times the cost required for the lowest security level. On the other hand, elliptic curve signature is dramatically faster, providing a performance of 7, 58 and 153 times faster than RSA for equivalent key strengths. For the verification operation, contrary to singing, the performance of the two cryptosystems reverses. RSA performs better than Elliptic Curve, however the difference between the two is not at all as dramatic as in the case of signing.

4.2 Macrobenchmark

In this section we evaluate the cryptographic schemes in a more complex scenario that involves realistic data sets and cloud workloads, as described in Sect. 3. We measure the total time required by a client to perform all the read and write operations on the input data set. For each entry of the data set, we randomly select an operation (either read or write) to follow the probability distribution defined by the cloud workload. Figure 5 shows our results for the mostly-small test set. We can notice that RSA performs worse on mostly-write and write-heavy workloads when the security strength increases. On the other hand, read-heavy and read-only workloads do not present this trend as the verification process of the RSA signature is cheap. The CTR-ECC cryptographic scheme shows always a good performance independently of the cloud workload or the security strength.

The results of our experiments for mostly-large sizes are shown in Fig. 6. Except for RSA that performs worse with mostly-write and write-heavy workloads, we observe that differences between cryptographic schemes reduce as read operations dominate more and more the workload. We notice that RSA outperforms ECC by a insignificant factor of 2% in read-only workload. We can also notice that the performance gap between the schemes based on CBC and the ones using CTR or GCM decreases almost proportionally with the number of write operations.

Similarly to mostly-large sizes, we observe for mixed-sizes (see Fig. 7) that RSA performs worse with mostly-write and write-heavy workloads and that the gap between the different schemes tends to reduce as the number of read operation increases.

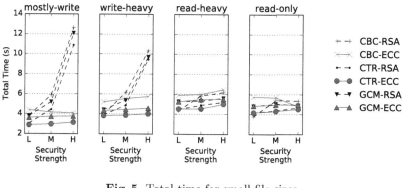

Fig. 5. Total time for small file sizes

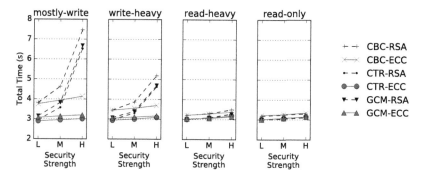

Fig. 6. Total time for large file sizes

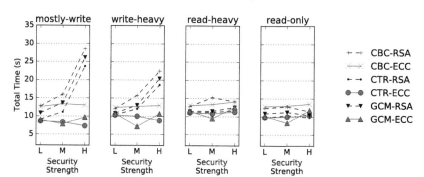

Fig. 7. Total time for uniform file sizes

4.3 Discussion

Our results show that CTR-ECC performs better in almost all usage scenarios. This scheme should be preferred if there is no prior knowledge on the workloads or data sizes.

However, we note that specific scenarios may require fine tuned schemes to maximize performances. Indeed, CTR-ECC performs better for mostly-writes and write-heavy workloads while CTR-RSA performs slightly better for read-heavy and read-only workloads. Furthermore, for read-only workloads CTR-RSA can be safely replaced by CBC-RSA, as their performances are very similar within this context. If information about data sizes is available, then a CTR-based scheme performs better as the data sizes increase.

When security is not a constraint, CTR-ECC and CTR-RSA are interchangeable as best performers. Contrary, when strong security strength is required, schemes relying on RSA should be avoided as they may induce severe performance penalties.

5   Related Work

Many previous work make use of cryptographic schemes for securing cloud storages. However, to the best of our knowledge, none of them report the result of a study to evaluate the rationale behind specific cryptographic choices. Some use of AES in CBC mode [3] while others use the CTR mode [18]. Furthermore, some even omit to describe the cipher mode they rely on [13,16]. Our benchmarking study shows that CTR outperforms CBC almost always and should be preferred. Moreover, we indicate that schemes using RSA for digital signatures [3,18] are suitable only for corner cases characterized among others by read-heavy and read-only workloads, and that ECC outperforms RSA in most usage conditions.

The costs of confidentiality, integrity and authenticity have been evaluated by Burihabwa et al. [5] within the cloud storage context. Besides a single cloud model, the study also considered the dispersal of confidential data over multiple storages by using erasure encoding. Although the study makes use of cryptographic primitives, there is no debate over different strength levels achieved by cryptographic keys, nor about the modeling of both the replayed test set and the read/write requests. Furthermore, the study makes use of AES in CBC mode coupled with RSA, a cryptographic scheme that, according to our findings, it is suitable only for read-only cloud workloads over mostly-small sizes.

A performance comparison study for digital signatures based on RSA and ECC has been addressed in a general context [12]. The authors propose the use of ECC for scenarios dominated by signing operations, while RSA have been proposed for scenarios dominated by verification operations. Similarly, the results of our study suggest the use of ECC for mostly-write and write-heavy workloads, and RSA for read-heavy and read-only workloads.

6   Conclusion

We have studied and compared, in this practical experience report, the performance of several cryptographic primitives that are widely used to implement security and privacy in public cloud storage. The objective of this experimental study was to compare the costs and effectiveness of cryptographic primitives for securing public cloud storage, and not to develop original schemes.

We conducted a wide range of experiments on six different cryptographic schemes both to measure their raw speed and their performance when used in a realistic cloud storage setup. Our observations notably highlight that the best scheme for a given situation, such as a write-heavy workload of mostly small files, is not necessarily the most appropriate for a different situation such as a read-only workload of large files.

We hope that our study will bring valuable insights and guidance to other researchers interested in using cryptography techniques for data storage in the cloud.

Availability. Our experimental framework and results are available in the open for use by the community at the following webpage: https://github.com/stefan-contiu/cloud-crypto-benchmark.

Acknowledgment. This work was partially supported by Scille and DGA under contract RAPID-172906010.

References

1. Cloud storage market worth 74.94 billion USD by 2021 - MarketWatch (2016). http://www.marketwatch.com/story/cloud-storage-market-worth-7494-billion-usd-by-2021-2016-09-06-72033123
2. Barker, E.: Recommendation for key management part 1: general. Technical report, National Institute of Standards and Technology, July 2016
3. Bessani, A., Correia, M., Quaresma, B., André, F., Sousa, P.: DepSky: dependable and secure storage in a cloud-of-clouds. In: Proceedings of the Sixth Conference on Computer Systems, pp. 31–46, April 2011
4. Bos, J.W., Halderman, J.A., Heninger, N., Moore, J., Naehrig, M., Wustrow, E.: Elliptic curve cryptography in practice. In: Christin, N., Safavi-Naini, R. (eds.) FC 2014. LNCS, vol. 8437, pp. 157–175. Springer, Heidelberg (2014). doi:10.1007/978-3-662-45472-5_11
5. Burihabwa, D., Pontes, R., Felber, P., Maia, F., Mercier, H., Oliveira, R., Paulo, J., Schiavoni, V.: On the cost of safe storage for public clouds: an experimental evaluation. In: 2016 IEEE 35th Symposium on Reliable Distributed Systems (SRDS), pp. 157–166. IEEE, September 2016
6. Chown, P.: Advanced encryption standard (AES) ciphersuites for transport layer security (TLS). Technical report (2002)
7. Cooper, B.F., Silberstein, A., Tam, E., Ramakrishnan, R., Sears, R.: Benchmarking cloud serving systems with YCSB. In: Proceedings of the 1st ACM Symposium on Cloud Computing, pp. 143–154. ACM (2010)
8. Dworkin, M.: Recommendation for block cipher modes of operation: methods and techniques. Technical report, DTIC Document, December 2001
9. Ferguson, N., Schneier, B.: Practical Cryptography, vol. 23. Wiley, New York (2003)
10. Ghemawat, S., Gobioff, H., Leung, S.T.: The google file system. In: ACM SIGOPS Operating Systems Review, vol. 37, pp. 29–43. ACM, October 2003

11. Gueron, S., Kounavis, M.E.: Intel® carry-less multiplication instruction and its usage for computing the GCM mode. White Paper, May 2010

12. Jansma, N., Arrendondo, B.: Performance comparison of elliptic curve and RSA digital signatures. University of Michigan College of Engineering, April 2004

13. Kamara, S., Lauter, K.: Cryptographic cloud storage. In: Sion, R., Curtmola, R., Dietrich, S., Kiayias, A., Miret, J.M., Sako, K., Sebé, F. (eds.) FC 2010. LNCS, vol. 6054, pp. 136–149. Springer, Heidelberg (2010). doi:10.1007/978-3-642-14992-4_13

14. Kerry, C.F.: Digital signature standard (DSS). FIPS PUB 186-4, July 2013

15. Koblitz, N.: Elliptic curve cryptosystems. Math. Comput. **48**(177), 203–209 (1987)

16. Li, M., Qin, C., Lee, P.P.: CDstore: toward reliable, secure, and cost-efficient cloud storage via convergent dispersal. In: USENIX Annual Technical Conference, pp. 111–124, July 2015

17. NIST: SHA3-Standard: permutation-based hash and extendable-output functions (DRAFT FIPS PUB 202). Technical report, May 2014

18. Popa, R.A., Lorch, J.R., Molnar, D., Wang, H.J., Zhuang, L.: Enabling security in cloud storage SLAs with CloudProof. In: USENIX Annual Technical Conference, vol. 242, May 2011

19. Seybert, H., Reinecke, P.: Internet and cloud services-statistics on the use by individuals. Technical report, Eurostat, December 2014

20. Tanenbaum, A.S., Herder, J.N., Bos, H.: File size distribution on UNIX systems: then and now. ACM SIGOPS Oper. Syst. Rev. **40**(1), 100–104 (2006)

21. Vrable, M., Savage, S., Voelker, G.M.: BlueSky: cloud-backed file system for the enterprise. In: Proceedings of the 10th USENIX Conference on File and Storage Technologies, pp. 19–19. USENIX Association, February 2012

22. Wang, X., Yin, Y.L., Yu, H.: Finding collisions in the full SHA-1. In: Shoup, V. (ed.) CRYPTO 2005. LNCS, vol. 3621, pp. 17–36. Springer, Heidelberg (2005). doi:10.1007/11535218_2

23. Zhao, R., Yue, C., Tak, B., Tang, C.: SafeSky: a secure cloud storage middleware for end-user applications. In: 2015 IEEE 34th Symposium on Reliable Distributed Systems (SRDS), pp. 21–30. IEEE, September 2015

24. Zhou, M., Zhang, R., Xie, W., Qian, W., Zhou, A.: Security and privacy in cloud computing: a survey. In: 2010 Sixth International Conference on Semantics Knowledge and Grid (SKG), pp. 105–112. IEEE, November 2010

Secure Cloud Micro Services Using Intel SGX

Stefan Brenner[1]([✉]), Tobias Hundt[1], Giovanni Mazzeo[2], and Rüdiger Kapitza[1]

[1] TU Braunschweig, Braunschweig, Germany
{brenner,hundt,rrkapitz}@ibr.cs.tu-bs.de
[2] University of Naples "Parthenope", Naples, Italy
giovanni.mazzeo@uniparthenope.it

Abstract. The micro service paradigm targets the implementation of large and scalable systems while enabling fine-grained service-level maintainability. Due to their scalability, such architectures are frequently used in cloud environments, which are often subject to privacy and trust issues hindering the deployment of services dealing with sensitive data.

In this paper we investigate the integration of trusted execution based on Intel Software Guard Extensions (SGX) into micro service applications. We present our *Vert.x Vault*, that supports SGX-based trusted execution in Eclipse Vert.x, a renowned tool-kit for writing reactive micro service applications. With our approach, secure micro services can run alongside regular ones, inter-connected via the Vert.x event bus to build large Vert.x applications that can contain multiple trusted components.

Maintaining a full-fledged Java Virtual Machine (JVM) inside an SGX enclave is impractical due to its complexity, less secure because of a large Trusted Code Base (TCB), and would suffer from performance penalties due to a high memory footprint. However, as Vert.x is written in Java, for a lean TCB this requires integration of native enclave C/C++ code into Vert.x, for which we propose the usage of Java Native Interface (JNI).

Our *Vert.x Vault* provides the benefits of micro service architectures together with trusted execution to support privacy and data confidentiality for sensitive applications in the cloud at scale. In our evaluation we show the feasibility of our approach, buying a significantly increased level of security for a low performance overhead of only ≈8.7%.

Keywords: Vert.x · SGX · Cloud security · Micro services

1 Introduction

Micro services are popular as they offer a new paradigm and many benefits such as flexibility, scalability, ease of development and manageability of applications [3]. Due to their scaling nature and flexibility, micro service architectures are mostly used in data centre and cloud scenarios where scale out capabilities are required to handle high load. However, trust issues still hinder the widespread adoption of cloud services and the deployment of sensitive applications processing sensitive data in the cloud [11,13].

© IFIP International Federation for Information Processing 2017
Published by Springer International Publishing AG 2017. All Rights Reserved
L.Y. Chen and H.P. Reiser (Eds.): DAIS 2017, LNCS 10320, pp. 177–191, 2017.
DOI: 10.1007/978-3-319-59665-5_13

With Software Guard Extensions (SGX) [4,12], Intel recently released a new technology for protecting applications from many—even physical—attacks such as the cold boot attack. SGX is an instruction set extension, released in the Skylake processor family, that allows the creation of Trusted Execution Environment (TEEs) inside the address space of an application. SGX TEEs are called *enclaves* and provide strong protection of code and data inside through encryption and integrity checks of their memory range directly by the CPU. This allows a strong adversary model and to limit the trusted computing base to the enclave code and the CPU package only, which is especially useful for sensitive data processing in the cloud. On currently available hardware, SGX is limited to a maximum of 128 MB of memory to be used for enclaves. This limitation requires to keep the memory footprint of enclaves as narrow as possible in order to prevent significant performance implications. Another important aspect with regards to security of TEEs is to keep their Trusted Code Base (TCB) as small as possible. This is due to the fact, that larger amounts of code usually lead to more exploitable security vulnerabilities [15].

Amongst others like *Spring Boot*[1], *Go Micro*[2], an excellent example for a renowned protagonist in the context of micro service development is Eclipse Vert.x [2]. The Vert.x tool-kit introduces the notion of *verticles* and supports the development of micro service applications. Furthermore, it provides a distributed event bus for its verticles to communicate with each other in a reactive fashion.

In this paper, we investigate the protection of data confidentiality in micro service applications by exploitation of the SGX technology, and chose the Vert.x tool-kit as an example micro service environment. Our contribution comprises the design of our *Vert.x Vault*, that allows the integration of slim SGX TEEs into the JVM-based Vert.x tool-kit, and demonstrates the feasibility of our approach, as well as an evaluation of its induced performance overhead.

A technical challenge to be solved in this work was the way of integration of native C/C++-based TEEs into the Java/Java Virtual Machine (JVM)-based environment of the Vert.x tool-kit. As we argued in earlier work [8], porting a full-fledged JVM into a TEE is not only a complex endeavour, but also violates common security principles such as the size and complexity of the TCB as well as the memory footprint of the TEEs which is highly performance-critical. Moreover, in this work we elaborate why the usage of SGX-based TEEs is a good fit for micro service applications.

In Sect. 2 we describe SGX and Vert.x as the cornerstone of our system. Next, in Sect. 3 we show the design of our *Vert.x Vault* followed by implementation details in Sect. 4. Afterwards, in Sect. 5, we present the benefits of our *Vert.x Vault* adopted in a critical infrastructure use case scenario. Finally, we measure the performance of our approach in Sect. 6 and conclude in Sect. 8.

---

[1] https://projects.spring.io/spring-boot/.
[2] https://github.com/micro/go-micro.

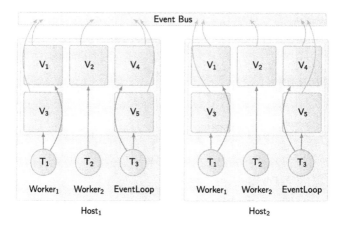

Fig. 1. Vert.x architecture and thread model (Verticles V_{1-5}, Threads T_{1-3}).

2 Background

In this section we describe the architecture, purpose, and main concepts of the Vert.x tool-kit. In addition, we give a short introduction to the SGX technology and describe the enclave life cycle and programming model.

2.1 Eclipse Vert.x

The rationale behind the concept of a micro service is to do one small thing and reduce complexity. In a micro service architecture, multiple of these services interact with each other and each of them has its very limited purpose. This allows the flexibility of development of such architectures, and also large development teams to collaborate simultaneously. Real applications of Vert.x can be for example REST services, or real time web applications[3].

According to its authors, "Vert.x is a tool-kit for building reactive applications on the JVM" [2]. In the context of Vert.x, micro services are called *verticles*, and are supposed to comprise a scarce, well-defined part of application logic. As Vert.x is a polyglot tool-kit for JVM-based languages, verticles can be implemented in various programming languages and interact across programming languages. Verticles communicate via the *event bus* that connects verticles even across machine boundaries were they can subscribe an "address" in order to receive callbacks once a message arrives for this address.

All verticles are scheduled via the *event loop* thread of Vert.x (one per physical CPU core), which delivers events to verticles. Supporting the idea of reactive applications, a verticle should never block this thread but implement blocking operations such as I/O operations in an asynchronous fashion. Long running tasks can be done in a *worker verticle* on a separate thread pool. Figure 1 illustrates the overall Vert.x system architecture and thread model.

---

[3] http://vertx.io/whos_using/.

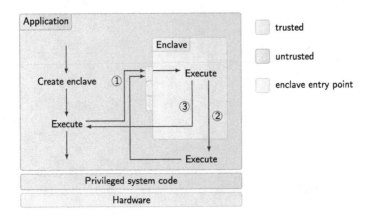

Fig. 2. Interaction between untrusted application and SGX enclave.

Currently, there is no support for trusted execution in Vert.x, however, the Vert.x engineers recently released a secure event bus implementation that provides protection of exchanged event bus messages using Transport Layer Security (TLS).

2.2 SGX

SGX [4,12] is a new instruction set extension by Intel, which has been released in the Skylake processor generation. It allows the creation of TEEs—called *enclaves*—inside the address space of user space applications. Enclaves are protected by the CPU package itself from a number of critical security threats: enclave memory is transparently encrypted and integrity-checked by the CPU, limiting trust to only the CPU package itself.

Entering and exiting an enclave is only possible via a defined enclave interface, that describes entry points and the allowed number of concurrent threads inside an enclave. Calls to enclave functionality are called enclave calls (ecalls), while calls from an enclave to outside code are called outside calls (ocalls). The enclave interface is described in a domain-specific language during development, which is also used to generate untrusted and trusted ecall and ocall stubs. Figure 2 illustrates the control flow of an ecall ①, an ocall ② and returning from an ecall to the untrusted code ③.

Enclave memory is backed by a range of normal DRAM—called Enclave Page Cache (EPC)—which is reserved by the firmware during the boot process. This memory range is managed by the untrusted operating system, while its contents are encrypted by the CPU package with a random key. Currently, SGX supports a maximum of 128 MB of EPC for all enclaves running on a system together. Memory demand exceeding this range requires the SGX driver to re-encrypt enclave pages and copy them to regular system memory causing a high performance impact.

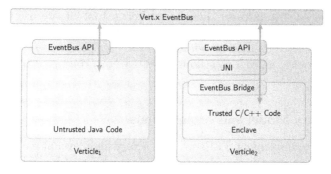

Fig. 3. Architectural Overview of *Vert.x Vault* showing two verticles connected via the Vert.x event bus and one of them containing an SGX enclave.

3 Design

With our *Vert.x Vault* we want to integrate TEEs into Vert.x applications such that the TEE developer can offload parts of the application logic to SGX enclaves. This allows usage of SGX for critical parts of the application logic while keeping most of it including the code base of Vert.x untrusted and not part of the TCB. Vert.x and SGX TEEs are a suitable fit, as the micro service paradigm matches the original idea of the SGX engineers to keep enclaves lightweight and small, and the ability of SGX to integrate multiple TEEs into a single user process.

Since Vert.x is written in Java and enclaves are written in C/C++, we propose integration of enclaves via Java Native Interface (JNI) into verticles. While the integration of a full-fledged JVM into an enclave would be possible, it is not favourable as it introduces a lot of complexity to the enclave and causes a drastic increase of the TCB, leading to a higher probability of exploitable security vulnerabilities and an increased attack surface. Furthermore, in the context of SGX this would lead to a significant performance penalty as the available enclave memory—limited to 128 MB on current hardware—would be exceeded. Exceeding the enclave memory causes the SGX driver to move enclave pages to regular system memory, requiring an expensive re-encryption of the pages [8].

An overview of our architecture is shown in Fig. 3, illustrating two verticles connected via the Vert.x event bus, and one of them containing an SGX enclave. As can be seen from the figure, a *secure verticle* is a verticle with an integrated enclave, that can be reached by other verticles via the Vert.x event bus. This enables the developer to design large micro service applications consisting of a mix of multiple untrusted and secure verticles. It is also possible to explicitly guide further isolation via process boundaries, as verticles can be deployed on specific hosts and multiple verticles can reside in the same JVM process.

The enclave which is integrated into a secure verticle, contains our Vert.x Vault as a C/C++ library offering an Application Programming Interface (API) to access the event bus directly from the enclave. In order to integrate the

C/C++-based enclave into the Java-based Vert.x tool-kit, we use a small JNI component to forward the *Vert.x Vault* calls to the original Vert.x API. By this, the enclave is able to register an address on the event bus and receive messages from other verticles, as well as sending messages to arbitrary addresses on the event bus.

3.1   Adversary Model and Assumptions

By using SGX to implement TEEs we gain a very high level of security allowing a very strong adversary model. We assume an attacker that has full access to the machines running Vert.x, including the firmware, Operating System (OS), and all system and user space software. Even physical attacks such as cold boot attacks can be allowed without violating the security guarantees that SGX provides. We assume a correct implementation of SGX and all cryptographic primitives.

3.2   Security Aspects

As already outlined, the size of the TCB influences the overall security of an application. Besides its complexity and the fact that syscalls can not be done in an enclave, this is the main security reason why a full-blown JVM should not be ported to run inside an enclave. Running a JVM inside an enclave would lead to both, a large TCB inside the enclave as well as a large memory footprint of the enclaves which negatively affects both, security and performance.

Hence, in our approach we aim at C/C++-based enclaves that execute only minimal parts of the application logic in the trusted environment. Partitioning the application logic to decide which parts of application logic are required to run inside the enclave and which not is the task of the developer. We demonstrated this approach—called *application partitioning approach*—for ZooKeeper, a complex Java-based coordination service [8], in an earlier work.

Running parts of application logic in an enclave, provides protection of confidentiality and integrity of data inside the enclave and the enclave code itself. However, once data is exchanged between and enclave and the untrusted outside world, data must also be protected in an adequate way; traditionally by using TLS between the two parties communicating. However, in case of SGX, the TLS endpoint must reside inside the enclave. In our *Vert.x Vault*, the enclave integrated into a secure verticle inherits the Intel SGX SDK features and can resort to the included cryptographic functions in order to protect data exchanged via the Vert.x event bus or with other secure verticles, respectively.

Enclave Interface. Another possible security aspect is the enclave interface, i.e. the amount and signature of ecalls. In general, there will be less security vulnerabilities with a more narrow enclave interface. Also, we wanted to keep the enclave interface generic in order to support any kind of application logic running in the enclave. The complete enclave interface is illustrated in Listing 1.1.

```
enclave {
  trusted {
    public void ecall_enclaveInit();
    public void ecall_deliverMsg(
      [in, size=lenCh] const char *channel, size_t lenCh,
      [in, size=lenMsg] const char *msg, size_t lenMsg);
  };
  untrusted {
    void ocall_register( [user_check] void* weak,
      [in, string] const char *channel, size_t len);
    void ocall_unregister( [user_check] void* weak,
      [in, string] const char *channel, size_t len);
    void ocall_send( [user_check] void* weak,
      [in, string] const char *channel, size_t len,
      [in, string] const char *msg,    size_t lenMsg);
    void ocall_broadcast( [user_check] void* weak,
      [in, string] const char *channel, size_t len,
      [in, string] const char *msg, size_t lenMsg);
  };
};
```

Listing 1.1. Enclave interface description.

We defined an enclave entry method which is called after the enclave is created. This allows the implementation of initialisation routines inside the enclave and to register to event bus addresses on secure verticle start-up and is analogous to the verticle's constructor method. Next, we implemented another method to deliver messages from the event bus to the enclave. Only within the enclave we distinguish the address on the event bus and deliver the message to the respective callback function.

Calls from the enclave to the untrusted context are also part of the enclave interface. Firstly, there are two methods for registering and de-registering an address on the Vert.x event bus. During registration, the enclave stores a function pointer in an internal (trusted) data structure to the user-defined callback function once a message is received for this address. In order to allow sending messages to the event bus, we implemented two ocalls to send and broadcast messages onto the event bus respectively.

3.3   Programming Model

A crucial requirement of our project was to give the enclave developer the impression of the Vert.x programming model inside an enclave. Consequently, we defined the notion of a *secure verticle* that essentially represents a verticle whose application logic is implemented inside an enclave. As a Vert.x application will usually consist of multiple verticles, the idea is to offload all sensitive application logic components to secure verticles that can interact with the other verticles via the event bus. In terms of the application partitioning approach from our earlier work [8], only application logic fragments that require direct plain text access to user data should be implemented as secure verticles, whereas all other parts should be untrusted verticles. This is compliant with our goal of minimising the TCB for a higher level of security.

Inside enclaves of a secure verticle, we want to give the developer a Vert.x-like programming model, i.e. reactive event-based callbacks. For this purpose, we mimic the Vert.x event bus API inside the enclave, and allow the enclave developer to register event bus addresses and receive callbacks for the registered addresses as well as sending messages to the event bus. By this, the secure verticles get integrated into the complete system of verticles of a full Vert.x application.

4   Enclave Integration and *Vert.x Vault* Features

The integration of SGX enclaves into Java applications in general, and into the Vert.x tool-kit specifically in this work, can be done using JNI. For this purpose we implement the interface that the enclave uses to interact with the event bus, as well as the one that Vert.x uses to forward incoming events to the enclave in JNI. In conjunction with stub code generated by the SGX Software Development Kit (SDK) supporting interaction of untrusted C/C++ code and the enclave code, this requires additional copies of the message buffers. We discuss their performance impact in our evaluation in Sect. 6.

In order to support multiple secure verticles coexisting in the Vert.x environment, we need to maintain an enclave identifier in the Java class representing the secure verticle, such that each secure verticle "knows" its associated enclave.

Furthermore, we want to enable one secure verticle to register multiple individual callback functions inside the enclave for different event bus addresses. This requires to maintain a distinct entry point inside the enclave for all incoming messages where a lookup happens in order to find the right callback function for this event. Including the deregistration of addresses on the event bus, all these features are implemented as part of our *Vert.x Vault*.

4.1   Bootstrapping and Remote Attestation

SGX enclaves inherently are not able to contain secrets when they are created, thus injection of secrets into enclaves must be done after a successful Remote Attestation (RA). Integration of RA into our *Vert.x Vault* architecture requires a generic untrusted component inside of each secure verticle that can create a "quote" of the enclave and publish it on the event bus to an administrator component. Along with a public key generated by the enclave, the quote can be used by an administrator to verify the secure enclave remotely and via the Vert.x event bus by using the Intel attestation service [4]. After a successful RA, the administrator can inject secrets into the enclaves of secure verticles.

4.2   Secure Event Bus

Recently, the Vert.x developers added the *secure event bus* to Vert.x, that allows the encryption of all messages on the event bus transparently to the verticles.

Essentially, the secure event bus provides TLS-based transport security of messages across machine boundaries. In order to be transparent to verticles, the integration of the secure event bus is done deeply inside Vert.x. Hence, the verticles can not notice the encryption or—in case of a secure verticle using our *Vert.x Vault*—move the encryption endpoints into the enclaves. For this reason, we consider the secure event bus orthogonal to the implementation of our *Vert.x Vault*. In order to integrate it with our secure verticles, the TLS endpoint of the secure event bus must be moved inside the enclave, requiring major changes to the internals of Vert.x. However, even without integration of the secure event bus with secure verticles, the latter can of course establish their own secure connections transparently to the event bus.

5   Use Case Scenario SERECA Project

In the context of the SERECA project, we demonstrate the opportunities coming from an integration of SGX with Vert.x through a suitable use case scenario: a cloud-based application for the monitoring of seven dams belonging to a water supply network [9]. This use case unarguably belongs to the Critical Infrastructure (CI) domain. CIs enclose assets essential for the functioning of all countries' fundamental facilities such as energy, telecommunications, water supply, and transport. Due to their importance in nations' sustainability, CIs are target of terrorist cyber-attacks, as demonstrated by recent events: "Black Energy"[4] in 2015, and "Havex"[5] in 2014. Security threats related to the disclosure or manipulation of sensitive data slows the migration of CIs to cloud technologies.

Through the cloud-based Water Supply Network Monitoring (WSNM) application, we want to prove that the combination of Vert.x with SGX—enabled by our *Vert.x Vault*—can represent a possibility to overcome CI's security concerns. The different tools provided by Vert.x enable the development of a reactive WSNM application based on micro-services having the following peculiarities: (1) Easily deployable among the dams and the cloud; (2) Highly scalable in front of sensors measurements peaks (3) Highly available in front of failures; (4) Highly performance in the process of sensors data collection, elaboration and provision. Moreover, the SGX extension allows the encryption/decryption and sealing of sensitive measurements by an *enclave* using a platform-specific key and while requiring to trust only the CPU package.

Figure 4 shows the overall architecture of the WSNM distributed application. On the dam-side, a *data collector verticle* interfaces, through a ModBus protocol, with a data logger equipment responsible for providing all the sensor data. Then, the acquired measurements are sent to the registered cloud-*verticles* through the Vert.x *secure event bus*. Thanks to this, messages are securely encrypted and signed. Only the involved receiver verticles, knowing the encryption key (AES) and integrity key (HMAC), can decrypt the message. In addition to a TLS secure

---

[4] https://ics-cert.us-cert.gov/alerts/ICS-ALERT-14-281-01B.
[5] https://ics-cert.us-cert.gov/alerts/ICS-ALERT-14-176-02A.

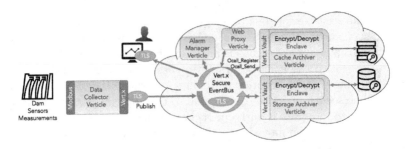

Fig. 4. Architecture of the dam monitoring application SGX-enabled

communication, a *Route-based* encryption is enforced. Senders and receivers do not indicate the key in the message. They use an equivalent configuration, which defines the key to be used for a specific address. In this way, they do not share key names, but agree on the address-key mapping.

On the cloud-side, four registered *verticles* receive data through the secure event bus and, based on their duties, take a specific action on it. Two of them are *secure verticles* and so make use of *Vert.x Vault* APIs seen in Sect. 3.3:

Cache Archiver Verticle (CAV): It is responsible for the storage of time-recent data into an in-memory system. Such a data is needed, e.g., by the alarm manager in charge of real-time analysis activities. The CAV is unarguably a *Secure Verticle* as the measurements it stores in memory must be encrypted. Therefore, the CAV registers itself from within the enclave to the Vert.x secure event bus through a *ocall_register*. Then, when new updates are received, the data—before being stored—is encrypted into the enclave. It can obviously happen that other *verticles* (e.g. the AMV) asks for that data. When this happens, a *ocall_send* is performed to provide the measurements to the interested verticle.

Alarm Manager Verticle (AMV): The alarm manager is in charge of signalling dangerous situations occurring on the dam infrastructure by enforcing a *Complex Event Processing (CEP)*, i.e., correlating different data sources to find events or patterns suggesting more complicated circumstances. To do that, the AMV needs to receive live data from the collector verticle and also temporarily store data in memory. For this reason, it communicates with the CAV through point-to-point messages exchanged through the secure event bus. The AMV, that currently operates on data securely stored, will be extended as a *secure verticle* to realize the CEP processing into an *enclave*.

Storage Archiver Verticle (SAV): Beside saving data for CEP processing purposes, it is also important to store measurements for historical trend evaluations into a persistent storage system. Even in this case it is important that stored data is encrypted. Hence, even the SAV is defined as a *Secure Verticle*.

Web Proxy Verticle (WPV): The final user operator has access to the monitoring application through a web-based dashboard, which reports real-time measurements, historical trends, and alarm notifications. Such a dashboard communicates with the back-end cloud application through the WPV, which can ask any verticle for data to be sent to the web browser based on the requests. The TLS-enabled transmission of sensitive data is realized through a Vert.x *secured SockJS bridge*—provided in the *secure event bus*—able to encrypt/decrypt data at application level using a key shared with the web browser.

6   Evaluation

In order to measure the performance impact of enclaves integrated into verticles using our *Vert.x Vault*, we wrote a benchmark tool in order to evaluate the performance of our prototype and present the results in this section. All measurements presented in this section were done with real enclaves and executed on SGX-capable machines with Core i7-6700 @3.4 GHz, 24 GB RAM, 256 GB SSD and 4x GbE.

6.1   Performance Measurement

The measurement scenario comprises three verticles deployed on two hosts: a sender verticle that sends requests and measures the response time and throughput on one host, and a regular and a secure verticle both running on the other host answering the requests. All communication between verticles is transferred via the Vert.x event bus using the Hazelcast cluster manager[6], which is the default cluster manager implementation of Vert.x. In order to get an impression of the performance impact of the usage of SGX in verticles, we exchange payloads of various size between the verticles and measure throughput and response time.

In a first experiment we investigate the level of concurrency that leads to optimal throughput by increasing the maximum allowed number of concurrent pending requests on the event bus in the sender verticle. We chose a realistic payload size of real Vert.x applications of 1024 Bytes for this experiment. The results of this experiment are shown in Fig. 5 which also includes the response times. As can be seen, the value of 128 pending requests leads to the highest throughput, while higher values do not significantly increase throughput.

We also measure the throughput of regular and secure verticles for various sizes of message payload using the aforementioned value of 128 concurrently pending requests that led to optimal throughput. Figure 6 illustrates the request throughput of our experiment for various payload sizes. It proves that secure verticles perform quite well, and in most of the cases reach a throughput almost as high as regular verticles. The same is true for the transmitted payload traffic on the event bus between the verticles, as can be seen from the same Fig. 6.

Finally, we measured the mean response time of requests for regular and secure verticles as illustrated in Fig. 7. The figure shows the additional processing time required to enter the enclave and copy the payload buffer in and out. As expected, in general the response time of secure verticles is higher than the one

---

[6] https://hazelcast.com/.

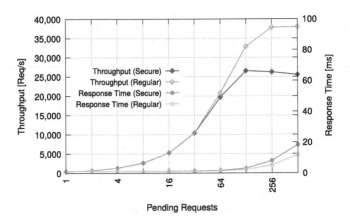

Fig. 5. Request throughput for various number of pending requests.

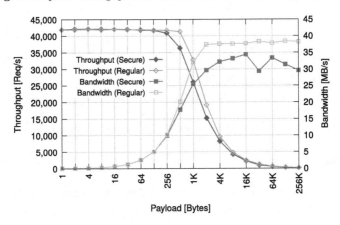

Fig. 6. Request throughput and traffic for various payload sizes.

of regular verticles. For very small payloads between 0–512 Bytes there is a *relatively* high overhead of ≈83.1%of secure verticles, while for larger payloads between 512 Bytes and 256 KB the relative overhead decreases to only ≈26.2%. We explain this by the constant overhead of entering and exiting the enclave which is relatively more notable for small payloads.

6.2   Size of TCB

As motivated earlier in this paper, we aimed at minimising the Source Line of Code (SLOC) inside the enclave (i.e. the TCB) in order to optimise both performance and security. While the Vert.x tool-kit's code base comprises thousands of SLOC, our *Vert.x Vault* only requires 69 lines of code inside the enclave in order to enable the enclave code to access the Vert.x event bus. Apart from this, the TCB naturally comprises the code by the micro service application devel-

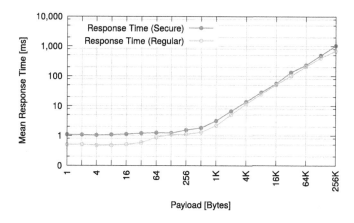

Fig. 7. Response times for various payload sizes.

oper, but the majority of code resides outside of the enclave and untrusted. This enables the developer to decide on a very fine-grained level what code is trusted.

7   Related Work

Haven [6] was the first system and supports execution of legacy applications unchanged in an SGX enclave. While running legacy applications in enclaves has many benefits, such as support for closed source applications, this feature adds a large amount of code to the TCB of the enclave, like a full library OS and other libraries. This eventually leads to a large memory footprint, which negatively influences the performance of the application on top of SGX.

SCONE [5] supports running secure containers based on Docker [1]. This approach reduces the memory footprint of the enclaves when compared to Haven, while still featuring a generic platform for the execution of secure containers.

Another type of related work is the field of partitioned applications, that are specifically paritioned applications to run most efficiently and with the least possible memory footprint on top of SGX. An example for securing complex cloud services by partitioning them for usage with SGX enclaves is SecureKeeper [7,8] featuring a partitioned Apache ZooKeeper [10] coordination service.

The communication of verticles on the Vert.x event bus is alike publish-subscribe systems. In this context, Pires et al. presented secure content-based routing with SGX [14]. Their system protects the subscription process of clients at data providers and the confidentiality of the data exchanged between them. In contrast, our *Vert.x Vault* not only enables protecting the confidentiality of exchanged messages between verticles, but also allows general-purpose sensitive data processing of inside secure verticles.

8 Conclusion

Micro service architectures are a modern way of writing scalable applications tailored for cloud environments. However, trust issues still hinder the adoption of cloud technology especially for sensitive applications handling sensitive data.

In this work, we showed an approach of integrating TEEs into the micro service tool-kit Vert.x. With our approach due to the usage of SGX, we gain a high level of security at a strong adversary model. Furthermore, we support the Vert.x programming model and control flow inside the TEE by mimicing its API. This allows interaction of trusted code with the Vert.x event bus.

Our prototype implementation demonstrates the feasibility of our approach, while the evaluation shows a very low performance overhead of only ≈8.7%.

Acknowledgements. This project received funding from the European Union's Horizon 2020 research and innovation programme under the SERECA project (Grand No. 645011).

References

1. Docker. https://www.docker.com/. Accessed 02 Jan 2017
2. Eclipse Vert.x. http://vertx.io/. Accessed 25 Jan 2017
3. What Led Amazon to its own microservices architecture. http://thenewstack.io/led-amazon-microservices-architecture/. Accessed 25 Jan 2017
4. Anati, I., Gueron, S., Johnson, S., Scarlata, V.: Innovative technology for CPU based attestation and sealing. In: Proceedings of the 2nd International Workshop on Hardware and Architectural Support for Security and Privacy (2013)
5. Arnautov, S., Trach, B., Gregor, F., Knauth, T.: SCONE: secure linux containers with intel SGX. In: 12th USENIX Symposium on Operating Systems Design and Implementation (2016)
6. Baumann, A., Peinado, M., Hunt, G.: Shielding applications from an untrusted cloud with Haven. In: Proceedings of the 11th USENIX Conference on Operating Systems Design and Implementation (2014)
7. Brenner, S., Wulf, C., Kapitza, R.: Running Zookeeper coordination services in untrusted clouds. In: 10th Workshop on Hot Topics in System Dependability (2014)
8. Brenner, S., Wulf, C., Lorenz, M., Weichbrodt, N., Goltzsche, D., Fetzer, C., Pietzuch, P., Kapitza, R.: SecureKeeper: confidential ZooKeeper using intel SGX. In: Proceedings of the 15th International Middleware Conference (2016)
9. Cerullo, G., Mazzeo, G., Papale, G., Sgaglione, L., Cristaldi, R.: A secure cloud-based SCADA application: the use case of a water supply network. In: Proceedings of the Fifteenth New Trends in Software Methodologies, Tools and Techniques, SoMeT 2016, Larnaca, Cyprus, 12–14 September 2016, pp. 291–301 (2016)
10. Hunt, P., Konar, M., Junqueira, F., Reed, B.: ZooKeeper: wait-free coordination for internet-scale systems. In: Proceedings of the 2010 USENIX Conference on USENIX Annual Technical Conference (2010)
11. Jayaram, K.R., Safford, D., Sharma, U., Naik, V., Pendarakis, D., Tao, S.: Trustworthy geographically fenced hybrid clouds. In: Proceedings of the 15th International Middleware Conference (2014)

12. McKeen, F., Alexandrovich, I., Berenzon, A., Rozas, C.V., Shafi, H., Shanbhogue, V., Savagaonkar, U.R.: Innovative instructions and software model for isolated execution. In: Proceedings of the 2nd International Workshop on Hardware and Architectural Support for Security and Privacy (2013)
13. Pearson, S., Benameur, A.: Privacy, security and trust issues arising from cloud computing. In: IEEE 2nd International Conference on Cloud Computing Technology and Science (2010)
14. Pires, R., Pasin, M., Felber, P., Fetzer, C.: Secure content-based routing using intel software guard extensions. In: Proceedings of the 17th International Middleware Conference (2016)
15. Synopsys, Inc., Open Source Report (2014). http://go.coverity.com/rs/157-LQW-289/images/2014-Coverity-Scan-Report.pdf

Adaptive Cheat Detection in Decentralized Volunteer Computing with Untrusted Nodes

Nils Kopal[1]([⊠]), Matthäus Wander[2], Christopher Konze[1], and Henner Heck[1]

[1] Applied Information Security, University of Kassel, Kassel, Germany
nils.kopal@uni-kassel.de
[2] Distributed Systems Group, University of Duisburg-Essen, Duisburg, Germany

Abstract. In volunteer computing, participants donate computational resources in exchange for credit points. Cheat detection is necessary to prevent dishonest participants from receiving credit points, without actually providing these resources. We suggest a novel, scalable approach for cheat detection in decentralized volunteer computing systems using gossip communication. Each honest participant adapts its detection effort dynamically subject to the number of active participants, which we estimate based on observed system performance. This enables minimizing the detection overhead for each participant, while still achieving a high preselected detection rate for the overall system. Systems based on majority voting usually produce at least 100% overhead, whereas our approach, e.g. requires only 50.6% overhead in a network with 1 000 participants to achieve a 99.9% detection rate. Since our approach does not require trusted entities or an active cooperation between participants, it is robust even against colluding cheaters.

1 Introduction

Cheating is a well-known problem in distributed systems that rely on the computers of volunteers, i.e. volunteer computing systems [2]. In such a system, the computers of volunteers are interconnected and build a large-scale distributed system for distributed computations. We call a complete distributed computation a job and a partial computation, typically performed by a single node, a subjob. Researchers often use volunteer computing in cases where there is no funding for sufficient computational resources within their research projects. Many volunteer computing projects have a charitable background, i.e. the search for cancer medicaments, AIDS research, water research, etc. We distinguish two different classes of volunteer computing: The first class is the classic volunteer computing, which is based on a client-server approach, e.g. the Berkeley Open Infrastructure for Network Computing [1] (BOINC). Here, a server manages the distribution of all subjobs. The combination of the corresponding subjob results leads to the result of the overall job. Participating nodes in the volunteer computing network request subjobs from the central server and deliver results to the central server. Clearly, if the server fails, the complete job computation stops since no new

L.Y. Chen and H.P. Reiser (Eds.): DAIS 2017, LNCS 10320, pp. 192–205, 2017.
DOI: 10.1007/978-3-319-59665-5_14

subjobs are assigned to requesting nodes. Additionally, a server requires maintenance which results in costs that have to be taken into account by researchers. The second class is decentralized volunteer computing, e.g. [9,14]. Here, no central server exists. The participating nodes have to self-organize distribution and assignment of subjobs and distribution and storage of results.

To offer incentives to participate in volunteer computing projects, i.e. motivate people to donate their computational resources, volunteer computing systems usually maintain lists of their participating users with respect to their computational work spent [1]. People who donate resources typically aim to improve their position on such lists, causing them to provide more resources.

Besides well-behaving users, there also exist cheaters in volunteer computing systems [3]. Such a cheater delivers false or only partial correct results to gain more credit points than they deserve. Correct results are essential for researchers, which requires a verification of results coming from untrusted and potentially unreliable volunteers. Otherwise, partly false results could impair the overall job result up to the point of invalidating the joint effort of hundreds or thousands of volunteers. There exist well-known anti-cheating techniques for client-server based volunteer computing [6]. These include redundant computation, majority voting, and sample testing, which are performed or initiated by the central and trusted server. In a decentralized network, there is no central authority that manages the distribution of subjobs. Thus, techniques like redundant computation and majority voting cannot be easily used.

In an untrusted, decentralized network, each node needs to devote a portion of their resources to detect and correct false results. As this reduces the overall speedup of computation, only a subset of results can be selected to be verified for efficiency reasons. Sample testing suffices to detect cheaters in search problem applications with close to 100% probability [15].

In this paper, we present a method for cheat detection in untrusted, decentralized volunteer computing networks based on sample testing. The method works on top of a gossip-based communication. It is immune to colluding cheaters, because each node performs its cheat detection independent of each other. We show that to meet a given detection rate, the overall cheat detection effort per network can be kept constant. With an increasing size of the network, this allows us to reduce the cheat detection effort per node without negatively impairing the detection rate. We thus propose to adapt the cheat detection per node dynamically subject to the size of the network, which can be estimated by each node individually by evaluating the current network workload. In sum, the **contribution** is a cheat detection method that dynamically adapts the verification effort to the total number of participating nodes in untrusted volunteer computing networks without the need of any additional messages.

The rest of the paper is organized as follows: First, in Sect. 2 we present our system model for decentralized volunteer computing. Then, in Sect. 3 we present our application scenario. Here, we base our model on a distributed cryptanalysis scenario. Additionally, we present our cheater classes and our cheat detection algorithm. We also present our definition of effort for computations and cheat detection. After that, in Sect. 4 we present our idea for an adaptive cheat detection method. In our evaluation in Sect. 5 we simulate the effort for cheat detection of a single computing node with fixed detection rates and effort. After that, we evaluate, on the basis of single nodes, the effort a complete network has to perform for cheat detection with fixed detection rates and effort. After that, we present an evaluation of our adaptive method. Then, in Sect. 6 we briefly present the related work in the field of cheat detection and prevention. We conclude our paper in Sect. 7 with a brief outlook on future work.

2   System Model

In a decentralized volunteer computing system, the knowledge of the participants is distributed using messages. Each participant can send messages directly to a certain number of other participants, which are called neighbors. Nodes disseminate knowledge by sending messages to their neighbors, which copy and forward them to their neighbors. Since such an approach leads to a high number of message transmissions, the amount of data that needs to be exchanged during a job computation has to be kept small. The basis for our gossip-based distribution is a network consisting of nodes. Each node is connected to randomly chosen neighbors. Nodes transmit the results of their subjob computations and their state of the overall job to their direct neighbors. Our distribution algorithms compute an embarrassingly parallel search problem (*search job*) with a result using a problem specific computation function. Such a search job can be parallelized by dividing it into independent subjobs, where each subjob can be computed by the same computation function. To get the overall result of a job, the results from all subjobs can be combined using a combination function. Furthermore, we assume that the combination function is associative, commutative, and idempotent. We assume that the size of the combination of two results equals the size of a single result. Since the jobs in our example scenario consist of several thousands, millions, or more subjobs, it is not possible to disseminate the state of each subjob. We use distribution algorithms [8–10], which divide the total computation space into subspaces. These subspaces are chosen small enough so that it can be disseminated in total. Nodes work in parallel on the same subspace. A node randomly selects a subjob, computes it, and sends the results to their neighbors. These merge all received results and forward them to their neighbors. Once the nodes finished a subspace, they move on to the next subspace until the job is complete.

3   Application Scenario

Our application scenario is the keysearching of a modern symmetric cipher, i.e. distributed brute-forcing an AES128 [4] encrypted text and searching for the decryption key. In our application scenario, we divide the complete search space ($\approx 2^{54}$ for passwords consisting of lowercase and uppercase characters, digits, and special characters) in subjobs, each consisting of $2^{20} = 1\,048\,576$ keys. To search through a single AES128 subjob, a node decrypts the given ciphertext using every key within the range of that subjob. The goal of the cryptanalysis is to find the correct decryption key. To rate the keys, a node uses the Shannon entropy [13] function H as a cost function. With natural language, i.e. the original plaintext, the entropy value is mostly at its minimum with respect to all decryption keys. After performing all decryptions, a node generates a toplist of the k "best" keys of a subjob. Those keys are the ones that decrypt the given ciphertext to the plaintexts with the lowest entropy. Each node does this for different subjobs. After finishing a subjob, the nodes send their results to their neighbors. They combine the toplist of each received subjob result to create a global toplist over all subjobs.

In our scenario, a cheater would not test all keys of an AES128 subjob. The cheater has the motivation to earn credit points to achieve a high rank in a volunteer computing network without doing all of the required work, while avoiding the detection by the system's countermeasures [1]. Thus, a cheater, in general, may compute only parts of a given subjob and only delivers partially (correct) results. The more of a subjob a cheater computes, the harder it is for a cheat detection algorithm to detect this cheater. This is based on the fact that the more results of a subjob are computed correctly, the less results are missing that could be detected. We refer to a cheater that only computes parts of a subjob as an *opportunistic cheater*. Opposed to that, a *disturber* submits garbage results just for the sake of vandalism. Disturbers can be easily detected with the same means as opportunists. *Colluding cheaters* coordinate their efforts to persist cheated subjob results in the network. In some systems, colluding cheaters have an advantage over solitary opportunistic cheaters, but this does not apply to our approach.

BOINC-based solutions use multiple computations of subjobs by different nodes and make a majority decision on the correct result. In [15], we developed an approach for the detection of cheated results within a distributed computing scenario introduced by an opportunistic cheater. The detection is based on two different approaches: *Positive verification* and *negative verification*. With positive verification, we verify the correctness of a subjob computation and with negative verification, we try to find other (better) results, which the delivering node omitted. If either positive verification fails or negative verification succeeds, we found a cheated result and we decline it. For positive verification, we assume that we can check the results in very short times. Clearly, this is true for an AES128 subjob since the decryption using all of the keys of the subjob toplist can be done very quickly.

To compare our decentralized cheat detection mechanisms and methods with the state-of-the-art solutions (client-server-based, i.e. BOINC) we need to estimate the effort that is needed for the computations and additionally the cheat detection mechanisms. First, we define the effort for a single subjob computation as $\mathcal{E}_{subjob} = 1$. Furthermore, the effort to compute i subjobs is $\mathcal{E}_{node}(i) = i \cdot \mathcal{E}_{subjob} = i$, which is i times the amount of effort needed for a single subjob. This is possible, since every subjob is, with respect to the needed computations, identical.

We define $\mathcal{E}_{Detect}(P_{Detect})$ as the effort needed for the computation of a detection algorithm with the detection rate P_{Detect}. For example, an effort equal to 0.5 means, that half of the subjob has to be recomputed to perform the cheat detection. Clearly, the effort function depends on the problem that is being computed by our volunteer computing network. Thus, the computation of $\mathcal{E}_{Detect}$ can not be generalized. In Sect. 5, we present an evaluation for the effort that is needed for the detection of cheated subjob results in a cryptanalysis scenario, i.e. keysearching for the key of a symmetric encryption algorithm.

4   Approach

In our approach, every node performs independently a partial cheat detection on every subjob result disseminated in the volunteer computing network. The approach needs no additional messages for executing the cheat detection. It is completely based on the assumption that every honest node provides its small part of cheat detection effort. This cheat detection effort is subject to a given fixed destination detection rate $P_{DetectNetwork}$ and the current workload of the network, to which our approach dynamically adapts to. We measure the workload in units of virtual nodes, which is a standard amount of processing power provided by a node. However, our approach is able to cope with heterogeneous nodes providing more or less workload than a virtual node. Each node performs the following steps in our cheat detection approach for each newly received subjob result:

1. Determine the number of virtual nodes $n_{Virtual}$ currently connected to the network with the method introduced below.
2. Compute the amount of virtual nodes r that the node represents itself.
3. Based on the amount $n_{Virtual}$ compute target detection rate P_{Detect} of node.
4. Perform cheat detection with the computed node detection rate P_{Detect} on each newly received subjob result with effort $\mathcal{E}_{Detect}$.

4.1   Determine Workload of Network

We now present a method to infer the workload of a node and of the whole volunteer computing network, which is necessary to determine the effort for cheat detection required. Each node administrates a list $L_{Timeframe}$ of finished subjob results within a sliding time window $Timeframe$. The list $L_{Timeframe}$ contains the received amount of subjob results of the node, the node's neighbors and all of their neighbors, which follows from the gossip-based dissemination of job results. The node divides the amount of subjob results $\#(L_{Timeframe})$ by the timeframe time $Timeframe$ to obtain the current $workload$ $W_{Network}$ of the network, i.e.

$$W_{Network} = \frac{\#(L_{Timeframe})}{Timeframe}. \tag{1}$$

To estimate the amount of nodes $n_{Virtual}$, we divide the workload $W_{Network}$ of the network by a constant virtual node workload $W_{VirtualNode}$, i.e.

$$n_{Virtual} = \frac{W_{Network}}{W_{VirtualNode}}. \tag{2}$$

Although we cannot compute the actual number of nodes or their workload, this virtual number of nodes suffices for our purposes. We assume that cheaters not only skip on result computation but also omit participation in the cheat detection process, since they have no benefit in doing so. We thus have to compensate for this amount by reducing the estimated workload by the amount of cheaters $C_{CheaterRate}$ that the system should be resistant against. Setting e.g. $C_{CheaterRate} = 0.05$, our approach achieves the target detection rate $P_{DetectNetwork}$ in a network with at most 5% of all claimed results to be cheated. If the actual amount of cheaters exceeds $C_{CheaterRate}$, the cheat detection still works but achieves a detection rate less than the anticipated $P_{DetectNetwork}$. The compensated amount of virtual nodes is thus

$$n_{Virtual} = \frac{W_{Network}}{W_{VirtualNode}} \cdot (1 - C_{CheaterRate}). \tag{3}$$

Each node now determines the number of virtual nodes r it represents with its own workload. It does so by dividing its current workload W_{Node} by $W_{VirtualNode}$, i.e.

$$r = \frac{W_{Node}}{W_{VirtualNode}}. \tag{4}$$

4.2 Perform Cheat Detection

Now that the node knows its computing power relative to the network's computing power, it computes the amount of effort it has to contribute so that the network reaches its target detection rate. Thus, it first computes the detection rate which a single virtual node has to add, i.e.

$$P_{DetectVirtualNode} = 1 - \sqrt[n_{Virtual}]{1 - P_{DetectNetwork}}. \tag{5}$$

After that, the node computes its node target detection rate based on that with the equation

$$P_{Detect} = 1 - (1 - P_{DetectVirtualNode})^r. \tag{6}$$

We combine the two equations to the following final single equation for the target node detection rate

$$P_{Detect} = 1 - (1 - P_{DetectNetwork})^{\frac{r}{n_{Virtual}}}. \tag{7}$$

Based on this computed local detection rate P_{Detect}, a node computes the verification effort $\mathcal{E}(P_{Detect})$ that it has to process, i.e. the amount that needs to be recomputed of each newly seen subjob result. This effort is also based on the type of cheater $T_{Cheater}$, the network has to be resistant again. A $T_{Cheater} = 0.5$

means, that the cheater only computes 50% of given subjobs. This target type of cheater is set by the user of our adaptive method. In our evaluation we empirically determine the function $\mathcal{E}(P_{Detect}, T_{Cheacter})$ for the 50% cheater. In other scenarios, this effort has to be either computed, if possible, or empirically determined by the user.

5   Evaluation

In this section, we first present our idea of two distinguished cheat detection classes: *Static* and *adaptive*. After that, we present the simulation of the effort of a single node in the static class. Then, we use the results of that simulation to evaluate the effort of a complete network based on the static class. After that, we present our method to let each node adapt its cheat detection rate and the needed mode effort with respect to the amount of nodes in the network. Doing so, we show how we keep the detection rate as well as the node effort constant.

5.1   Detection Classes

We differentiate cheat detection in two different classes: The *static class*, and the *adaptive class*. In the static class, a network or the nodes of the network perform cheat detection with a static, i.e. fixed, detection rate P_{Detect}. Thus, a node performing cheat detection on a received result has the probability of P_{Detect} to detect, if the result is not correct, i.e. cheated. In the next section we show, that this static detection class does not scale in a decentralized network since the increasing effort $\mathcal{E}_{Network}$ for detection reduces the speedup to an upper limit. With the *adaptive class* the nodes of a network adapt their detection rates P_{Detect} and effort $\mathcal{E}_{Detect}$ according to the amount of nodes within the network. We furthermore use the simulation result of a single node to estimate the correlation between effort and detection rate in the adaptive class.

5.2   Cheat Detection in the Static Class for a Single Node

We base our simulation on the AES128 scenario presented in the last sections. In our simulation, we let the simulator search for the 10 "best" AES128 keys in a cryptanalysis job. Thus, a simulated cheater that only searched through 50% of the keys of a subjob would only find 5 of these keys on average. Then, to simulate the detection of the cheater, a real node would first positively verify the best list, i.e. check the entropy-values of each entry. Clearly, all the entropy values within our simulation best list are correct, thus, we omitted this step in the simulation. After that, a node would randomly try to find "better" values, i.e. keys with lower entropy values. For that, we used different amounts of detection effort ranging from 0.0001% to 100%. We simulated the cheat detection performed by a single node with different cheaters with respect to the cheated amounts of computations. A cheater omits between 10% and 90% of all keys of a subjob computation. It selects the keys, for which it actually does computations randomly. The cheat detection node randomly selects a dedicated amount of AES keys out of the subjob space to find lower entropy values, i.e. doing negative verification. In Fig. 1 we show the results of our simulations. For each point in the graph, we did 10 000 simulations and calculated the average value over all simulation runs. The graph shows different amounts of cheated values starting from 90% (black line) going down to 10% (purple line). A cheater with 90% means that the cheater omitted 90% of the computations. In our graph, it can be seen that with higher amounts of negative verifications, i.e. the node effort (abscissa), the detection probability, i.e. the detection rate (ordinate), also increases. With an effort value $\mathcal{E}_{Detect} > 7\%$ our node would detect nearly every cheated subjob. Clearly, 7% of effort, i.e. recomputation of 7% of each subjob, is way too high for a real-world usage. But since not only one node performs cheat detection, but also all n nodes do, we can decrease the effort and detection probability at every node as shown in the next sections.

5.3 Cheat Detection Effort in the Static Class of a Complete Network

If only exactly one node would perform a single detection run on each subjob, in the previous section we evaluated that we need a recomputation of nearly 7% (random selections) out of every subjob in the best case to perform cheat detection as seen as black line (90%) in Fig. 1. Here, the maximum value is reached at nearly 7%. For determining the real effort of a decentralized network, we evaluated three different scenarios (A, B, and C) with different static detection probabilities P_{Detect} (from high to low) and corresponding node efforts $\mathcal{E}_{Node}$. We show the different detection probabilities and effort rates in Table 1. We extracted these values out of our simulations, as shown in Sect. 5.2. The basis for our computations is a volunteer computing job that consists of $j = 2^{32}$ different subjobs. First, we computed the effort $\mathcal{E}_{Client-Server}$ that a client-server solution, for example BOINC, would need for the cheat detection:

$$\mathcal{E}_{Client-Server} = 2 \cdot \mathcal{E}_{Node}(j) \tag{8}$$
$$= 2 \cdot \mathcal{E}_{Node}(2^{32}) \tag{9}$$
$$= 2^{33} \tag{10}$$

This amount of computations has to be performed in total by all the client-nodes in a client-server based volunteer computing network. Clearly, the value is inde-

Table 1. Different scenarios - detection probability and effort of a single node

Scenario	Detection probability P_{Detect}	Effort $\mathcal{E}_{Node}$
A (high)	1.22%	≈0.1271895%
B (medium)	0.46%	≈0.0490371%
C (low)	0.06%	≈0.0129130%

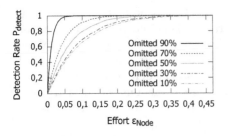

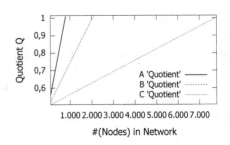

Fig. 1. Node effort simulation (Color figure online)

Fig. 2. Effort quotient Q

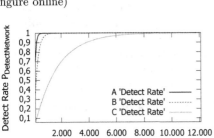

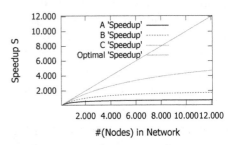

Fig. 3. Detect rates $P_{DetectNetwork}$

Fig. 4. Speedup S (Color figure online)

pendent from the amount of nodes, since the distribution of subjobs to the nodes is done by the server. We then computed the amounts for our three different scenarios with variable numbers of nodes. We show the result of these computations in the Fig. 2. For comparison with the client-server case, we computed the *quotient* Q of the client-server case effort (*numerator*) and the decentralized cases (*denominator*) effort. A quotient of 1 means, that the network's effort is the same as the client-server's effort. For example, the effort $\mathcal{E}_{Decentralized}$ for scenario A with $P_{Detect} = 1.22\%$ and an assumed amount of nodes count $n = 700$ is:

$$\mathcal{E}_{Decentralized} = \mathcal{E}_{Node}(j) + (n \cdot \mathcal{E}_{Detect}(j)) \tag{11}$$

$$= 2^{32} + (700 \cdot 0.001271895 \cdot 2^{32}) \tag{12}$$

$$= 8\,118\,891\,612.85 \tag{13}$$

We now calculate the quotient Q of the client-server case $\mathcal{E}_{Client-Server}$ and the scenario A case:

$$Q = \frac{\mathcal{E}_{Decentralized}}{\mathcal{E}_{Client-Server}} = 0.944691034 \approx 94,45\% \tag{14}$$

Thus, a decentralized network (with parameters as in case A) needs $94,45\%$ of the computations that a client-server network needs. Then, we computed the corresponding detection rate $P_{DetectNetwork}$ of such a network. To compute that detection rate, we used the detection rate of a single node P_{Detect}:

$$P_{DetectNetwork} = 1 - (1 - P_{Detect})^n \tag{15}$$
$$= 1 - (1 - 0,0122)^{700} \tag{16}$$
$$= 0.999814512 \approx 99.98\% \tag{17}$$

With scenario A the detection rate is nearly 100% - only one out of 1 000 cheated subjobs would remain undetected on average in a network. Clearly, in a real volunteer computing scenario, we assume that there would never be a thousand cheated results disseminated in the network. By increasing the effort of a single node the detection probability of the network can also be increased. We also show the different detection rates of our scenarios in Fig. 3.

Finally, we computed the speedup S of our scenarios. The speedup of a distributed system is the amount of parallel computed subjobs. If a network consists of n nodes the speedup is optimal if n different subjobs are processed in parallel. We computed the speedup S with the following equation

$$S = \frac{\mathcal{E}_{Node}(j)}{\mathcal{E}_{Decentralized}} \cdot n \tag{18}$$

where j is the total amount of subjobs, $\mathcal{E}_{Decentralized}$ is the total effort of the decentralized network, and n is the amount of nodes in the network.

We depicted the speedup graphs of our scenarios with different amounts of nodes in Fig. 4. As a result of our evaluation it can be seen that with increasing the amount of nodes but keeping a constant effort $\mathcal{E}_{Node}$ for cheat detection at every node, the speedup is restricted to an upper bound. For scenario A this upper bound is ≈ 340, for B this upper bound is $\approx 1\,750$, and for C this upper bound is $\approx 4\,750$. Additionally, we added the optimal speedup (green line) to the graph. Here, the speedup S is equal to the amount of nodes n. Speedup values higher than these bounds cannot be reached with constant $\mathcal{E}_{Detect}$ values.

5.4   Our Adaptive Method

In this section, we present the evaluation which we performed with a simulator that implements the static and the adaptive cheat detection. In this evaluation we combine the adaptive method presented in Sect. 4 with the estimation of node amount of Sect. 4.1 needed for the adaptive method to create a prototype. The simulation time is represented in 'ticks'. A simulated subjob is 'computed' by a node waiting a defined amount of ticks, i.e. 'subjob duration'.

The simulated network is defined by the amount of nodes and their neighbors, the computational power of the nodes, cheater rates, cheat detection rates, cheat detection effort, etc. For cheaters and their corresponding detection effort $\mathcal{E}_{Detect}$, we used the $T_{Cheater} = 0.5$ cheater, i.e. a 50%-cheaters, as shown in Fig. 1. We extracted the detection rate and effort values and created a mapping function for our simulator.

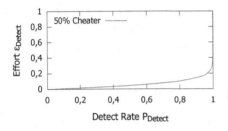
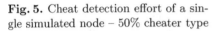

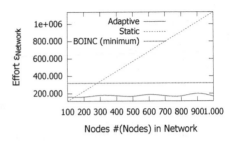

Fig. 5. Cheat detection effort of a single simulated node – 50% cheater type

Fig. 6. Cheat detection effort – static vs adaptive cheat detection vs BOINC (Color figure online)

With our simulations we show that our adaptive method outperforms the static cheat detection with respect to the effort needed by the nodes for performing the cheat detection. Furthermore, our simulations show that the static class does not scale with increasing amount of peers. Additionally, we show that the adaptive method needs less effort for cheat detection than a BOINC-based system needs.

We simulated different networks with sizes between 100 and 1 000 nodes, each node having 5 neighbors. Our simulator performed a simulation of a distributed job comprising of 320 000 subjobs. For the static cheat detection class, we set the detection rate of a single node $P_{DetectNode}$ to 5%, which results in an estimated $P_{DetectNetwork}$ of 99.4% for 100 nodes. We set the amount of cheaters in each network to 5% who cheat with 5% of their subjobs. Thus, 0.3% ≈ 800 of all subjobs disseminated within the simulation network were cheated on average. Furthermore, we set the virtual node workload for our algorithm to 0.2, thus, a virtual node finishes 0.2 subjobs in each simulation iteration. The real simulated nodes finished a subjob in 5 simulation ticks. We set the window of our algorithm to 10 ticks.

We present the results of our effort simulations in Fig. 6. With the static approach, the effort increases proportionally to the number of nodes (red, dashed line). This is caused by the fact that each node performs cheat detection on every subjob result distributed in the network. The adaptive algorithm (blue, solid line) adapts dynamically to the amount of nodes in the network, keeping the effort at a rate around 162 000. This is about 50.6% of the overall amount of computed subjobs. A BOINC-based system (black line) would compute each subjob at least twice to enable majority voting, resulting in a minimum of 100% additional effort for the cheat detection. Directly compared to BOINC the quotient Q is $Q = \frac{\mathcal{E}_{OurMethod}}{\mathcal{E}_{Client-Server}} \frac{162\,000+320\,000}{320,000+320,000} = 0.753125$. I.e. our system needs ≈75% effort compared to a client-server system with majority voting needs, i.e BOINC.

In Fig. 7 we depicted the cheat detection rates of the static and the adaptive methods. Additionally, we computed the detection rate of BOINC with colluding cheaters. BOINC achieves 99.7%, because there is a chance that BOINC gives the same sub job to two colliding cheaters, which results in an overlooked cheated

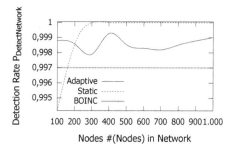

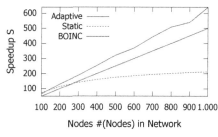

Fig. 7. Detection rate – static, adaptive, BOINC (Color figure online)

Fig. 8. Speedup – static, adaptive, BOINC (Color figure online)

sub job result despite redundant computation. The static method (red, dashed line) keeps a detection rate of 100%, but as already shown does not scale with respect to the effort. The adaptive method (blue, solid line) reaches a detection rate between 99.8% and 100%. The target detection rate was 99.9%, which is reached on average. Collusion among cheaters does not affect the detection rate, because each subjob result will be checked for correctness by each honest node, unlike e.g. with majority voting (Fig. 5).

We finally present a comparison of the achieved speedup S of the static class, the adaptive class, and BOINC. We computed the speedup as shown in Sect. 5.3. In Fig. 8 we show that the adaptive method performs best keeping the speedup at the highest rate (blue line). Close to this, we see BOINC (black line). We furthermore see, that the static class reaches a speedup limit close to 210 which confirms that the static method does not scale.

6   Related Work

Prior work has considered cheat detection and cheat prevention in distributed computing, which includes volunteer computing. There are attempts to secure volunteer computing and grid computing by introducing mechanisms to either validate the correctness of results received from participants or by making it hard or impossible to cheat on given jobs. In [7], Golle and Mironov describe their idea of uncheatable distributed computations. They show two different security schemes, a weak and a strong one, that defend against cheating participants. The weak one depends on 'magic numbers' and the strong one depends on a supervisor and so called 'ringers'. Both schemes have in common that participants have to find either these magic numbers or the ringers to get rewarded for their done work. The main difference between their solution and ours is the organization of the computations. They use the supervisor who assigns subjobs to nodes. In our scenario, we have no central management since our network is completely unstructured and decentralized. Moca et al. present in [11] a method for distributed results checking for 'MapReduce' [5] in volunteer computing. They use a distributed result checker based on majority voting. Furthermore, they developed a model for the error rate of 'MapReduce'. Compared to our solution, which only needs recomputation of very small parts of subjobs, their method is based on majority voting. Thus, their nodes have to redundantly compute complete subjobs. Hence, the total amount of recomputations is at minimum 2 to apply majority voting on their results. In this paper, we show that our method needs considerably less recomputations compared to their method. Zhao and Lo show their scheme 'Quiz' in [16], which inserts indistinguishable quiz tasks with verifiable results to a distributed job. They outperform the method of the replication of jobs in terms of accuracy and overhead under collusion assumptions. Compared to our solution, they need a central server that assigns the quiz tasks as well as the regular tasks to the clients. With our solution, we do not need a central server since every node in the network performs a small part of detection work. Sarmenta presents in [12] his sabotage-tolerant mechanisms for volunteer computing. He shows a method called 'credibility-based fault-tolerance' where he estimates the conditional probability of (sub/job)-results and workers being correct, based on the results of voting, spot-checking and other techniques, and then he uses these probability estimates to direct the use of further redundancy. Compared to our solution, they use a work pool-based master-worker model where the master assigns subjobs to workers. Here, the master randomly assigns redundant subjobs to workers. Compared to majority voting based techniques, their method reduces the total amount of recomputations, but also increases the chance of non-detected cheated subjob results. Our method also reduces the needed amount of recomputation but still keeps a very high detection probability with small network and node effort.

7   Conclusions

We introduced a cheat detection method for decentralized, gossip-based volunteer computing networks. The method is suitable for ad-hoc computations without setting up a central server. Nodes do not need to trust each other, which makes the method robust against colluding cheaters or cheaters who decide to abuse their acquired reputation. We are targeting opportunistic cheaters, which are attempting to collect the same reward as well-behaving users, e.g. credit points. However, cheaters provide job results that are incorrect and incomplete.

The method works by sample testing each job result that is disseminated in the network. With a static cheat detection effort per node, the scalability is limited as the system approaches an upper bound on the speedup with an increasing number of participating nodes. We thus adapt the cheat detection effort subject to the workload of the network, which is determined by each node based on the number of results disseminated in the network. This allows us to achieve a given target detection rate efficiently, e.g. 99.9% with only about 50.6% recomputations of subjobs. As we have shown with our simulations, such a decentralized sample testing is more efficient than a server-coordinated majority voting like e.g. being used by BOINC. In future work, we will analyze how cheat detection results can be used to exclude cheaters from our system and reduce the detection effort by doing so. Furthermore, we will examine how such a node exclusion can be used by attackers to remove well-behaved nodes.

References

1. Anderson, D.P.: Boinc: a system for public-resource computing and storage. In: Fifth IEEE/ACM International Workshop on Grid Computing, pp. 4–10. IEEE (2004)
2. Anderson, D.P., Fedak, G.: The computational and storage potential of volunteer computing. In: Sixth IEEE International Symposium on Cluster Computing and the Grid, CCGRID 2006, vol. 1, pp. 73–80. IEEE (2006)
3. Anderson, D.P., Korpela, E., Walton, R.: High-performance task distribution for volunteer computing. In: First International Conference on e-Science and Grid Computing, p. 8. IEEE (2005)
4. Daemen, J., Rijmen, V.: The Design of Rijndael: AES-the Advanced Encryption Standard. Springer, Heidelberg (2013)
5. Dean, J., Ghemawat, S.: MapReduce: simplified data processing on large clusters. Commun. ACM **51**(1), 107–113 (2008)
6. Domingues, P., Sousa, B., Moura Silva, L.: Sabotage-tolerance and trust management in desktop grid computing. Future Gener. Comput. Syst. **23**(7), 904–912 (2007)
7. Golle, P., Mironov, I.: Uncheatable distributed computations. In: Naccache, D. (ed.) CT-RSA 2001. LNCS, vol. 2020, pp. 425–440. Springer, Heidelberg (2001). doi:10.1007/3-540-45353-9_31
8. Kopal, N., Heck, H., Wacker, A.: Simulating cheated results acceptance rates for gossip-based volunteer computing. Int. J. Mob. Netw. Des. Innov. **7**(1), 56–67 (2017)
9. Kopal, N., Kieselmann, O., Wacker, A.: Self-organized volunteer computing. In: Organic Computing: Doctoral Dissertation Colloquium 2014, vol. 4, pp. 129–139. kassel University Press GmbH (2014)
10. Kopal, N., Kieselmann, O., Wacker, A.: Simulating cheated results dissemination for volunteer computing. In: 2015 3rd International Conference on Future Internet of Things and Cloud (FiCloud), pp. 742–747. IEEE (2015)
11. Moca, M., Silaghi, G.C., Fedak, G.: Distributed results checking for MapReduce in volunteer computing. In: 2011 IEEE International Symposium on Parallel and Distributed Processing Workshops and Phd Forum (IPDPSW), pp. 1847–1854. IEEE (2011)
12. Sarmenta, L.F.: Sabotage-tolerance mechanisms for volunteer computing systems. Future Gener. Comput. Syst. **18**(4), 561–572 (2002)
13. Shannon, C.E.: Prediction and entropy of printed English. Bell Syst. Tech. J. **30**(1), 50–64 (1951)
14. Wander, M., Wacker, A., Weis, T.: Towards peer-to-peer-based cryptanalysis. In: IEEE 35th Conference on Local Computer Networks (LCN), pp. 1005–1012. IEEE (2010)
15. Wander, M., Weis, T., Wacker, A.: Detecting opportunistic cheaters in volunteer computing. In: 2011 Proceedings of 20th International Conference on Computer Communications and Networks (ICCCN), pp. 1–6. IEEE (2011)
16. Zhao, S., Lo, V., Dickey, C.G.: Result verification and trust-based scheduling in peer-to-peer grids. In: Fifth IEEE International Conference on Peer-to-Peer Computing, P2P 2005, pp. 31–38. IEEE (2005)

Blockchain Based Access Control

Damiano Di Francesco Maesa[1](✉), Paolo Mori[2], and Laura Ricci[1]

[1] Department of Computer Science, University of Pisa, Pisa, Italy
damiano.difrancescomaesa@for.unipi.it, laura.ricci@unipi.it
[2] Istituto di Informatica e Telematica, Consiglio Nazionale delle Ricerche, Pisa, Italy
paolo.mori@iit.cnr.it

Abstract. Access Control systems are used in computer security to regulate the access to critical or valuable resources. The rights of subjects to access such resources are typically expressed through access control policies, which are evaluated at access request time against the current access context. This paper proposes a new approach based on blockchain technology to publish the policies expressing the right to access a resource and to allow the distributed transfer of such right among users. In our proposed protocol the policies and the rights exchanges are publicly visible on the blockchain, consequently any user can know at any time the policy paired with a resource and the subjects who currently have the rights to access the resource. This solution allows distributed auditability, preventing a party from fraudulently denying the rights granted by an enforceable policy. We also show a possible working implementation based on XACML policies, deployed on the Bitcoin blockchain.

Keywords: Bitcoin · Blockchain · Access control · XACML

1 Introduction

Access Control systems are used in computer security to regulate the access to critical or valuable resources such as data, services, computational systems, storage space, and so on. The rights of subjects to access resources are typically expressed through access control policies, which are evaluated at access request time against the current access context. In Attribute-based Access Control (ABAC) [1], policies consist of a set of conditions over the attributes which describe the features of the subjects, resources, environment, etc., involved in the access request. Among the subject attributes there could be, for instance, his ID, the ID of the company he works for, his role in this company, the name of the projects assigned to him, his physical position, the number of resources he is currently using, and so on.

Some scenarios require that access rights can be transferred from a subject to another for some reasons. For instance, a user could sell its access right to another user. Another example is the one where an employee of a company who was supposed to perform a given computation on a Virtual Machine delegates

L.Y. Chen and H.P. Reiser (Eds.): DAIS 2017, LNCS 10320, pp. 206–220, 2017.
DOI: 10.1007/978-3-319-59665-5_15

the execution of this task to another employee, who needs to access that same Virtual Machine.

Moreover, the evaluation of the access control policy in order to decide whether the requested access to a resource can be executed is performed by a party which is trusted by (the owner of) that resource, but it could be not trusted for the subject of the request who, instead, would like to be guaranteed against unduly denial of access. For example, the Access Control system can run directly on a server of the owner of the resource. In fact, the party which actually evaluates the policy and enforces the result on the resource could maliciously force the system to deny the access to a subject although the policy would have granted it. Hence, in this scenario there is the need for the subjects to have a mean for verifying which policy has been enforced when they performed an access request which has been denied.

This paper proposes an approach based on blockchain technology to represent the right to access a resource and to allow the transfer of such right among users. The proposed approach is validated by a preliminary implementation exploiting the Bitcoin framework.

The paper is structured as follows: Sect. 2 presents a background on blockchain technology and Bitcoin as well as a survey of related works on the subject at hand, while Sect. 3 gives a brief overview of our proposed novel approach. In Sect. 4 we describe the architecture of the access control scheme proposed and Sect. 5 presents our real world implementation example. Finally, Sect. 6 discusses the conclusions and presents our future work.

2   Background and Related Work

A blockchain is a distributed, always available, irreversible, tamper resistant, replicated public repository of data. It allows trustless users to agree on an immutable and auditable piece of data without third party interaction. In other words, blockchain technology allows to build an append only secure database relying on a distributed consensus protocol to decide what valid new data to add in a distributed manner.

Historically blockchain technology was first introduced to support cryptocurrencies and, up to date, cryptocurrencies are still its main field of real practical application, even if several proposals in other fields are being studied. The first blockchain was used by the Bitcoin cryptocurrency protocol [2] and today Bitcoin is still the most popular and widespread example of blockchain technology adoption. This is why we have decided to provide an implementation of this paper proposed approach on this particular protocol.

Bitcoin, as other cryptocurrencies, exploits the blockchain as a public ledger to store value exchanges called 'transactions'. This ledger is divided in blocks where each single block is a collection of non conflicting transactions. The linking between blocks is achieved by saving the hash of the header of the previous block in the header of the next block of the chain. To make each block header (and so its hash) dependent from all transactions contained in that block, the root of the (implicit) Merkle tree [3], built from the block transactions hashes is included in the block header. Deciding which block to add to the ledger at each step is resolved by a distributed consensus algorithm called 'Nakamoto consensus' that relies on HashCash Proof-of-Works [4].

From a data point of view, the Bitcoin blockchain can be seen simply as a list of transactions. Transactions are created to exchange funds between users, represented by their addresses. An address is a double hash (firstly SHA-256 [5] is applied and then Ripemd-160 [6]) of a public key derived from a ECDSA key pair [7]. Addresses (and hence public keys) are used by users to send and receive payments, while the corresponding private keys are used to provide proofs of ownership (through digital signatures). Creating new addresses is as cheap as creating new ECDSA key pairs, so each user can create and use multiple addresses. Moreover, users are incentivized to use different addresses since the pseudonymity given by addresses is the only (weak) anonymity protection in Bitcoin.

Since the entire state of the system is only defined by the list of transactions saved in the blockchain, transactions are the only mean to manage funds. Funds can be divided or aggregated only by being spent. Transactions are multi input and multi output, hence a transaction may withdraw funds from more than one address and can transfer funds to more than one output address. Furthermore each input is signed by the owner with the private key corresponding to the address spending the funds. A transaction can also specify a voluntary fee to cover the expenses of the validation process. This fee is meant as an incentive for users to take part in the consensus protocol mentioned previously. In a transaction, each output can be seen as a couple (amount, receiver address). Each input specifies, instead, where to withdraw the funds, i.e., the previous transaction (through its hash) where the funds were created. The Bitcoin protocol uses a not Turing complete stack based scripting language, and scripts are (mostly) used in transactions to specify conditions needed to redeem the funds of that transaction. It is beyond the scope of this paper to analyze in detail Bitcoin scripting language, we will only mention its features relevant to this work in Sect. 5. Finally we note that new transactions are created by any user and notified to the community with a gossip style broadcast message on the P2P Bitcoin network.

According to [8] even if blockchain technology is mostly well known for applications in cryptocurrencies such as Bitcoin, it can be used outside of the monetary domain as well, for instance to trace the origin and transformation in a supply chain. [9] shows how blockchain can be exploited to create decentralized, shared economy applications that allow people to monetize, securely, their things to create more wealth. [10] observes that the ability to have a globally available, verifiable and untamperable source of data provides anyone wishing to provide trusted third party services the ability to do so cheaply and robustly.

3   Proposed Approach

In this paper we propose to use blockchain technology to represent the rights to access resources and to transfer them from one user to another. In particular, we propose to store the representation of the right to access a resource in a blockchain, allowing the management of such right through blockchain "transactions"[1].

The main advantages of the proposed approach are:

- the right to access a resource can be easily transferred from a user to another through a blockchain transaction created by the last right owner, without the intervention of the resource owner;
- the right is initially defined by the resource owner through a transaction, and all the other transactions representing the right transfers are published on the blockchain. Hence, any user can inspect them at any time in order to check who currently holds the rights to perform a given action on a given resource. Consequently, a user who had its access request denied, can check whether the entity in charge of verifying the existence of the required right actually made the right decision.

A common way of expressing access control rights is through Attribute-Based Access Control (ABAC) policies. Roughly speaking, an attribute-based access control policy combines a set of rules expressing conditions over a set of attributes paired to the subject, to the resource or to the environment. The rules are conjunctively or disjunctively combined and they must be satisfied accordingly in order for the access right to be granted. A well-know policy language allowing to express ABAC policies is the eXtensible Access Control Markup Language (XACML), defined by the OASIS consortium [11].

The actors of our reference scenario are the resource owner, say P, (unique for each resource) and a number of subjects, S_i. The resource owner is the entity who has the control of the policy for each of its resources, say R_j, and it creates, updates and revokes such policies. Note that we consider for simplicity that the policy issuer is also the corresponding resource owner. The subjects hold the rights to perform actions on resources, as specified by the respective policies. The subjects can transfer the action rights specified by policies, even by refining or splitting them (as explained in Sect. 3.1).

Hence, our approach requires that P and S_i perform distinct actions, independently one from the others. The policy issuer takes no part in the policy rights exchange, and, similarly, the subject currently owning a right takes no part and needs not to be online when the policy issuer modifies the policy (even if this action might of course affect the subject right).

---

[1] In the following, we refer to cryptocurrency style blockchains, because they are the main application of blockchain technology currently implemented. Consequently, we assume to have transactions, which are typical of cryptocurrencies. However, cryptocurrencies are just one of the possible applications of blockchain technology. In those cases, we have to define proper transactions to implement the approach we propose.

3.1 Policy Creation, Update, and Revoke

The policy which defines the access rights on the resource R is defined by the resource owner P, and it is stored in the blockchain through a new transaction called Policy Creation Transaction (PCT). After its creation, a policy can be updated by P any number of times and, at the end, it can be revoked, i.e., canceled.

In our approach, the policy consists of:

- the condition which defines the ID of the subject to whom the policy grants the access right;
- the conditions which define the sets of values allowed for the attributes of the subject, resource and environment for the access to be granted.

In other words, the resource owner decides the subject to whom it wants to initially grant the access right and a set of conditions that must hold to grant the access. In our scheme we allow these conditions to be properly modified by the right holders when they transfer these rights to other users. By *properly modify* we mean that the current right holder is allowed to:

- add new conditions in AND with the conditions already defined in the policy;
- split the set of values allowed for an attribute by an existing condition C of the policy in two (or more) sets by defining proper disjunct conditions, C_i and C_j. i.e. the set of attribute values which satisfy C_i OR C_j is the same set of values which satisfy C, and there is no value of the condition attribute which satisfies both C_i and C_j.

We note that adding conditions (done by a right holder) is not the same as executing policy updates (doable only by the policy issuer). Since the conditions added to the policy by right holders are combined with the existing ones through an AND operator, the resulting overall policy can only be more restrictive than the original one. This means that the original policy conditions cannot be violated. During a policy update step, instead, the meaning of the policy can be completely changed. This is correct since the policy issuer is the only one that can update a policy. We also remark as the conditions added by a right holder are added incrementally for each exchange of rights, so they cannot be modified by the new right owners. This is correct since a right owner should be allowed only to restrict the rights it wants to transfer, not to expand them.

For the sake of simplicity, we suppose that each policy concerns one subject ID only. This is not a limitation, because when P wants to grant the access to a resource to several subjects, it can simply produce a distinct policy for each one of these subjects. Moreover, in our approach we suppose that each policy includes one rule only, and this rule includes all the conditions of the policy, properly combined with AND and OR logic operators.

We remember that a blockchain can be seen as a distributed append-only database replicated among all the users. This means that every piece of data added to the blockchain cannot be subsequently removed and it will constitute a permanent burden on the entire network. This is the reason why, when defining a new protocol, we should try to minimize the amount of data saved on the blockchain, storing essential information only. The problem with our approach is that the standard policy language XACML is a very verbose formalism and policies can be relatively big. Storing policies in XACML format directly on a blockchain will result in a serious space occupation problem.

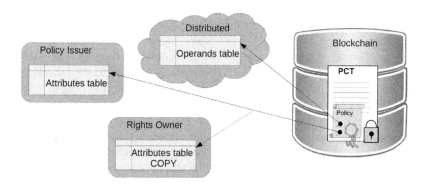

Fig. 1. Proposed hybrid policy storage approach.

The easiest solution would be to store in the blockchain only a link to an external source containing the policy, coupled with a cryptographic hash of the policy itself to make it tamper proof. For example, the blockchain could save only a tinyurl or a torrent descriptor pointing to an external source hosting the actual policy (written in a standard format as, for example, XACML) [12]. The advantage of this solution is obviously to minimize the quantity of information to be stored on the blockchain, since the space occupation of the policy is constant independently of the policy size. The main disadvantage is that policies themselves are stored outside of the blockchain, thus not benefiting of blockchain technology advantages (i.e. availability, security, etc.).

Our approach (shown in Fig. 1) adopts an hybrid solution between saving in the blockchain the entire policy or just a link to it. We chose to store policies directly in the blockchain but coded in a custom built efficient format that favors compression and avoids information repetitions.

First we rewrite a policy expressed directly in ABAC format as a list of basic conditions over attributes. Each condition can be written as three pieces of information:

- the right attribute name;
- the operand connecting right and left term;
- the left term that can be either an attribute name or a constant value (possibly a set of constant values).

Conditions are combined through the logic operator AND/OR to form a unique condition.

If we want the policy storage to be scalable in the size of the policy we would want each of the above listed informations of a condition to be represented with constant size. The logic connector of the policy is of course easy to codify with one bit (0 for OR and 1 for AND). To try to compress the rest of the condition as much as possible we want to compress both attribute names and operands in a fixed size field (for example one byte). To compress operands we can define a protocol defined table of symbols representing the mapping between every possible operand usable in a policy and a numerical code. This map would be maintained at protocol level (open source) and updated with new usable symbols during future protocol versions. We can then follow a similar approach to map attribute names to a short numerical value. The difference is that attribute names are different between users and so the mapping have to be defined by the policy issuer. The attribute mapping is a publicly available mapping of attribute names (identifier in the verbose XACML format) with one unique code of fixed size (for example one byte). The list to be validly published (and accepted by other users to be used in policies) must be signed by the issuer. This public key/identity should be the same used to create new policies using such mapping in the blockchain. A cryptographic hash of this list is then inserted in every policy using the attributes of the list. Such hash is necessary to know what mapping is being used and it prevents the policy issuer from creating a new mapping, potentially changing the meaning of an already existing policy. The policy issuer could still delete the mapping at a future point (since it is stored locally and not on the blockchain), so it is recommended for the user buying the rights derived from a policy to locally save the corresponding mapping. In case of future dispute the right owner can prove that the mapping is correct because the hash matches and the policy issuer cannot deny to be the mapping creator because of the signature attached to the mapping.

We note that this solution allows to save verbose informations about an attribute off the chain, so without space constraints. For example we can save the attribute values type, making the type of operand non ambiguous (i.e. for example differentiating an equality over integers from an equality over strings).

If we adopt this solution, the left term of the condition is the only one of potentially variable length. If it is a parameter name it can be represented as a reference to an entry of the issuer attribute table as for the right term, but if it is a constant value we need to represent it directly, eventually in a compressed format. Furthermore, since we know the type of the attribute (expressed in the verbose attributes table) we can save the values in a suitable format. For example we would save a number or a date in a numerical representation rather than in its string representation.

3.2   Right Transfer

A relevant feature of our approach is that the right to access a resource R can be transferred from the subject who is the current right holder, say S_i, to another subject, say S_j, through a custom data structure stored in the blockchain, called

Right Transfer Transaction (RTT). Each RTT must contain a (direct or indirect) link to the policy whose rights are being exchanged. It is worth noting that the only parties involved in a RTT are S_i and S_j, the RTT is created by S_i, and so the intervention of the owner of the resource is not required during any rights transfer.

When transferring its right through a RTT, S_i can modify the mutable conditions regulating its right only by restricting them. For instance, supposing that a changeable condition defined by the resource owner (or by the previous right owner) states the access can be performed from 9.00 AM to 5.00 PM, S_i could transfer this right to S_j by restricting the access time from 9.00 AM to 1.00 PM. S_i can also split its right in two (or more) parts, and transfer a part of it to a subject, and the other part to another subject. With reference to the previous example, S_i could transfer the access right from 1.00 PM to 5.00 PM to a third subject S_h.

We note that the subjects are only owners of rights to perform actions, in general they have no other right neither on the policy nor on the resource. We also remark that the subjects are able to freely exchange action rights between themselves without any interaction with the policy issuer. That implies that the policy issuer (in general corresponding to the resource owner) has no knowledge in advance of which subjects will be the policy right beneficiaries (even if it can of course model a subject prototype by specifying the correct attributes conditions to be satisfied inside the policy).

We also note that policy updates from a resource owner can potentially change the meaning of a policy. This means that subjects can gain rights on a certain resource that can be later changed by the policy issuer, but, since the blockchain never forgets and timestamps both the right transfer and the policy updates, those changes are manifest and traceable.

4   Architecture of the Proposed Framework

The architecture of the framework we propose for the enforcement of blockchain based access control, shown in Fig. 2, is based on the XACML reference architecture [11], which has been integrated with blockchain technology. Specifically, in order to allow the enforcement of blockchain based access control policies, we customized the Policy Enforcement Point (PEP) and the Policy Administration Point (PAP). The resulting workflow is hence an extension of the standard one.

When requesting to perform an action on the resource, beside the IDs of the subject, of the resource, and of the action, the PEP must also retrieve an additional information to unequivocally link the subject S_i with a RTT in the blockchain. As an example S_i might be required to sign a challenge nonce with the private key corresponding to the identity it used to get the access rights in the RTT. This is no different from a classical authentication scheme in a classical access control scenario. All those informations are properly included in the request which is passed to the Context Handler (CH). The CH is in charge of managing the workflow of the decision process, interacting with all the other components of the authorization system.

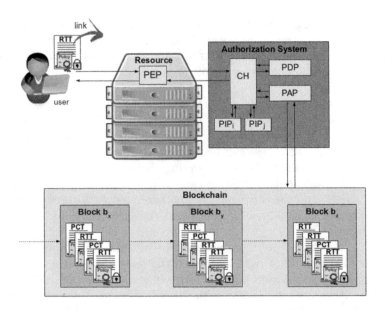

Fig. 2. Architecture of the Blockchain based access control framework.

First of all, the CH sends the request to the PAP. The PAP extracts the RTT link from the request, and retrieves from the blockchain this RTT and all the other RTT related to this policy, as well as the initial policy and the related policy updates issued by the resource owner. The PAP combines the retrieved data to produce a standard XACML policy, and sends this policy back to the CH.

Once the security policy has been reconstructed from the blockchain and verified, its evaluation against the access request follows the process defined by the XACML standard and described in [11]. Briefly, the CH asks the Policy Information Points to retrieve the relevant attributes, it embeds these attributes in the original request, and it passes the policy and the new request to the Policy Decision Point (PDP), which evaluates it and returns to the CH the decision: permit or deny. The CH then forwards the decision to the PEP, which enforces it on the resource by executing the request or not.

5   Bitcoin-Based Implementation

This section describes an example of how the proposed model is deployable in a blockchain technology model. In particular, we developed a proof of concept implementation scheme based on the Bitcoin blockchain. Aim of this section is also to show how our protocol can be immediately deployed on top of an already existent real world blockchain, as the Bitcoin blockchain is, without any modification to the underlying blockchain implementation required. As an example we report in Fig. 3 a real PCT Bitcoin transaction we broadcasted in the Bitcoin network as publicly visible from the site https://blockexplorer.com.

In our scenario firstly a resource owner creates a new policy. Then, an arbitrary number of policy updates and right transfers can be executed, where each of the two actions can be performed independently of the other one. Finally the resource owner can revoke the policy. In our implementation each step (policy creation, policy update, policy revoke or right transfer) is performed atomically by a single Bitcoin transaction.

5.1 Storing Data

As described in Sect. 2, the Bitcoin blockchain was designed to be used as a distributed ledger to manage a very specific kind of data: transactions. In other words, the Bitcoin blockchain was not designed to store arbitrary data. To overcome this limitation, we employ two commonly used methods based on Bitcoin transactions scripting language to store arbitrary data on the blockchain: the OP_RETURN script op code and the MULTISIG transactions (either through a MULTISIG output script or a multisignature P2SH output) [13]. Without going in further details we only note that our implementation automatically chooses the method to be exploited without the need of user intervention. Whatever storage method we use the policies and conditions data is encoded in a compressed custom format that follows the hybrid approach showed in Sect. 3.1.

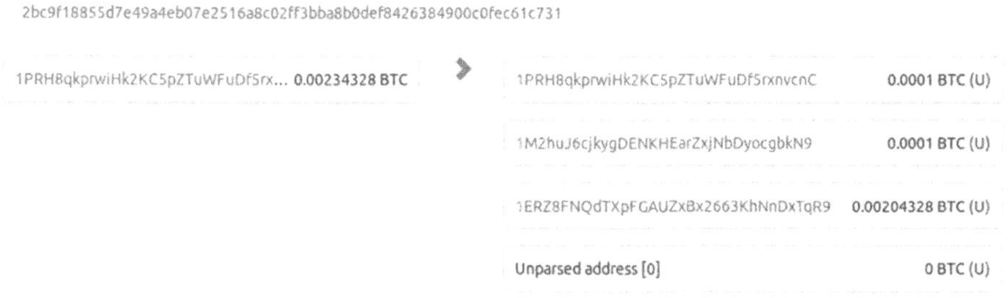

2bc9f18855d7e49a4eb07e2516a8c02ff3bba8b0def8426384900c0fec61c731

1PRH8qkprwiHk2KC5pZTuWFuDf5rx... 0.00234328 BTC	❯	1PRH8qkprwiHk2KC5pZTuWFuDf5rxnvcnC	0.0001 BTC (U)
		1M2huJ6cjkygDENKHEarZxjNbDyocgbkN9	0.0001 BTC (U)
		1ERZ8FNQdTXpFGAUZxBx2663KhNnDxTqR9	0.00204328 BTC (U)
		Unparsed address [0]	0 BTC (U)

Fig. 3. A real example of PCT in our Bitcoin-based proof of concept implementation.

Since each step is performed exploiting a Bitcoin transaction, each step has a price, i.e., the price of the underlying transaction, defined as the transaction fee paid by the transaction, which is dependent on the transaction size [14]. So we can evaluate the cost of a step as the size of the underlying transaction necessary to perform it. Every Bitcoin full node also keeps in its main memory a data structure to keep track of all unspent transactions outputs (UTXO), so if we include a big output in a transaction (e.g. by including a big multisignature output) this will also encumber precious main memory space of all the users. Finally, we point out that during each step the transaction price is payed by the beneficiary of the action. For policy creation, revoke and update transactions the price is payed by the policy owner (that is the one benefiting from such operations), while for a rights exchange the price is payed by the buyer (since the buyer is the one who will benefit from the rights).

To embed data in a transaction we first need to create a Bitcoin transaction and so we need value to be exchanged. To build transactions we will use fixed amounts of BTC to represent *tokens*, using an approach similar to the Colored-Coins proposal [15]. We call them tokens because the value they represent will be used in transactions to carry data through the connected scripts, so we are not interested in the monetary value they represent but rather on the information they carry (visible only to those who take part in our protocol). The actual trade value of such tokens is completely independent from their nominal value (i.e. the number of BTC they represent). The fixed amount chosen for a token should be low enough so that it is easy to be owned by any user (otherwise only rich users could take part in the protocol) and its economical value is not relevant compared to its protocol specific value, but also high enough so that it can be transacted freely between users (above the dust limit [16]). In our current implementation we chose 0.0001BTC that corresponds to few euro cents at the exchange rate at the time of writing. We will indicate this value as *CommonAmount* in the rest of this paper.

5.2   Policies Management

Policy Creation. A new policy is issued by the resource owner by creating a new Bitcoin transaction with one or more inputs and two or three outputs. Each of the first two outputs will create a new token, so it is paying out the value of CommonAmount. The only purpose of the inputs is to provide enough funds to create these two tokens and so should include any number of resource owner funds so that $\sum(input\ values) \geq 2 * CommonAmount + fee$. The first two outputs are mandatory, and their structure is defined by the protocol, while the third output is optional, and it represents the change address for the resource owner to keep the unspent input. The order of the first two outputs is important (it can not be changed):

- the first output creates the token that will be subsequently used to perform rights exchanges among subjects. It is credited either to an address that will be used by the policy issuer to sell the action rights to the first subject, or to the first subject directly.
- the second output creates a token containing as data the policy encoded in our custom format. This token is credited to an address controlled by the resource owner and it will be used by the policy issuer to update/revoke this policy in the future.

When the resource owner creates this transaction, the network is notified and, eventually, this PCT will be inserted in the blockchain. If the policy is too large to be included in the second output data field, the policy issuer creates a normal PCT and then creates a chain of policy update transactions (as explained later) to include all the information required. We note that the policy creator does not have to wait for the PCT to be included in a block before starting to create policy update transactions, since he is the owner of all input and output addresses in both policy creation and update transactions and, consequently, there is no risk of double spending attempts. In the end, this means that a very long policy will generate several transactions and, consequently, it will be simply more expensive for the owner (due to more fees to pay).

Policy Update/Revoke. At any time the policy issuer can update or revoke a policy it created before. To do so, it creates a new transaction spending the second output of the creation policy transaction if the policy was never modified before, or spending the output of the last update policy transaction if the policy was already updated at least once. Obviously, only the policy issuer can create those transactions because it is the only one that can spend the corresponding output.

- *Update:* the update transaction has two (or more inputs). The first input corresponds to the previous update or PCT output and the additional inputs are meant to provide the value necessary to be spent as fees to pay for this transaction. The transaction has one or two outputs, the first one carries on the token of the previous policy update or creation step, while the second one is only used as change address to collect the money left after paying the transaction fees. The update token contained in the first output is used to store the data containing the policy update informations.
- *Revoke:* to revoke a policy, the policy issuer must spend the related token (even to himself), i.e., it must use it as value instead of using the embedded information. To this aim, it just creates a transaction spending the input corresponding to the previous update or PCT. This effectively destroys the token, thus canceling the policy.

5.3   Rights Exchange

To allow the exchange of access rights between two (or more) subjects we assume the existence of some kind of marketplace (or any way of exchanging messages between users) where subjects interested in selling or buying action rights take part. We also note that, since each policy and its updates are publicly visible in the blockchain, each subject can first check a policy to verify the actual rights it is buying. The right exchange between two subjects is achieved through the participation of the subjects in a message exchange protocol to allow them to jointly build and sign the RTT. Main goal of the message exchange is to guarantee that both subjects sign the RTT only after checking that it fulfills the exchange agreement. The RTT is basically a transaction where the token representing the access right is passed from the current subject to the new one and, in exchange, the new subject accredits some money (expressed in BTC) to the current owner. Furthermore the token can be enriched by the old owner with new data to refine the policy conditions and it can be divided in different tokens (as explained in Sect. 3.1). We have seen in Sect. 5.2 that the right transfer token is created initially by the resource owner in the policy creation transaction, this means that the resource owner is the first one to sell the rights to a subject.

Note that the fact that rights are represented by a token, coupled with the fact that every output can be spent only once, guarantees that the same rights can be transferred only once. Note also that the subject that has currently the policy action rights can also decide to destroy those rights. To do so it only needs to spend the corresponding token as if it was just normal value (using the same process explained previously used by the policy owner to revoke a policy). This is semantically correct since the current owner has payed for the rights and so it can do with them whatever it wants. It could as well decide to never sell the rights again, which is the same for the other users as if it had destroyed them. The advantage is that the resource owner can see from the blockchain when a subject rights token has been destroyed, and so it could choose to revoke the old policy and issue a new one. We also note that revoking a policy or destroying subject rights actively removes the policy data heavy outputs from the UTXO (see Subsect. 5.1) of all the users, so any policy stops encumbering the network once it is not active anymore.

5.4   Policy Evaluation

Let us suppose that a policy granting access rights to the resource R has been created and updated m times, and that this right has been transferred among subjects n times. This means that the blockchain includes a PCT, say pt, defined as in Sect. 5.2 with a chain (actually a tree in case of rights splits) of n RTT defined as in Sect. 5.3 originating from the first input of pt and a single chain of m policy update transactions originated from the second output of pt.

When the PEP receives a request, it only receives a link (for example a cryptographic hash) to the last RTT, say rt, and this is the only information it needs to pass forward in a request to the CH (see Sect. 4). Given a request the PAP can access the blockchain and navigate backward the chain of n RTT from rt all the way back to pt, collecting at each step the additional conditions added by right owners. Once the PAP has reached pt it can read the policy from the blockchain. Then it traverses forward the chain of all m policy update transactions, updating the policy accordingly with the data read at each update step. Once it has the fully updated policy it can add the restricting conditions inserted by right owners and read during the RTT chain traversal. At the end of this process the PAP has derived the completely updated policy in a standard format ready for evaluation by the PDP.

Note that the above policy reconstruction can be done by anyone, given a RTT, since all the informations are publicly visible in the blockchain. This is particularly important for the interested subjects that can retrieve the same way the updated policy from the blockchain and then decide whether to buy the rights for themselves or not.

6   Conclusions

This paper defines an approach to create, manage and enforce access control policies exploiting blockchain technology. The main advantages of this approach are that the policy is published on the blockchain, thus being visible to the subjects of the scenario, and that the access rights can be transferred from one user to another simply through a blockchain transaction. The approach has been validated through a reference implementation based on Bitcoin.

We plan to extend our work to study how to better embed an access control system in blockchain technology. In particular we are studying the possibility of using smart contracts to obtain self enforcing policies. We are exploring how to formulate the classical access control scheme (see Sect. 4) as a smart contract that can be stored and executed in the blockchain to automatically evaluate and enforce policies. Moreover we plan to improve our approach in order to also manage multi-rule XACML policies and policy sets. We are also currently studying the privacy implications of our approach and how to mitigate them.

References

1. Hu, V.C., David, F., Rick, K., Adam, S., Sandlin, K., Robert, M., Karen, S.: Guide to attribute based access control (abac) definition and considerations (2014)
2. Nakamoto, S.: Bitcoin: A peer-to-peer electronic cash system (2008)
3. Merkle, R.C.: A digital signature based on a conventional encryption function. In: Pomerance, C. (ed.) CRYPTO 1987. LNCS, vol. 293, pp. 369–378. Springer, Heidelberg (1988). doi:10.1007/3-540-48184-2_32
4. Dwork, C., Naor, M.: Pricing via processing or combatting junk mail. In: Brickell, E.F. (ed.) CRYPTO 1992. LNCS, vol. 740, pp. 139–147. Springer, Heidelberg (1993). doi:10.1007/3-540-48071-4_10
5. NIST, U.: Descriptions of sha-256, sha-384 and sha-512 (2001)
6. Preneel, B., Bosselaers, A., Dobbertin, H.: The cryptographic hash function ripemd-160 (1997)
7. Johnson, D., Menezes, A., Vanstone, S.: The elliptic curve digital signature algorithm (ECDSA). Int. J. Inf. Secur. **1**(1), 36–63 (2001)
8. Pilkington, M.: Blockchain technology: principles and applications. In: Xavier Olleros, F., Zhegu, M. (eds.) (2015)
9. Huckle, S., Bhattacharya, R., White, M., Beloff, N.: Internet of things, blockchain and shared economy applications. In: International Workshop on Data Mining and IoT Systems (DaMIS 2016), pp. 461–466. (2016)
10. Mainelli, M., Smith, M.: Sharing ledgers for sharing economies: an exploration of mutual distributed ledgers (aka blockchain technology). J. Finantial Perspect. **3**, 38–69 (2015)
11. OASIS: eXtensible Access Control Markup Language (XACML) version 3.0, January 2013
12. Zyskind, G., Nathan, O., et al.: Decentralizing privacy: using blockchain to protect personal data. In: 2015 IEEE Security and Privacy Workshops (SPW), pp. 180–184. IEEE (2015)

13. Hidden surprises in the Bitcoin blockchain. http://www.righto.com/2014/02/ascii-bernanke-wikileaks-photographs.html. Accessed 24 Feb 2017
14. Bitcoin Wiki. https://en.bitcoin.it/wiki/transaction_fees. Accessed 24 Feb 2017
15. Bitcoin Wiki. https://en.bitcoin.it/wiki/colored_coins. Accessed 24 Feb 2017
16. Current Standard for Dust Limit. https://github.com/bitcoin/bitcoin/blob/v0.10.0rc3/src/primitives/transaction.h#l137. Accessed 24 Feb 2017

Author Index

Printed in the United States
By Bookmasters